AFRICANS IN PAKISTAN

AFRICANS IN PAKISTAN

JÜRGEN WASIM FREMBGEN

with contributions by
Sheedi Yaqoob Qambrani, Aliya Iqbal Naqvi,
and Hasan Ali Khan; photographs by Akhtar Soomro

AFRICA WORLD PRESS

TRENTON | LONDON | CAPE TOWN | NAIROBI | ADDIS ABABA | ASMARA | IBADAN | NEW DELHI

AFRICA WORLD PRESS
541 West Ingham Avenue | Suite B
Trenton, New Jersey 08638

Copyright © 2022

All rights reserved. No part of this publication may be reproduced, stored in a retrieval system or transmitted in any form or by any means electronic, mechanical, photocopying, recording or otherwise without the prior written permission of the publisher.

Book design: Dawid Kahts
Cover design: Ashraful Haq

Cataloging-in-Publication Data may be obtained from the Library of Congress.

ISBNs: 9781569027950 (HB)
        9781569027967 (PB)

Dedicated to

the Shidi people and to those Baloch and
Sindhis whose ancestors migrated
from Africa to present-day Pakistan.

Contents

Preface by Shihan de Silva Jayasuriya	ix
Author's Note	xi
Acknowledgements	xiii
Note on Presentation	xv
An Anthropologist's Introduction	xvii

I   Africans in Pakistan as the 'Other': Prejudices, Stereotypes, and Scholarly Viewpoints
    Introduction   1
    Forgotten, Overlooked, and Sidelined   3
    Discriminated Against: Racist Stereotypes   4
    Lifting the Curtain: Scholarly Viewpoints   12

II Regional Settings and Identities: On the Complex Picture of People of African Descent
    Introduction   19
    Living Spaces and Settlements   20
    Ethnonyms and Ethnic Labels   24
    Language Diversity   32
    Identities   34

III Historical Perspectives: From Africa to the Coastal Belt of Makran and Sindh
    Introduction   39
    Legendary Descent   40
    Early Contacts between Africa and South Asia   42
    The Zanj Rebellion
    [by Aliya Iqbal Naqvi and Hasan Ali Khan]   45

Baloch Confederacies and the Assimilation of People of African descent into the Baloch Nation [by Aliya Iqbal Naqvi and Hasan Ali Khan]	47
Slavery	49
Africans in Positions of Authority	59
Oral Traditions of Migration	65

IV Socio-economic Life: Subsistence and Social Organization

Introduction	77
Family and Kinship	79
Subsistence and Poverty	81
Social and Political Organization	87

V Religious Traditions: Saints, Shrines, Rituals, and Sufi Orders

Introduction	93
Bava Ghor and the Pantheon of African Saints	96
Major Shidi Shrines in Karachi	100
Secondary Shidi Shrines in Karachi	104
Shidi Shrines and Abodes of Sufi Saints in Interior Sindh	107
The Shidi mēlā at Mangho Pir [by Sheedi Yaqoob Qambrani and Jürgen Wasim Frembgen]	108
The Power of Rituals I: Remembering Benevolent Saints	125
The Power of Rituals II: Warding Off Malevolent Spirits	129
People of African Descent in the Rifa'i Sufi Order [by Aliya Iqbal Naqvi and Hasan Ali Khan]	134

VI Facets of Culture and Everyday Practices: From Music and Dance to Sports and Pastimes

Introduction	145
The muggarmān and Other Musical Instruments	147
Music Making and Entertaining	150
Sports	156
Everyday Pastimes	162

Afterword	167
Bibliography	171
Contributors	189
Photography Credit	191

Preface

Jürgen Wasim Frembgen's well illustrated account draws together anthropological and historical knowledge on a large African diaspora in South Asia. Descriptions of ritual shrine behavior reveal Frembgen's ethnographic strength and research into liminal academic spaces. Performances entwined with Sufi traditions bring the presence of Shidis to the fore connecting them to the wider Indian Ocean World and to neighboring India. Drawing together knowledge of over ten years in the field in Pakistan, Frembgen writes as an outsider who has become an insider.

The field of Afro-diasporic Studies has grown over the last twenty years and scholarly interest has grown since I co-edited *The African Diaspora in the Indian Ocean* with Richard Pankhurst also published by African World Press with contributions from a group of pioneering scholars. Afro-descendants in Pakistan are lost amidst a landscape of two hundred and twenty million and Frembgen's book should generate further interest in the dispersal of Africans to Asia, a result of both free and forced movements over centuries. Whilst informing the scholarly community, the book contributes to the wider discourse on the easterly movements of Africans.

Shihan de Silva Jayasuriya, PhD, FRAS
Visiting Fellow, University of Cambridge
Senior Research Fellow, Institute of Commonwealth Studies, School of Advanced Study, University of London
Visiting Professor, Ritsumeikan University, Kyoto

Author's Note

In anthropology, all 'culture' is the product of human thought. In simple words the term can be understood as 'the sum of all manifestations of people's life.'[1] Less descriptively, it is a system of giving meaning to life, a 'sense system,' which covers the reciprocal relations between people and environment as well as between individual and society. It includes concrete everyday practices and learned routines as well as the casual, unfinished, and ambiguous aspects of human existence, the ups and downs of ordinary life, the pleasures and tribulations. Of course, this notion of culture as a complex whole also contains indigenous history relevant for the present. And to put it bluntly in terms of our topic: culture is a concept which has, of course, nothing to do with 'race' (see Chapter I).

Drawing thus on cultural and social anthropology grounded in ethnography, I try to describe and explore the traditions and lifeways of African-descended populations in south Pakistan, a local diasporan setting still not sufficiently studied, and to identify distinctive features of their culture(s). Uprooted from their original homelands, the descendants of former slaves, soldiers, and seafarers, but also of free men and women, are so-to-speak 'people-in between' whose identities became fragmented in the course of history. Even today, they are often taken for foreigners in a country in which they have lived for centuries – in their own country. They constitute a significant minority living on the fringes of multiethnic Pakistan – mostly impoverished, socially deprived, and politically disempowered. Because of the lack of a commonly accepted collective name for these different diasporic groups, I designate them descriptively as 'Africans in Pakistan' and alternatively as 'Pakistanis of African descent' (avoiding mostly the term 'origin' as it may be misleading; 'origin' being a relative category), although they themselves do not use these umbrella terms and are also not called as such by others in Pakistan.

This study is a tribute to them and an endeavor to understand their cultural traditions and practices and, in particular, their indigenous religion from within, as lived reality, taking into account that it is shaped by the historical circumstances of trans-oceanic migration. Comparing their history and culture with those of their sisters and brothers in neighboring India and Iran makes it possible to trace differences and variations and examine what they have in common. This book is not meant exclusively for fellow scholars, but also intended to be read by the educated younger generation of Africans in Pakistan. If it helps them to value their distinct translocal cultural traditions, their 'voices' understood as reminiscences of distant African lands embodied, for instance, in saints, spirits, songs, and drums, it will have achieved its aim and object.

Endnote

1   This very short characterization of culture coined by the German ethnologist Adolf Friedrich (1914-1956) builds on the canonical descriptive formulation of 1871 by Edward Burnett Tylor (1832-1917), the founder of British anthropology. Tylor drew on the term and concept of culture developed by the German philosopher Johann Gottfried von Herder (1744-1803), in many ways the father of modern anthropology (cf. Müller 2003: 16-18). Later Franz Boas (1858-1942) introduced the term in the USA and became the founder of Cultural Anthropology.

Acknowledgements

This study owes its existence to many people with African roots in Pakistan who opened their minds and hearts to me, enabling me to learn about their traditions. In particular I am indebted to the support of two renowned public figures and local dignitaries of African descent in Karachi, namely the late Hajji Ghulam Akbar Shidi (d. 2019) and Sheedi Yaqoob Qambrani, to whom I am deeply indebted (Figs. 2-3).[1] Ghulam Akbar was a respected ritual leader, spokesman of his community, and political activist who lived in the Baghdadi quarter of Lyari (Karachi). Likewise Yaqoob Qambrani, President of the 'Pakistan Sheedi Ittehad,' is a respected social activist and political leader living in Baldia (Karachi). He co-authors a subchapter with me on the rituals of his community performed annually at the shrine of Mangho Pir (in Chapter V). I must also acknowledge Goethe Institute in Karachi for funding the English translation of Yaqoob Qambrani's unpublished Urdu manuscript to which I occasionally refer in the present work (see also my comments in the respective section on scholarly viewpoints in Chapter I). Furthermore, I want to express my sincere thanks to many people living in the metropolitan city of Karachi as well as in Hyderabad and smaller towns, like Tando Bago, Sujawal, and Sehwan, who patiently listened to and answered my questions during shorter and longer conversations. To protect privacy, I have either changed their names or I use abbreviations, such as 'Baba,' 'Apa,' 'Hajji,' M.B.' or 'Nawab.' I feel grateful to all of them for their cooperation and for welcoming me in their midst.

My special thanks go to my friends Akhtar Soomro and Aslam Khwaja, with whom I regularly discussed the findings of my fieldwork. They were always sources of generous advice and enriched me with their insights. Akhtar is an experienced photojournalist born and raised in Lyari (Karachi) who generously shared his immense knowledge about Africans in Pakistan with me. He also contributed the vast part of the photographs illustrating this volume taken over many years; those of people in a state of rapture during the annual festival at Mangho Pir could only be taken by arrangements kindly made by Hajji Ghulam Akbar Shidi and 'Apa.' Akhtar's keen interest in the cultural traditions of Africans in Pakistan is in documenting a world that is in danger of disappearing (Fig. 60). Aslam is a renowned intellectual and noted researcher who writes on the social and political life of Sindh. He worked as reporter and sub-editor for several leading Sindhi daily newspapers and also does translations in Sindhi, Urdu, and English.

Apart from Yaqoob Qambrani, I invited two historians from Karachi, Aliya Iqbal Naqvi and Hasan Ali Khan, to contribute. Their texts on the Zanj rebellion, the role of the Baloch confederacies in 'integrating' people of African descent into their ethnicity, and the affiliation of this people with the Rifa'i Sufi order not only supplement, but in fact fill the painfully felt lacunae in this volume. The book is much enriched by Aliya's and Hasan's contributions.

Endnote

1 Their photographs are shown in Frembgen 2020: 158. Both dignitaries also figure prominently in a 23 minute-long Urdu documentary on the 'Life of Pakistani Black People': www.youtube.com/watch?v=KujrrVeZp2U (last accessed on 7 September 2020).

Note on Presentation

For the transliteration of terms from Urdu, Persian, Arabic, Sindhi, etc., I use a simplified system with italicization and the spare use of diacritical marks, such as differentiating long and short vowels through macrons (short stroke marks above Latin vowels) and indicating a nasal with a tilde.

Having witnessed for years the fatal dominance of English in today's academic discourse, I wish to remind the reader that there is not just one 'world language' because every language has its own perspective on this world. In fact, the overemphasis on English flies in the face of the much touted academic multilingualism and renders scholarly discourse superficial through simplification. Therefore, I request the reader to allow me a few words of explanation for the spelling of indigenous terms, here especially of the ethnonym 'Shidi' (*shīdī*). Nowadays the name Shidi, denoting the major group of people of African descent examined in the present study, is often spelled 'Sheedi.' Many writers, journalists, and even scholars use this philologically incorrect orthography with a double *e* derived from colloquial English, thereby repeating misspellings frequently found in colonial travel literature (such as 'Seedees'; see, for instance, Napier 1845: 37). This follows the 'English-ized' or 'globish' script now common almost worldwide, especially in journalistic works and novels, whose spread is accelerated by new electronic media. If someone writes 'Sheedi,' then she or he should in consequence write in plural 'Sheedees' too and, for instance, also 'Soofee,' 'Peer,' 'Beebee,' 'Hubshee,' 'fukeer,' 'loongee,' 'doodh putti,' 'Hindoo,' 'Sheeas,' 'Sindee,' or 'Kurrachee'. In fact, such spellings were found across writings published over the last decades, thereby relinquishing any academic standard for adequate transliteration. I wonder why the scholars in question do not use dictionaries any more or follow the method of the *Encyclopedia of Islam* to find transliterations for local terms. With respect to the misspelling 'Sheedi,' even colonial officials, whose English

orthography is otherwise archaic, such as Richard F. Burton, recommended the philological transliteration *Sīdi* (1877: 103-104). Similarly, Thomas Postans (1843: 74) and Edward H. Aitken for the Gazetteer of Sindh (1907: 180) both wrote *Sidi*.

Nevertheless, to aid the reader's understanding of this book, apart from transliterated indigenous words, I adhere to the current English spelling of names and local terms by including the use of the plural s. In addition, I use conventional forms of orthography for geographical terms, such as 'Punjab' (for *Panjāb*) and 'Muscat' (for *Masqat*), and for Arabic terms, such as Ulama, Pir, Sunni, and Shi'a, which have found their way as loanwords into most Western languages. While total consistency is impossible, as an anthropologist I have attempted to stay as close to original colloquial pronunciation as possible.

Unless otherwise specified, throughout the text given dates correspond to the Common Era.

An Anthropologist's Introduction

Based on notes from my fieldwork diary (Sehwan Sharif, a small town and pilgrimage centre in interior Sindh; Saturday, 31 July 2010):

The day begins with the twitter of birds and the distant noise of traffic under a pale-grey sky.

After breakfast I wander around dusty-grey clusters of houses and visit a dervish lodge. The air is dry and the heat already sweltering. On my return I walk through the main bazaar of the Sabzwari neighborhood; by chance I meet a local Sindhi historian, Nazir Husain Soomro. We begin to chat. He knows about my interest in rituals and performances during the *'urs* (literally 'marriage,' mystical nuptial of the soul with God) of Pakistan's most popular Sufi saint Lal Shahbaz Qalandar. It is my eighth visit to Sehwan. The elderly scholar tells me that he just came across some dark-skinned people (he calls them Shidis and Makrani Baloch) and remembered that on each of the three main days of the *'urs* festival they would customarily take out their own processions with music and dance. On the first day they would greet Bodla Bahar, the Qalandar's most beloved disciple, and on the second and third day they would go to the shrine of the Red Sufi. 'Something special,' he emphasized. Today it is the eighteenth of the Islamic month of Sha'ban, the second day of the *'urs*. If I would be interested in seeing their procession, I should visit the Makrani neighborhood after *'asr* prayers. He also mentioned the name of a person behind whose house the procession would start, situated not far from the main road.

In the scorching afternoon heat I enter a narrow lane leading to a cluster of houses, a poor neighborhood. In front of a small local mosque I see some older men, dark-complexioned and with short curly hair; my first encounter in Pakistan with people with obviously African roots. Two tall single-headed drums strike my attention. They resemble drums used in Uganda, Congo, and parts of East Africa for healing ceremonies. One of the bystanders explains

Africans in Pakistan

that these four-footed drums are called *muggarmān*. These drums have a body made from mango wood and a single drum head of camel skin. Close by, two men squatting on the floor are busy warming the covers of circular frame drums (*daf*) by holding the drum heads made of goat skin towards the flames of a small fire.

Afterwards the drums are placed upright on the ground, standing on their frames. The heads of the tall four-footed ceremonial drums, whose body is wrapped with a green piece of cloth, are also held towards the fire, carefully keeping just the right distance. After a while, more people assemble – white-bearded dignitaries as well as young men, the older dressed in white with embroidered Omani caps or Muscati *kulāh*s on their head and sandals on their feet, the younger dressed in various colors. Some wear European trousers, one with a baseball cap, the others bareheaded, all barefoot. A round metal tray with a folded cloth, a green- and red-colored *chādar*, later to be ritually placed on the tomb of the Qalandar, is held over an incense-burner to purify it. A group is formed, about fifteen men, three or four elders, the rest youngsters, apparently mostly of African descent, the rest probably Baloch. Some of the young processionists now wear a prayer cap. The group is led by Hajji Ghulam Mustafa, a prominent leader of the Qadri-Rifaʻi Sufi order and a guardian of oral African traditions as I come to know (Fig. 1).

Fig. 1   Khalifa Hajji Ghulam Mustafa reciting hymns during a procession around Makrani neighborhood; ʻurs of La l Shahbaz Qalandar, Sehwan (July 2010)

xviii

He starts to sing, obviously praise-poetry in honor of Prophet Muhammad. Then he opens a rough book with hand-written verses and starts to recite and sing *sifātaiñ*, words eulogizing the qualities of God, followed by a hymn for the great Qalandar. All the others repeat the verses in responsorial style. Then the group slowly moves on, singing and playing the frame drums. A little behind, the second group follows, led by Ghulam Nabi, a member of another Sufi order, the Qadri-Qalandariyya. At the head of each group is a boy carrying a standard with a green- and red-colored flag and a finial of the Shiʿa type made of cheap metal, after him another boy carrying the metal tray with the *chādar* to be presented to Laʿl Shahbaz Qalandar. Both processional groups slowly move through the mainly Baloch neighborhood and stop three times at a mosque and two courtyards.[1]

In each group there is a young man who carries the *muggarmān*, places it on the ground when the group comes to a stop, and starts to play African rhythms. I can feel the warm bass tones and the repetitive rhythmic patterns; a powerful sound, fascinating, and unheard during all my previous travel in the country; a penetrating and irresistible sound which transports me to distant African lands. I succumb to the allure of the exotic, of images carried with me for a long time. This seems the heartbeat of people of African descent in Pakistan which leads into the deep recesses of their emotional experience. (Later I learned that the sound of this sacred instrument is believed to be the voice of the ancestor saint Bava Ghor, a voice filled with the power of the past.)

In addition to the young men tapping the *muggarmān*, four boys play frame drums, from time to time handing them over to others. On and on goes the singing by the leader and the chorus. Spectators distribute sweets and offer money which they consecrate by circling the notes over the heads of singers and musicians. In one of the courtyards a woman begins to dance, but stops after a short while, then a young man falls into an ecstatic devotional dance. First he weeps, standing with both hands folded on the back, his head lowered, then he puts his hands on the neck from behind; after a few moments he gets down on his knees, body leaned forward, supporting himself with both hands on the ground, and starts whirling his head. Suddenly he gets up and starts jumping, in quick and 'hot' rhythms, hurling his arms into the air. Is he possessed by a spirit or in a state of rapture experiencing the presence of the Qalandar? Finally, both processional groups step out from the neighborhood onto the main road leading to the Qalandar's shrine and are immediately absorbed by the milling crowd of pilgrims.

Postscript from a subsequent visit to Sehwan Sharif on 23 November 2010:

Naïvely I hoped to meet the Shidi people of the procession again, to be able to talk to them at ease outside the rush of the *'urs*, thinking they would live in town. When I visited the neighborhood called Makrani, I learned that there are only three Shidi households here. The participants in the procession observed in summer, however, all came from Karachi. The young man who explained this to me was extremely friendly, a warmhearted character, to whom I took a liking immediately. His name was M.B. Baloch. He is the one who smoothed the path for me to discover the world of Africans in Pakistan, and the first to tell me about their life in Lyari, an old working-class area of Karachi. Within Lyari Town, they were particularly concentrated in Baghdadi, the heart of Lyari, situated right behind historic Lea Market. Baghdadi is named after Abdul Qadir Jilani, the great Sufi saint of Baghdad and founder of the Qadiriyya, the largest mystic order of the Muslim world. After offering me *sēl machchī*, hot and spicy salted fish, served with bread made from rice flour, M.B. provided me with names of prominent members of his community in Karachi, such as Hajji Ghulam Akbar Shidi (Fig. 2) and Sheedi Yaqoob Qambrani (Fig. 3). Moreover, he told me that the younger brother of his mother-in-law was a magic healer, a 'Baba,' who treats patients possessed by evil spirits. He offered to contact the Baba over the phone and so I spoke to him. Another door was opened and a few days later I visited this gentleman in Baghdadi, a sympathetic middle-aged person, heavy-limbed, with an open face. We had tea at a nearby Pathan restaurant on Shidi Village Road, embarked on a lively conversation, and later strolled through the unpaved inner lanes of his quarter, a grey brick and concrete urban agglomeration. My scholarly interest was alerted and my journey into a new chapter of research could begin, thanks to moments of serendipity in the holy city of Sehwan.

As mentioned in the introductory note, people of African descent constitute a significant minority in Pakistan. As their total population is not recorded through a separate census and accurate numbers are therefore not available, demographic estimates vary considerably, ranging between tens of thousands, hundreds of thousands up to about one million.[2] My own estimation, extrapolated from numbers given by several authors and my own data collected in the field, totals approximately 300,000 people with African roots.[3] Primarily, they live in the lower Indus Valley in the province of Sindh, especially in Karachi, as well as in the coastal regions of

Introduction

Fig. 2   Hajji Ghulam Akbar Shidi at the 'urs of the saint Bava Ghor; Kharadar makan, Karachi (July 2011)

Fig. 3   Sheedi Yaqoob Qambrani with Faqir Muhammad Bilal (right) and the latter's son (middle); Baldia, Karachi (November 2014)

Makran in Balochistan. There, they constitute the third largest subgroup.[4] In comparison, the Sidis (pronounced 'Siddi' in Hyderabad/Deccan) of Indian Gujarat were said to number about 20,000 in the early twenty-first century (a number which must be much higher now). Their total population in India may be around 35,000 or more today.[5]

Despite this considerable number of people of African descent in Pakistan, in general their presence is hardly noticed. In the south of the country, where they are more visible, they are stigmatized because of their skin color (Chapter I). After clarifying how the descendants of chiefly Sub-Saharan Africans are perceived today, how they are otherized through racist ascriptions, stereotyping, and inferiorization, I discuss their living spaces and settlements, ethnonyms, and languages as well as identities (Chapter II). Whatever these various small-scale diasporic communities call themselves, the main analytic focus of the present volume is on those among them who try to retain their traditions and identity, particularly those who still venerate their African ancestor saints. This marked cultural trait in tandem with other patterns, such as ways of thinking, expressing emotions, and manners of behavior, forms a particular configuration shared especially by the Shidi community. 'Shidi' (*shīdī*) is derived from the Arabic word for Sayyid ('lord' or 'master'), in plural Sayyidi, a term lending in principle dignity to people who migrated from Africa whether as slaves or freemen, dock workers or seafarers.[6] In North Africa, 'Sidi' has long been a title given to Sufi saints. Nevertheless, the root of this word, *swd*, means 'black' (cf. *hajr aswad*, the 'black stone' of the Kaaba) and denotes any 'thick collection of things,' thus *sawād* means 'wealth and large population.'[7]

As the text unfolds, its subject, Africans in Pakistan, will also be referred to as 'our people' to avoid mentioning each time the various ethnonyms in use, some of which carry derogatory connotations (such as 'Shidi' as a racial slur for 'Blacks' among tribal Baloch). This is also done to convey the sense of participant observation which has informed this work.[8] 'People' is of course a broad category which implies plurality, referring to various classes, ethnicities, and divergent opinions. In Chapters III to VI, together with my co-authors Yaqoob Qambrani, Aliya Iqbal Naqvi, and Hasan Ali Khan, I elaborate on their history, society, and religion as well as some expressions of their vibrant and fascinating indigenous cultures which have been retained to this day. Music and dance in particular not only indicate their African heritage but prove the enormous power of resistance inherent in folk culture vis-à-vis the onslaught of global modernity. In this way, the present study tries to discover the cultural values and ideals of the African diaspora in Pakistan with a particular focus on subaltern Sufi-related ritual practices as performed in Karachi.

My research is informed by the methodological tool of a mild (not ideological and not decontextualized) cultural relativism with its ethical emphasis (respecting cultures as being in principle of equal value, not prejudging them, accepting cultural otherness)[9] and emic perspective (trying to understand cultures from the insider's perspective). It takes an historic-empirical approach with regard to the overall theme augmented by ethnographic evidence including sketches of life stories. The study is based on ethnographic fieldwork conducted since 2010 in the course of eighteen short field-trips to various parts of Sindh with a focus on the megacity of Karachi.

These sequential visits allowed me to establish good contacts with 'our people' (henceforth in this book written without quotation marks), to overcome suspicion towards an outsider, and, thanks to my initial introductions, to find friends. In addition to this primary research, the book is based on academic and wider secondary literature from which I frequently quote. Nevertheless, my work is far from exhaustive and is imperfect, as are all ethnographies. For instance, as a male participant observer, I could not access the close-knit networks of women during religious rituals and mundane celebrations, although I managed to talk to women on several occasions. Furthermore, all conversations were conducted in Urdu which went well insofar as the people I talked to were fluent in this language, but of course a command of Sindhi, Balochi, or Gujarati would have allowed deeper insights.

In 2020, I called for the diverse cultures of people of African descent in Pakistan 'to be recorded, documented and researched in-depth.'[10] The present study is not a definitive account, but can only be considered a first step in investigating these cultures which are particularly rich with respect to rituals, music, dance performances and sports. It is an attempt to situate this marginalized people within the social fabric of Pakistan. More empirical and archival research needs, of course, to be done. Hopefully, this book will generate further scholarship.

Endnotes

1   See photographs No. 25 and 26 in Frembgen 2020: 162.
2   Fatah 2005: 113 (estimation of some hundreds of thousands by the late Dr Adam Nayyar, a renowned Pakistani anthropologist). Khalique notes: 'The largest diaspora communities of approximately 40 – 50,000 live in the province of modern day Sindh (Pakistan)' (Khalique 2009: 9). In 2002, Helene Basu estimated around 30,000 in Sindh (as quoted in Campbell 2008: 52)

and in 2003 around 40 – 50,000 (Basu 2003: 223). In addition, we need to take into account the large number of people with African roots living on the Makran coast. Concerning Balochistan, Omar Hamid Ali thus writes: 'It has been estimated that at least a quarter of the total population of the Makran coast is of African ancestry [...] that is, at least 250,000 people living on the southern coast of Pakistan [...] can claim East African descent' (Ali 2011: 19). Referring to the Census of India from 1921, Pastner comments about the Nakib, 'generally believed to be descended from a population of East African slaves' (p. 31): 'Historically there have been far more Nakibs [...] in Makran than in any other district of Baluchistan. In 1907, about 27,000 were enumerated in Makran' (Pastner 1971: 32; cf. Gazetteer Balochistan 1906: 560, 562). As far as the former principality of Kalat is concerned, we come to know that: 'The system of slavery was so much encouraged under the Khānate rule, that even today seventy per cent of the Kalāt population consists of slaves [...]' (Sardar Khan Baluch 1958: 176). Likewise, in 1901, the number of people of African origin in Las Bela, then an independent state and now a district of Balochistan, was given with '7,898 souls' (Gazetteer Las Bela: 62). Rumana Husain notes that 'according to various sources, there are approximately 5,000 Sheedis living in Karachi' (2010: 20). The travel writer Alice Albinia mentions the exaggerated number of 'one million or so Sheedis' (2008: 53).

3 This is also corroborated vaguely by Qaimkhani (1996, p. 64: 'hundreds of thousands of people of African descent') and more precisely by Paracha (2018: 70), namely approximately 250,000 estimated in the year 2012.
4 Sultana 1996: 30.
5 Lodhi 1992: 83 (the author writes 250,000, but I believe this must be a misprint); Basu 1995: 75 (estimation: about 6,000); Basu 2005: 178 (mentioning 20,000) Basu 2008 b: 230 (estimation: about 20,000); Campbell 2008: 52 (referring to an estimation by Basu in 2002 of 10,000 people); Prasad & Angenot 2008: 207 (mentioning 20,000 to 30,000).
6 Basu 2005: 177.
7 Ahmed 2010: 298-299. In India the honorific title 'Sidi,' used in Arabic to denote descendants of Prophet Muhammad, was taken by aristocratic soldiers of African descent as their *nisba* (name referring to the place of birth, clan or caste, or to religious affiliation and even occupation), for instance in the case of the naval admiral Sidi Yaqut Khan. Cf. Basu 1995: 58 (endnote 6); Qaimkhani 1996: 64; Baptiste 2008: 122-123; Basu 2008: 9 (footnote 8); De Silva Jayasuriya 2009: 21-22; Paracha 2018: 69.
8 In this I follow O'Brien's study on Punjabi Christians (2012: 39, note 2; cf. 11-12).
9 See, for instance, Richardson 1975: 523.
10 Frembgen 2020: 154.

Africans in Pakistan as the 'Other': Prejudices, Stereotypes, and Scholarly Views

Introduction

Open any book on Pakistan, read any chapter introducing its peoples and ethnic groups, and you are unlikely to find any mention of people of African descent. At best there might be a hint in a footnote. Most scholarly works written by anthropologists and historians on the African diaspora in the Indian ocean region focus on the Sidis of Gujarat and other parts of India, although Pakistan is home to most people with African roots in South Asia. The little that has been written thus far on Africans in Pakistan is of varying quality; either focused exclusively on historical sources, poorly researched and biased in one way or the other, or focused on very detailed formulation of research questions. And there are scholarly articles thick in theory but poor in ethnography; other material has not been officially published and remains 'grey literature.' Newspaper reports frequently cover the spectacular Mangho Pir festival, celebrated by the Shidi community at a shrine on the northern outskirts of Karachi in honor of the saint Hajji Sayyid Sakhi Sultan, better known as Mangho Pir. Apart from that, few people in Pakistan know that there exists a Shidi community as well as other groups with African roots. Many Karachiites belonging to the upper and middle classes do not seem to be aware of their fellow citizens often having been reduced to servitude in the past.

Fig. 4   A middle class Shidi family, Karachi (November 2010)

Although in Islam racism is frowned upon, this does not mean that in social reality it does not exist. Also in Pakistan there is an asymmetric distribution of power between major ethnic groups on the one hand, such as Punjabis, Pakhtun/Pathan, Urdu-speaking Mohajirs, Sindhis, Baloch and so on, and on the other hand dark-skinned marginalized groups, such as people of African descent in the south of the country and descendants of indigenous tribal groups in Sindh and the Punjab – the typical Other perceived as and made to feel as outsiders. As a result of this Othering, we come across constructions of 'Blacks' and 'the Dark' in value opposition to those of a lighter, 'wheatish' skin color. My friends living in low income areas or in poor dwellings in Lyari, Baldia, the slum of the Machar Colony, and other neighborhoods of Karachi, as well as in various parts of interior Sindh, have ample stories to tell about stigmatization and discrimination in daily life based on their African somatic features. They are made subjects of ridicule, considered ignorant and wild, and are not given respect. The underlying stereotypes informing the opinions and attitudes of many Pakistanis towards our people will be deconstructed below in a subchapter.

Not without reason has it been argued that anthropologists studying such communities can hardly avoid portraying them as the Other, as they per se acknowledge differences in cultures and peoples, and are thus guilty of a kind of 'positive discrimination.' I am aware of this dilemma.

Chapter 1

Forgotten, Overlooked, and Sidelined

Before saying a few words on how people of African descent have been described and analysed in academic literature on Pakistan, let us examine at how they are perceived in some general pseudo-anthropological works as well as in travelogues and articles written by journalists.

In the days when Pakistan was still a destination for courageous foreign tourists and travelers, those among them with a keener interest in the country and its peoples consulted, for instance, the generally informative APA guide book edited by Tony Halliday. Writing about Karachi, the anthropologist Christine Cottam refers in passing in one sentence to people from Africa, calling them 'Habshi' and uncritically repeating the local folk legend that this term was derived from the name of the Hab river (which is, of course, nonsense) marking the border between Sindh and Balochistan.[1] 'Habshi,' derived from the Arabic word *habash* (plural *ahabish*) for the Habesha, the highlanders of Abyssinia/Ethiopia, has often been used to designate 'Black' slaves of African descent in Indo-Muslim history.[2] Although its etymology is not clear, the original meaning of the word could be 'gatherers of incense.'[3] While in Pakistan and India the *nisba* 'Habshi' usually carries less negative connotations than other ethnic identifiers and labels (discussed more closely in Chapter II), it is used pejoratively too, depending on the situation and locale.[4]

Another voluminous travel book showcasing Pakistan and its culture, edited in English by Mohamed Amin, does not mention our people at all.[5] Opening lavishly illustrated coffee table books on Pakistan, one learns, for instance, about the 'Negroid features' of the Makrani fishing community,[6] while the more scholarly *Pakistan. Past & Present* published in commemoration of the birth of the founder of Pakistan, also including a section on 'The Land and the People,' has within its 282 pages not a single word to say about Africans living for centuries in this country. In one prestigious worldwide monograph series, the volume on Pakistan with 555 pages edited by Mohammad Usman Malik and Annemarie Schimmel, again devotes only one sentence to the 'Negroid features' of the Makrani people.[7]

We should keep in mind that we are talking about an ethnic group comprising probably 300,000 people or even more. It is therefore disturbing to note that this sizeable minority has been almost completely overlooked. This is the case for instance in two well-known German encyclopedias, picked up for a random sample in my library, namely works dealing with 'peoples of the world' and 'peoples of the fourth world.'[8] Although the renowned encyclopedia on 'South Asian Folklore' discusses the immigration of South

Fig. 5   Old Shidi lady at Mangho Pir, Karachi (July 2010)

Fig. 6   Muhammad Arab, a peasant from village Kado near Tando Bago, Sindh (February 2018)

Asians to Africa under the heading 'Diaspora, Africa', there is no entry about Africans who migrated to South Asia.[9] Likewise, in his voluminous *Pakistan. A Hard Country*, the political scientist Anatol Lieven, who traveled extensively in the country, does not mention our people, probably because they are not a major ethnicity.[10] Consequently and with good reason, the renowned ethnographer and humanist Khurshid Qaimkhani, who worked for the betterment of underprivileged Muslims and Hindus in Pakistan, opens the chapter on Shidis in his book *Bhataktī Naslaiñ* (The Nomadic Peoples) with the words: 'In Pakistan, perhaps only a handful of people are aware that in this country there are hundreds of thousands of people of African descent who have lived here for centuries.'[11] Lack of knowledge is often the reason for prejudice.

In short, as far as these written sources are concerned, our people are at best sidelined, characterized as exotic with a focus on their African physiognomy, or simply overlooked.

Discriminated Against: Racist Stereotypes

As in other parts of the Middle East and South Asia, in Pakistan the physical difference of Africans is essentialized and usually perceived to signify a displeasing Other, instigating contempt, ridicule, and social exclusion – in short, mean attitudes trying to empower oneself by denigrating others.[12] This inferior treatment of our people has led to a deeply felt pain. In general, people in Pakistan make space for the pain of others and show compassion. Nevertheless, racism exists and is an insidious disease, so it is pointless to talk about 'less harmful forms of racism' in comparison to other countries.

The term 'race' was coined by the French physician and traveler François Bernier in 1684. In the nineteenth century, it was understood as the biological continuity of an ethnic group. There was a heated debate between the preachers of mankind's 'racial unity' and 'racial plurality'. Since then, in combination with Darwinian concepts of evolution, race has become a highly problematic categorization as it was used to legitimize exploitation and to preserve the good conscience of liberal Europeans who supported colonialism. In the Anglo-Saxon world, the word 'race' is nowadays used in the sense of a social construct, stripped of its main biological components. There it has other layers of meaning and connotations than in continental Europe where the term is heavily loaded due to its historical context. In Germany, 'Rasse' (race) was central to the vocabulary of National Socialists who understood it solely as a biological reality. Instead of 'races,' it is more neutral to speak of 'populations' or 'ethnicities.' For a German, like the chief author of the present study, to speak of 'Rasse' (race) would be crossing the boundary between science and ideology. The discourse in Germany is probably best summarized as: 'The concept of race is the result of racism and not its prerequisite.'[13]

Franz Boas (1858-1942), the German-American father of cultural anthropology, had already emphasized that 'races' do not exist; that variations within such categories, however they are defined, would be more than between such 'imagined races.'[14] Today we know that genetic differences are too marginal to differentiate 'races'. In any case, the use of the term 'race' pretends to draw sharp lines between groups, but in fact strengthens existing hierarchical beliefs of cultural difference. Although the term is above all socially defined, categories of 'race' do correlate to a certain degree with the genetic origins of groups. Nevertheless, with respect to Pakistan and other postcolonial states, the term 'race' has been misused to create a social and political typology by projecting prejudices upon People of Color and to classify populations into racist categories. At least from the perspective of a European, the term just serves the low instinct to stigmatize others.

Racist stereotypes, which poison society, are age-old and widespread across the world and need not be discussed here in depth. Already in ancient complex societies like Sumer and Babylon, the difference between people of the upper and lower strata was expressed in terms of 'the white' and 'the pure' on the one hand and the 'Blacks' or those with 'black heads' on the other.¹⁵ It is therefore sufficient, but also revealing, to quote one of the most prominent figures in the intellectual life of his time, the medieval Islamic philosopher and historian, Abu Ali Ahmad Miskavayh (932-1030), who wrote about practical ethics and humanity.¹⁶ In his *al-Fauz al-Asghar* (The Small Book on Greetings), he disparagingly denotes 'Black Africans' (*al-zanj*, plural *zunūj*, a term used for Bantu-speaking people living on the Swahili coast and in Zangbar/Zanzibar) as 'Negroes' and being slaves by nature who would live almost like beasts and would only be slightly better than apes.¹⁷ With these abusive words, Miskavayh only expressed the current view of his day, negatively imagining 'Blacks' and 'Blackness' contrary to Qur'anic teachings. In his world history *al-Muqaddima*, the famous Arab historian and sociologist, Ibn Khaldun (1332-1406), followed in line describing the 'bestial character' of dark-skinned people.¹⁸ Also in medieval Persian writings from the tenth to the fourteenth centuries, there are extremely negative images of people of color, essentializing them as ugly, stupid, untruthful, excessively merry, and sexually unbridled; most sources, however, do not mention them at all.¹⁹ Similarly, in the European 'Enlightenment period', or the 'Age of Reason', the word 'Negro' suggested barbaric primitivism marked by Black skin color which symbolized sin and damnation. 'Enlightened' Europe with its belief in moral progress created the concept of 'scientific racism' in combination with ideas on human evolution and perfectibility. The works of European thinkers were, in fact, used to justify colonization and racial genocide whereby Black bodies were and still are treated as objects.

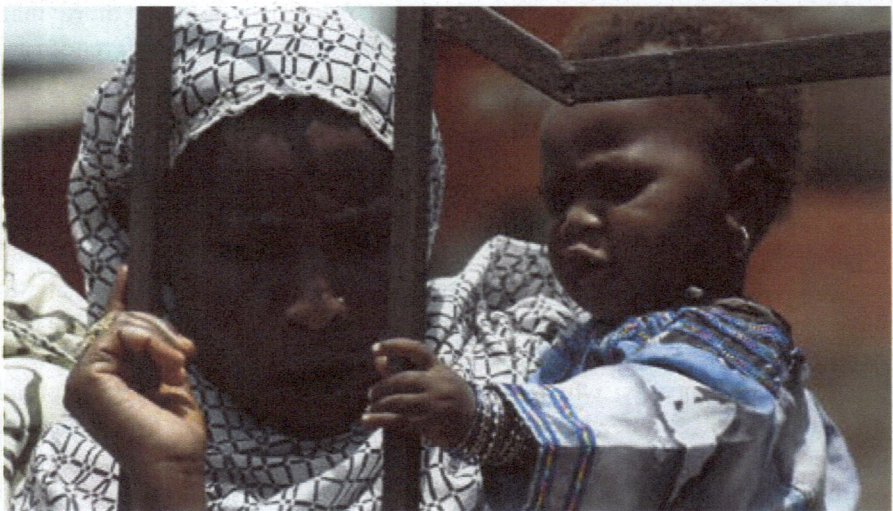

Fig. 7   Mother and child, Karachi (May 2005)

At times in Pakistan, the ethnographer comes across outrageous incidents and shocking commentaries when the race card is played, and 'race is used as an excuse' to explain socio-cultural differences. For example, during my earlier fieldwork in the western Himalayan region of Indus Kohistan the local fair-complexioned Kohistani people contemptuously called dark-complexioned people from the Punjab 'Blacks', associating bad character with this color. At times, Pakhtun also use the word *kāliā*, a racial slur, for Punjabis. In Pakistani society in general, darker complexion is often considered inferior. The authors of a recent investigation on Pakistani women's perceptions regarding skin color found that 'Black or overly Black skin tone in males is less approved and appreciated,' and emphasized: 'A Black skin toned person is many a time teased for being Black because such tone is not esteemed in this culture.'[20]

In fact, what we find nowadays is a kind of 'pigmentocracy,' in the sense of a clear preference for fair skin tone firmly entrenched in social belief. It rules daily life from Pakistan to Thailand where models and actresses proudly present their bleached skin in advertisements and advise prospective brides to stay out of the sun. Skin lightening creams and fairness products dominate the beauty industry in today's consumerist society, now also targeting underprivileged classes of people. The religious studies scholar John O'Brien observed: 'Pakistanis are addicted to skin-lightning creams, some of them injurious to health. No one seems to mind that advertisements on TV and large billboards promoting these products are blatantly racialist.'[21]

The travel-writer Alice Albinia insightfully talked about the daughters of a Shidi community leader in Badin (Lower Sindh) whose family is per se proud of their Blackness: '[…] even they at times succumb to the monolithic Pakistani ideal of beauty. When the eldest daughter comes to be married, every evening for weeks leading up to the ceremonies, she bleaches the skin on face, hands and feet (those parts of her body which will be visible beneath her wedding garments). A pale bride is an obligation for the family – even if everyone knows it is fake. "It is only for the marriage photos," she says apologetically; "otherwise I will be laughed at for my Blackness".'[22] Today girls who are about to get married sometimes even get whitening injections. This colorism is a form of systemic racism deeply entrenched in South Asia and elsewhere.

The young artist Sammi Baloch (a pseudonym), born to a family of 'Black Baloch' (as she says) originally from Gwadar, describes the racist taunts she experienced in England, where she grew up, as well as in Pakistan: 'Every other summer as children, we travelled to my parents' respective homes in Karachi, my dad hailing from the ghettos of Lyari and my mother from poverty-ridden Malir. Both areas are predominantly Baloch (often also spelled 'Baluch'), mostly Black and severely deprived. In the summer of 2004, I was sitting with my cousins when someone pointed out that I was only slightly lighter compared to one of the others, but my hair was nicer. It was a good thing, she remarked that my hair was not still curly like in my baby photos. Then I would have looked more "Raghi" ['bad blood'], like my cousin, who looked "Somali." No one knew that I was endlessly combing out my curls and blow-drying my hair so it could stay straight; in fact, when I got older I would have semi-permanent hair extensions attached so I could hide my curls. They began to taunt my "Somali"-looking cousin and call her names.'

The author adds that skin tones and beauty were constantly discussed among friends and family and finally she confesses: 'I can't remember a time where any of my uncles or aunties ever called me beautiful. "You're light enough not to complain, but dark enough not to marry." These words were said to me in passing once and they stuck to me like glue at the time.'[23]

The ideal correlation between the elite and pale skin (*sāf rang*) probably dates back to the subjugation of dark-complexioned Dravidians by the light-complexioned Aryan invaders and colonizers from Central Asia. In this context, the anthropologist Richard Murphy, who did fieldwork in Pakistan, wrote: 'In Hindu society the fact that lower caste people and untouchables are usually dark skinned is often explained by reference to their supposed Dravidian descent. In Pakistan, similarly, dark skinned people (Christian sweepers, for example) are said to be descended from low caste Hindu converts. Fair skin, on the other hand, is often taken as evidence of Muslim Arab or Central Asian ancestry.'[24] Likewise, O'Brien, who worked on the oppressed caste of dark-skinned Punjabi Christians, drew a line between them and the occupational 'untouchable' group of sweepers in the pre-Aryan Indus Valley civilization and their links to later Hinduism.[25] In Hindu myth the goddess Parvati changes into Gauri, the Golden Girl, to please her light-complexioned husband Shiva.[26] On the subcontinent, racialized thinking was already rooted in the ancient Rig-Veda and filtered into the caste system, later reinforced by European notions of racial hierarchies in times of British colonial rule. Today, Pakistani women and men with 'dusky' skin often feel humiliated as they face the firmly entrenched fairness bias in society. In India, the 'Dark is Beautiful' campaign tries to battle undisguised color prejudices in explaining people that dark skin simply developed in people as an adaptive response to tropical sun.

This obsession with fair skin, apparently shared by the majority of people in Pakistan, forms the backbone of the racist stereotypes faced by

Chapter 1

Fig. 8   Shidi woman in colorful dress at Mangho Pir, Karachi (July 2010)

the indigenous colored population of Karachi and other parts of Sindh and Balochistan as well as in the Punjab. Thus, ethnic groups have been ranked according to physical traits, especially skin color, throughout history. Referring to Baloch of African descent, the eminent Pakistani scholar on social and political affairs, Feroz Ahmed (1940-1997), notes: 'The darker among them are worse off, for the purity of their skin is directly correlated with the failure to climb up socially.'[27]

A telling example of racist stereotyping with 'barbarous' overtones is Sardar Khan Baloch's comment on the Nakib, descendants of slaves brought from Africa, who were made to serve the chiefs of the Gichki Baloch tribe in Makran. He writes: '[…] the Nakibs, in case of whom darkness was and is the dominating hue of the external man both in dress and complexion. Black are their faces, black their dress, they usually paint black their teeth with a permanent dye, even like black animals and to crown their speciality, they are black in deeds. Their refined manners to a great extent cover a truly grand faculty for deceit and debauchery.'[28]

Here the Baloch chief adopts the key element of racist ideology – the assumption of allegedly 'mental' qualities of race. He further elaborates on slave trade with Africa since the seventeenth century: 'The Darzādās, Nakībs and other servile classes in Makurān peculiarised with flat noses, crisped hair, thick protruding lips and colour black as soot, are the descendants of Negro slaves [...].'[29]

Similarly, in conversation with Karachiites belonging to different social strata, from the well-educated elite living in posh localities of Clifton and Defence to simple laborers around Lea Market, Civil Lines, and Soldier Bazaar, people started smiling, grimacing, or responding with a condescending overtone when asked about African-descended communities living nearby. They sometimes pejoratively call their dark-skinned neighbours *dādā* ('grandfather'), a term associated with black skin (*kālā jild*) and frizzy hair (*gungriāle bāl*), *ghulām* ('slave'), *naukar* ('servant'), *syāh* ('black'), or, even worse, insult them as *lūsī* ('thick-lipped') or *laghūr* ('langur monkeys').[30]

In particular, the shapes of their noses and lips and their curly hair are a regular object of ridicule. Thus, Yaqoob Qambrani tellingly notes: 'The dominant people say about our curly hair that it is because we have stolen a sheep belonging to the Prophet Muhammad (peace be upon him) and that he had cursed us therefore.'[31] 'Hajji' narrated to me how he was once mistreated by police upon his arrival in Lahore. Suspecting that he was an African spy, policemen ran their fingers through his hair several times during interrogation and could not get over how curly it was. Telling me about this form of suppression and harassment, which may seem innocent to some observers, and other microaggressions, he ended saying that it would be best to stay at home in Lyari where such things would not happen. These examples show an essential feature of racism, namely to mark certain bodies as inferior by differentiating them from superior ones in order to justify domination.

As far as racist mockery is concerned, the son of my friend 'Baba,' who stayed for a while in the Middle East, told me that he used to work together with Sudanese people. Being aware that *as-sudān* is the plural of the Arabic word *al-aswad* (meaning 'Black'), he asked them how they were treated, for instance, in Egypt where they had earned their livelihood before. He learned that in Cairo they would degradingly be called 'peanuts without shell.' In the 1970s, a dark brown sweet became popular in the city of Multan in south Punjab, since then widely called in Pakistan *Habshī hālwā*; a sweet by the same label is sold in India. *Habshī hālwā* is related to the alleged virility of Africans and said to improve 'performance.'[32] The term itself carries similar racial undercurrents to the French expression *tête de nègre* ('Negro's head') for a chocolate marshmallow. Known in France since the late nineteenth century, this sweet was popularised in Germany in the early twentieth century and translated as *Mohrenkopf* ('Moor's head') and later also called *Negerkuß*

('Negro's kiss'). In Syria it is known as 'slave's head.' In the south German province of Bavaria, a mix of cola and light, fizzy beer made of wheat and malt is served in bars by the name *Neger* ('Negro').

The racist context of *tête de nègre*, *Mohrenkopf*, and *Neger* finds an echo in incidents of ridicule reported by Yaqoob Qambrani from schools in Sindh. He notes: 'Till 1978, the biased behavior towards our children in schools was a major problem in getting education. The lesson with the pronunciation of the letter *shīn* in Sindhi syllabus was specially degrading for us and the impact of it on our children cannot be described in words. In that lesson the phonetics of this letter was accompanied by comparing us Shidis with a matchstick.'[33]

A wealthy and smart businessman residing in Defence earnestly proclaimed when asked about the indigenous people of African descent in Karachi: 'They and their women are all mentally deficient because they take all sorts of drugs.' Listening to such stereotypes and sweeping generalizations, stemming from ethnocentric arrogance, over-estimation of the self plus a clear racial mindset, of positioning a 'pure' 'we' against a 'dirty' 'us', left me speechless. The gentleman in question continued commenting on the Shidis' strong and long back teeth as a physical criterion differentiating them from 'real' Baloch (cf. Chapter II). His friend added that 'these people are all loafers and lead a life of idleness as they used to be slaves.' In Hyderabad I spoke to Sindhi and Baloch women who praised the physical strength and sexual potency of 'Black men,' but also ascribed immorality to them. In fact, promiscuity has long been a negative stereotype attributed to them.[34]

In everyday life it happens that people avoid sharing a meal with our people because they think they would become 'impure' (*nā-pāk*). This belief may be a remnant of the Hindu caste system with its ban on commensality, but it also shows a shocking lack of knowledge. My friends from the Shidi community told me heart-breaking incidences of utter disregard, abuse, and mistreatment only because of looking physically different. Thus, in a class of forty pupils, there were three Shidi boys. After wiping the blackboard, the teacher out of the blue painted chalk across the face of one of them using the dirty duster. This is only one drastic example of how our people are often the target of racial bias. It evokes age-old prejudices expressed in racist sayings by such famous Persian poets as Firdousi (d. 1020 or 1025/26), who wrote 'the Zangi will not turn white by washing,' and Sa'di (d. 1292), who wrote 'nor will a bath make the Zangi white.'[35]

Yaqoob Qambrani highlighted another aspect of everyday discrimination in an interview: 'When anyone from our community boards a public transport bus, everyone else tries to keep at a distance. We are not blind to how others look and treat us.'[36] Moreover, I learned that a feudal lord in Sindh highlighted the status of Shidis in saying: 'They are born to serve us. They have to sit on the ground. When my sons go to school, their satchels are of course carried by a Shidi boy.' The use of taunts and derogatory speech when addressing people of African descent is highlighted again by Sammi Baloch: 'The most brutal word of them all for me is "Raghi" which loosely translates as "Black/Bad Blood," a word that tormented me throughout my childhood.'[37] While the responsibility to avoid racist attitudes lies primarily with the individual, such cases of abuse and belittling indicate a climate of systematic structural oppression.

While wandering around streets and markets in Karachi, I frequently encountered laborers of African descent who seemed intimidated and vulnerable. Often they receive little or no respect in their daily lives. They may internalize feelings of inferiority in reaction to the overall stigmatizing society in which they live and work, where often the inhuman becomes normal. In general, however, the treatment dark-skinned people have to endure in Pakistan is not comparable to parts of the Anglo-Euro-American world where systemic racism ranges from subtle and visceral forms to open hostility.[38]

Lifting the Curtain: Scholarly Viewpoints

In contradistinction to the stereotypes discussed above and to written sources (overviews and works of more general character) with their shortcomings in viewing our people from a historical and anthropological perspective, a few quite informative and unbiased articles on Shidis have been published by Pakistani journalists.[39] For instance, one insightful chapter was written by the historian and columnist Nadeem Farooq Paracha on the people of African descent in Lyari, the largest, in parts slum-like working class settlement of Karachi.[40] Likewise, the chapter entitled 'Ethiopia's First Fruit' in Alice Albinia's travelogue *Empires of the Indus* (2008) is instructive as far as the history and culture of Shidis is concerned. It is especially meritorious that the author could draw on the autobiography of Muhammad Siddiq Musafir, referred to in more detail in Chapter III. Albinia's work proves that travel writing is not necessarily a lowbrow genre as often seen by scholars. The well-illustrated and well-researched book *Karachiwala*, written and published in 2010 by Rumana Husain, also starts with extensive sympathetic portrayals of Shidi and Makrani people in the city.[41] Finally, the German writer Ilija Trojanow has given Shidis a voice in his novel on the life of the

Chapter 1

Fig. 9 Shidi woman donning an indigo-dyed shawl, Karachi (January 2017)

Fig. 10 Pir Bakhsh, a Shidi dignitary and teacher in Tando Bago, Sindh (February 2018)

British explorer, officer, and colonialist Sir Richard F. Burton in the figure of 'Sidi Mubarak Bombay.'[42]

As far as the purely academic body of work on the anthropology and history of Shidis is concerned, there are some excellent books and articles on the African diaspora in the Indian Ocean world in general and on the East African slave trade to Asia in particular, as well as on the veneration of Shidi Sufi saints in parts of west India.[43] Additionally, there is a magnificent book of photographs on the Sidis of Indian Gujarat including a well-written introduction.[44] These works will be referred to in the present volume.

Compared to India, research on Pakistanis of African descent, particularly on Shidis, has been rather neglected. Part of 'grey literature' and therefore hard to trace is a paper kept in the archive of Lok Virsa in Islamabad from 1976. Although the author pursues a scholarly approach, he depicts the 'ebony-skinned, thick-lipped man with a head of extremely curly hair' as 'funny,' as 'wretched people' and condemns them with a final blow stating 'the Shidi is a homosexual.'[45] Such use of judgmental adjectives reflects a general tendency in South Asia and thus not only belongs to the matrix of the white man's colonial gaze. In 1989, Feroz Ahmed published an excellent pioneering article on 'Africa on the Coast of Pakistan,' and in 1999, the socio-linguist Shemeem Burney Abbas conducted some interviews with female musicians of the Shidi community in Karachi Mori, a village situated close to Jamshoro in interior Sindh.[46] There is also an unpublished M.Sc. thesis in anthropology from Quaid-i-Azam University Islamabad dated 2006 as well as a little booklet on the role of Shidis in Sindhi history, originally written as a BA thesis and also not easily accessible.[47]

Originating from seven readings in Urdu recorded by my friend Akhtar Soomro, Sheedi Yaqoob Qambrani's unpublished treatise on his people stands out as a voice from within, reflecting and defending the perspective of the all too often overlooked people of African descent, also ignored by historians in Pakistan. In the present volume I have, with his permission, included the insightful subchapter on the Shidi festival at the shrine of Mangho Pir augmenting it with further ethnographic material.[48] Qambrani is a literate guardian of Shidi culture who presents native interpretations of its traditions (Fig. 3, 60). He rightly calls for the recognition of Shidis in Pakistani society. Of scholarly merit is the work done by several anthropologists such as Carroll and Stephen Pastner on Makrani Balochistan. There exist references to groups of people with African ancestry doing menial jobs, Farhat Sultana's observations on spirit healing in Makran, Sabir Badalkhan's short but insightful account on African music in coastal Balochistan, and in particular Helene Basu's article on 'ritual kinship performances of the African diaspora' focusing on the *'urs* celebration of Mai Mishra in Karachi.[49] Basu, who has done fundamental work on the Indian Sidi community in Gujarat, convincingly argues that the memory around 'Africa' as their place of origin is of major importance in all ritual performances involving music, dance, gestures, related to the veneration of African ancestor saints. In this way African identity is constructed through processes of common remembering grounded in the body.'[50] The author shows that the cult of both male and female saints developed in response to values of the host society and represents a 'subcultural context constructed by the African diaspora.'[51] Recently, I published a visual essay with descriptive notes which provides a brief glimpse into the everyday life of the Shidi community in Karachi.[52]

Endnotes

1   Halliday 1990: 144.
2   Basu 2003: 225; De Silva Jayasuriya & Pankhurst 2003b: 8; De Silva Jayasuriya 2009: 21-22.
3   Baptiste 2008: 121.
4   Basu 1995: 14, 43, 56, 57 (endnote 3).

5   Amin 1992.
6   Amin & Willetts & Hancock 1982: 230 ('The Makranis [...] have pronouncedly Negroid/Hamitic features [...]'). Cf. also Janmahmad 1982: 72 ('Arab traders brought Negroes [...]'; 'All the slaves belonged either to the indigenous population of Negroes [...]') and Qazi 1988: 15-16 ('The Negroes [in Sindh] [...] are very good dancers'). Such pejorative statements were, of course, common in the colonial period, see for instance: Burton 1877: 104 ('Zanzibar negroids'), 103-105 (this paragraph is tellingly entitled 'The Negro dance'); Hughes 1877: 138 ('Negro slaves are numerous [...] at Sonmiani'), 45 (referring to slavery throughout Balochistan, the author mentions male and female slaves and writes: 'The greater number are Sidis, or Negroes from Maskat [...]').
7   Malik & Schimmel 1976: 166 ('Die Makrani [...] die oft negroide Züge haben [...]').
8   See, for example, the otherwise comprehensive Bertelsmann dictionary *Die Völker der Erde* (Gütersloh & Munich 1992) as well as the encyclopedia *Völker der Vierten Welt* (Munich et al. 1981).
9   Mills & Claus & Diamond 2003: 148-150. In this encyclopedia only half a sentence is found on the 'Siddis or Habshis' in the context of the entry 'Roma (Gypsy)' (p. 522). In addition, the Abyssinian saint Bava Ghor is mentioned briefly (p. 393).
10 Lieven 2011.
11 Qaimkhani 1996: 64.
12 This is also emphasized by Malik (2002, p. 12) in his report on religious minorities in Pakistan.
13 This is the wording of the Jena declaration on 15 September 2019, publicized on the 112th meeting of the German Zoological Society in Jena, Germany (in fact, at the University of Jena the zoologist and philosopher Ernst Haeckel [1834-1919], the 'German Darwin,' formulated his ideas on 'human races' later promulgated by the Nazis). The scholars of biology and palaeogenetics stated that there is not a single gene in man justifying 'racial' differences, not even a single base pair among 3.2 billions of base pairs in the human genome. In reality borders are fluid.
14 Boas 1922: 94.
15 Müller 2020: 10.
16 Jamal al-Din 1994.
17 Harvey 1992: 41. For a detailed discussion of the negative image of 'Blacks' and 'Blackness,' see Baptiste 2008: 136-159. Cf. also Fartacek 2014: 577.
18 N'Diaye 2010: 49.
19 Southgate 1984: 8-26; cf. Gholi & Ahmadi Musaabad 2015 (focusing on negative prejudices on people of color in Sa'di's *Gulistan*).
20 Zubair & Ali & Akhtar 2020: 409, 411.
21 O'Brien 2012: 41, footnote 47; cf. Albinia 2008: 61.
22 Albinia 2008: 68.

23 Baloch 2020.
24 Murphy 1994; cf. Kooria 2020: 353.
25 O'Brien 2012: 17-21, cf. 26 (on serving men of the 'black race'), 66 (on 'dark-faced' Chuhras); cf. Harris 1971: 115-116.
26 Doniger 1980: 93, 98, 111.
27 Ahmed 1989: 27.
28 Sardar Khan Baluch 1958: 235, cf. 176.
29 Sardar Khan Baluch 1958: 182. Also in colonial government records it is stated about the Darzadas and Nakibs of Makran: '[…] many of them show signs of African blood in the short curly hair and thick lips. Their skin is a dark copper colour and not uncommonly quite black' (Gazetteer Balochistan 1906: 565).
30 Cf. for instance the negative portrayals of Africans in current populist narratives and in consequence the racial behavior towards Africans, especially Nigerians in India; thus, Niha Masih writes: 'Africans in India live with racism every day. Slurs such as "monkey" and "kalu" (black) are literally thrown at them; they are often asked whether they eat human beings. African men are perceived to be drug dealers, and women are seen as prostitutes' (2017: 1). Cf. also Pozdena 1978: 58; Fabietti 1996: 8; Badalkhan 2008: 277.
31 Qambrani 2017: 16.
32 Robbins & McLeod 2006a: 248, ill. no. 314 (see caption).
33 Qambrani 2017: 13.
34 Cf. Basu 1995: 56.
35 Southgate 1984: 10.
36 Shadi Khan Saif 2020.
37 Baloch 2020.
38 For a discussion on racism in South Asia, see Kooria 2020. The author notes an unwillingness to acknowledge the issue of racism in this region and in general across Asia, 'where questions of racism are not even conceded, let alone addressed concretely' (Kooria 2020: 352).
39 For example: Rashdi 1992; Qureshi 1993; Fatah 2005.
40 Paracha 2018: 69-78 (chapter entitled 'Their Man from Africa').
41 Husain 2010: 15-26.
42 Trojanow 2006: chapter on East Africa, nearly throughout pages 368 to 505.
43 For example: Harris 1971; Basu 1995; Basu 2008; De Silva Jayasuriya & Pankhurst 2003a; Catlin-Jairazbhoy & Alpers 2004; Robbins & McLeod 2006a; Prasad & Angenot 2008; De Silva Jayasuriya 2009; Ali 2011.
44 Sheth 2013. For contemporary pictures of Afro-Iranians, see the photo-book by Ehsaei (2015), for historical ones from Qajar Iran, see Khosronejad 2017.
45 Rahman 1976: 17; cf. Basu 1995: 47; Basu 2000: 265-266.
46 Ahmed 1989; Abbas 2002: 36-46.
47 Rahman 1976; Nizamani 2006; Khalique 2009.
48 These readings by Yaqoob Qambrani, which were partly based on written notes compiled from sources in Urdu and Sindhi (published by Siddiq Musa-

fir and Qaimkhani, see bibliography) as well as on his own knowledge about different topics of Shidi history and culture (such as the role of the ritual drum *muggarmān* and on the 'urs of Mangho Pir), were encouraged by me and recorded in several sessions in 2014 by Akhtar Soomro in the form of interviews conducted at Karachi Press Club. In 2016, I was able to raise money for the English translation of these recordings through the Goethe Institute in Karachi. I especially thank Stefan Winkler, then director of the institute, for his kind help and keen interest in my research on Africans in Pakistan. Aslam Khwaja did the translation into English in 2017. The manuscript in question is henceforward referred to as: Qambrani 2017.

49 See the articles by Carroll and Stephen Pastner listed in the bibliography; Sultana 1996; Badalkhan 2008; Basu 2000 (the author conducted field-research on the Shidis of Sindh during a period of three months in 1994 and 1995).
50 Basu 2000: 265.
51 Basu 2000: 266.
52 Frembgen 2020.

Fig. 11   Young women in Lyari, Karachi (November 2010)

2

Regional Settings and Identities: On the Complex Picture of People of African Descent

Introduction

In my attempt to obtain an overview of the distribution of our people in Pakistan, I primarily rely on oral information gathered in conversations, considering the paucity of written sources. People with African roots are widely dispersed over Sindh and littoral Balochistan; some may have also settled in Punjab and Khyber Pakhtunkhwa.[1] Although more detailed information can be given about their living spaces and settlements in Karachi, this is almost impossible with respect to other parts of Sindh and particularly to Balochistan, a region almost inaccessible to foreigners in recent decades. The picture is equally complex as far as various ethnonyms as well as regional and ethnic identities are concerned. One of my esteemed interlocutors in Karachi, 'Nawab,' emphasized in response to my questions that 'of course, not all people with an African physiognomy belong to the Shidi community and not all of them venerate African ancestor saints.' Many people with African roots are Baloch like himself, he said, or Sindhi-speaking Khaskelis, but all of them would be descendants of the Abyssinian Hazrat Bilal, the first *mu'azzin* (mosque official who announces the call to prayer) of Prophet Muhammad, and hence Habshis. As far as their physical appearance is concerned, they show a wide range of variation in skin color and facial features indicating different places of origin in Africa, from Ethiopia further south to east and central Africa.[2]

Following the anthropologist's scholarly interest in internal differentiation of populations, this chapter first tries to present an overview of the regional distribution of Africans in Pakistan before discussing the problematic issue of ethnonyms and ethnic labels as well as language diversity and identities.

Living Spaces and Settlements

Today the port city and trading center of Karachi is probably inhabited by about 25 million people. Originating as a village of fishermen, it grew since the eighteenth century into a small town then considered of little importance. When occupied by soldiers of the British colonial empire in 1839, its population was estimated at around 14,000; in 1856, it had already increased to almost 57,000, and in 1881 reached a total of 68,000.[3] Throughout the twentieth century, particularly after the Partition of the subcontinent in 1947, the city attracted huge numbers of refugees from India as well as migrants from all over Pakistan. Subsequently, it became the hub of commercial activities and grew exponentially into one of the largest cities of the world. In vernacular Urdu, this city of migrants is often called *gharīboṅ kī māṅ*, 'mother of the poor.'

People of African descent, who merged into the cosmopolitan urban jungle of Karachi, live mainly in Lyari, a huge, densely populated, and impoverished suburb of dock laborers, industrial workers, and craftsmen situated just outside the ancient walled city areas of Kharadar ('salt-water gate') and Mithadar ('sweet-water gate') chiefly inhabited by merchants. This inner-city working-class settlement near the seaport is the oldest in Karachi, named after a seasonal river on the city's western boundary or more precisely after the *lyār* trees growing there in the olden days.[4] In the words of the sociologist Haris Gazdar, Lyari 'was literally a settlement inside the delta of the old river. When the river occasionally rose in flood, the settlement would be inundated.'[5] Lyari is also proudly called by its inhabitants *Karāchī kī māṅ*, 'mother of Karachi.' Today, Lyari Town (the official name since 2001) has a population of around 1.5 million.[6] It is a melting pot of peoples and cultures; since the late nineteenth century, many people migrated in the wake of famines from Iranian Balochistan, Makran, Las Bela, and the erstwhile princely state of Kachchh (Kutch) in Indian Gujarat. As a considerable number of our people live in Lyari, it is sometimes also called 'Little Africa' or 'Karachi's Harlem.'

Adjacent to Lea Market, a historic landmark constructed by the British engineer Measham Lea in 1927 at the crossing of seven major roads, there is the old Shidi Goth, a former urban village today considered to be part of the Lyari quarter of Juna-Kumharwara. This rather narrow and elongated space located between Lea Market and Ath Chowk was the original home of African people; many still live there, for instance around two major shrines of their ancestor saints. In the southeast it borders on the quarter of Chakiwara and in the northwest on 'Shidi Village Road,' an important artery of Lyari congested by heavy traffic, above all buses shuttling between Karachi and different parts of Balochistan. Opposite is the quadrangular-shaped quarter of Baghdadi, so-to-speak the heart of Lyari and home of most of our people in the city. Like the adjacent quarters, it was founded around 1875; originally a *bastī* (urban slum-like settlement), it is now in terms of size a small town within Lyari.[7] It consists of several intimate neighborhoods such as Juna-Baghdadi, the oldest part, with '*Arabī Shīdī masjid* and little Bumbasa (Mombasa) street, as well as Seypilen (Saifi Lane), Umarabad, Qasarqandi (named after Qasr-e Qand, a place in Iranian Balochistan), Khushkalat, and Basra Colony.

Apart from Baghdadi, our people also live in the adjacent quarters of Shah Baig Lane, Singu Lane, Gul Muhammad Lane, and Musa Lane which first appear on maps after 1895; one year before Lyari was ravaged by the plague.[8] Inhabitants of Baghdadi still remember from their forefathers that 'in the past,' or in the second half of the nineteenth century, the Arabic sea still reached close to the western border of their settlement, up to (Atma Ram) Pritam Das Road, now called (Shah Abdul Latif) Bhitai Road. Hence the new Lyari quarters of Daryabad and Nayabad, both situated on the borders of Baghdadi towards the ocean, were developed in the 1930s and 1940s on land reclaimed from the sea. In Nayabad, for instance, there are some thirty to thirty-five families whose ancestors came from Africa. Shidis also settle in the neighborhood of Gazdarabad in Ranchore Lines as well as in Soldier Bazaar. However, many of our people live in low-income areas on the outskirts of Karachi such as Baldia Town, Seydabad, Mohajir Camp, Agra Taj Colony, Yusuf Goth, Gudni Goth, Moach Goth, and Hab Chowki. They are all situated in the western part of the city not far from Mauripur, the harbor, and the large industrial zone, as well as in Mangho Pir (around 500 people)[9] in the northwest and in Malir (Chaman Colony) in the east. 'Habshi Colony' in Baldia Town was settled in the early 1970s and originally consisted of about 250 houses.

As for housing conditions, people told me that in the beginning they lived in mud huts with thatched roofs. This echoes the British explorer, officer, and orientalist Sir Richard Francis Burton's (1821-1890) description in 1851 that 'the native town is a miserable collection of wattle huts and mud houses, clustering round the ruined walls of a native fort.'[10] In the words of Latif

Baloch, a renowned journalist from Lyari, 'until the sixties, the houses of Lyari were made of tamarisk wood and mud. Bricks and mortar houses were few and far between [...]. The majority of houses were without electricity.'[11] Gradually, in the course of the second half of the twentieth century, huts and makeshift houses were replaced by solid (*pakkā*) houses of stone or unplastered concrete blocks, some small and single-storied, others larger. In the 1970s and 1980s, Lyari saw a construction boom. Those who had become wealthy started to build five- to seven-story blocks with apartments rented out to people with low income.[12] However, many of our people still live on subsistence level in small airless accommodations with sackcloth partitions between rooms.

To map Africans living in other parts of Sindh, we next look at Hyderabad, the ancient capital of the province. There is a small Shidi Goth or Quarter, inhabited by about thirty to forty families near the quarter of Qasimabad. More Shidis are said to live scattered across the city as well as in nearby Tando Qaisar. Another settlement, with 1,253 people according to census data, is part of the predominantly Baloch village of Rajo Nizamani close to Tando Muhammad Khan, a town southeast of Hyderabad.[13] Apart from Hyderabad, the town of Tando Bago (with about 30,000 inhabitants), situated in the southeast of Lower Sindh, is known to have a sizeable Shidi community. When I visited Tando Bago on 12 February 2018 accompanied by my friend Aslam Khwaja, local Shidi dignitaries told us that there were some one thousand families of their community who were settled mainly in the first and second section of the town consisting of altogether nine sections (*wards*). Considerably smaller in number are Shidi communities in Sujawal, a town situated in the south of the province not far from Tando Bago. There fifty to sixty families live in the neighborhood of Haqqabad.

In the small town of Bulri, the 'Black population' is estimated at around eighty to ninety families, in Bhit Shah about forty to fifty families, and in Umarkot twelve to fourteen families. From information gathered through friends and acquaintances as well as personal observation, I received the impression that there are many towns and villages throughout Sindh with at least a small population of people with African roots, such as Kotri, Sehwan, Matli, Mirpur Pathoro, Pir Patho, and even remote villages in the Thar desert and small towns like Mithi, Kunri, Naukot, and Islamkot.

Chapter 2

Fig. 12   Girl in Balochi dress; Lyari, Karachi (January 2017)

As mentioned, not much information is available about our people living in Balochistan, the vast land situated between the Iranian plateau and the Indus plains, particularly in the coastal region of Makran (the Pakistani portion alone covers an area of about 23,000 sq. miles) and in Las Bela. In antiquity, the hot, sandy Makran is said to have been inhabited by the 'Icthyophagoi,' 'fish eaters,' encountered by Alexander the Great. Some later historians deduced the origin of 'Makran' from Persian *māhī-khōran*, although this etymology is not accepted by philologists; in fact, a Dravidian origin of this word, namely 'Maka,' seems more likely.[14] While Makran was a sub-division of the Khanate of Kalat for two centuries, it became a Baloch princely state under the rule of local chiefs in the colonial period. In 1948, at the time of accession to Pakistan, the Nawab of the Gichki tribe was declared Wali of Makran.[15] The region is located at the crossroads of multiple cultural influences: from the ancient indigenous Indus Valley culture to nomadic Baloch tribes who migrated from northwest Iran. Regular contacts were also maintained with Arabia (especially Oman) and Africa.

A large part of the population living along the sea coast and in the arid interior has African roots. Farhat Sultana notes: 'The third major subgroup in coastal Makran consists of the Sheedi and Ghulam who are the descendants of Black slaves […].'[16] Feroz Ahmed specifies: 'There, anywhere from 10 to

20 percent of the population has clear African features, while even a larger number with lighter skin have an African admixture.'[17]

According to the anthropologist Nina Swidler: 'About 30 per cent of the population of Makran are landless labourers. Known as *hizmatkar* ['dependents'; author's note, JWF], they are the descendants of slaves brought from East Africa, war captives, and perhaps some impoverished Baloch as well.'[18] This landless group of menial workers also included fishermen, craftsmen, story-tellers, and domestic servants.[19] As argued by Aliya Iqbal Naqvi and Hasan Ali Khan, the influx of people of African descent could have already started in the ninth century after the Zanj rebellion in southern Iraq (see the respective subchapter in Chapter II). This historic incident might have played a critical role in the initial settlement of free Africans along the Balochistan littoral.

Makran alone has a 200-mile coastline and throughout history played a key role in maritime trade in the Persian Gulf and Indian Ocean. This region, with its many small harbor towns and maritime villages was a bridge between Iran, the Indian subcontinent, and Oman all the way to Zanzibar and Mombasa. However, people of African descent also live in oasis settlements in the hinterland of Makran, for instance in Panjgur and Kech, in Kharan (north of Makran, formerly a quasi-independent tribal area belonging to the Khanate of Kalat), in Kalat in interior Balochistan, as well as in Las Bela (both former native princely states).[20]

Ethnonyms and Ethnic Labels

In the following section, ethnonyms and exonyms, self-designations and ethnic labels, as well as names with derogatory connotations imposed by others on populations with distinctive African features, will be discussed. It goes without saying that, apart from self-designations, labels always remain problematic. Although, in the words of the American anthropologist Miles Richardson, 'no matter how hard we try we cannot escape labeling and being labeled. Labeling is as much a part of us as shells are a part of turtles.'[21]

From an anthropological point of view, it must be emphasized that the terms in question, at present common in the south of Pakistan, are not to be understood as strict ethnic identifiers. As the category 'Habshi,' already explained in Chapter I, simply denotes people with African roots, rather than referring to any particular ethnic group, it is not listed here again. The nomenclature examined below refers to historically and linguistically differentiated diasporic communities. Self-designations therein clearly mirror the struggle over identity. We observe that in empirical reality mixture, overlapping (as a natural state in this world), and permeability play an important role. Thus, particularly among the population of the Makran coast, there is a remarkable fluidity and openness in accepting African descent and cultural heritage.

The first and foremost ethnonym used in Sindh is 'Shidi' and refers to members of the Shidi *jam'āt* (community, congregation). Their leaders, such as the late Hajji Ghulam Akbar Shidi, understand this term as a *nisba* and hence an ethnic marker emphasizing their African roots. Likewise, Yaqoob Qambrani is proud to be Black and to be a Shidi.[22] He uses 'Shidi' in a self-empowering gesture as a title attached to his given name as was done for centuries.[23] Throughout Sindh, African communities in general call themselves and are named by others 'Shidi' or 'Shiddhi,' in Makran also 'Siddi.' There is, for instance, in Karachi an organization by the name 'Kathiawadi Shidi Muslim Habshi Jamaat' (in Baldia), a Gujarati-speaking group with the self-designation 'Shidi Jamnagarwale' (based in Musa Lane), as well as other social and political organizations using 'Shidi' as marker of their ethnic identity. Thus, similarly to the Jews, they have not decided to rename themselves or to veil their origins.

Nevertheless, in conversation, Hajji Ghulam Akbar Shidi and other spokesmen of their community admitted that the term 'Shidi' throughout Sindh is associated with inferior social status and often used as a term of abuse with connotations of being 'Black,' 'African,' or a 'slave.'[24] He added that it was even used as a swearword of medium or strong intensity, especially in Karachi. Thus, because of its association with slavery, it is perceived by many people of the community as a pronounced racial classification. Although 'Shidi' is the original self-designation of our people carrying strong historic connotations to Africa, it remains a highly contested term.

In Sindh, there are people of African descent using the self-designation 'Khaskeli,' literally meaning 'special service' (*khās kēl*). Khaskelis are regarded as a Sindhi *zāt* (caste-like group) consisting of several subgroups, one of them with obvious African roots. At times the latter also call themselves Shidis. Some of those with whom I had the chance to talk in interior Sindh as well as in Karachi explained that because of their African physiognomy they must have come from Africa in the past, although they had no memory of this. Many said that their forefathers migrated from Las Bela to different parts of Sindh including Karachi. They speak Sindhi. Most are poor or belong to the lower middle class. Most of them may have had a slave background and worked as servants for local rulers.[25]

Feroz Ahmed calls the Khaskelis an 'indigenous slave or near-slave' *zāt*.[26] This colonial emphasis on slavery has to be taken with a pinch of salt as we do not possess concrete information on the personal lives of those people reaching the country now known as Pakistan. As further examined in our chapter on history by Aliya Iqbal Naqvi and Hasan Ali Khan, slavery is only one of several historical factors that contributed to the presence of our people in what is now the south of Pakistan. Thus, we can assume that free men and women of African descent also migrated to Makran and Sindh after the Zanj rebellion in southern Iraq.

Apart from that, Khaskelis and Baloch with African roots settled on the Makran coast which remind us of the historian Shihan de Silva Jayasuriya's general observation that 'assimilation, largely through intermarriage, has made it difficult to distinguish Africans from other ethnic groups. Successful cultural assimilation makes it difficult to identify Asians with African ancestry today' and (in cases such as those described above) 'assimilation has led to a blurring of "Africanness" and migrants have lost their "otherness".'[27] Thus, more than other groups of African descent, Khaskelis constitute an amalgam. When I asked some of them in Karachi as well as in Bhit Shah and Hyderabad, they said that they did not know anything about Bava Ghor and other Shidi saints, but would pay allegiance to various Sufi saints. However, all of them venerate Hazrat Bilal.

As they have often lost or suppressed African cultural traditions, Shidis do not consider them as part of their *jam'āt*. Khaskelis often even deny any African connection (in this way resembling other urban marginal communities, such as the Ghorbat in Afghanistan who deny their origins in peripatetic, nomadic groups) and instead emphatically claim their identity as Sindhis. Keeping in mind prejudices and stereotypes towards dark skin-color and their obvious African roots, this process of cultural assimilation surely helped them integrate into their host society. To clarify their ancestry, we may designate them as 'Afro-Sindhis' (see below for a brief discussion of such umbrella terms).

Many of our people living in Karachi, particularly in Baloch-dominated Lyari, come from Makran and Las Bela in Balochistan and identify themselves as Baloch. Examining this eagerness to adopt local Baloch ethnic affiliation and to become assimilated into Baloch tribal communities, one needs to take into account – at least with respect to those who were deported as slaves from Africa – that their self-worth was severely shattered and needed to be restored and redeemed. They wanted to look forward and not to be burdened with the past. They also must have been mentally overwhelmed by dominant

Baloch culture after they reached the rugged Makran coast, its hinterland of deserts and mountains and its searing heat. With the passage of time and as a concomitant of Baloch nationalism, which has downplayed tribal identities since the 1930s, people of African origin were accepted as Baloch in large part because they speak Balochi.[28] Sabir Badalkhan emphasized with respect to Makran: 'The Black population is completely absorbed in the Baluch ethno-linguistic group.'[29] Hence they avoid the ethnonym 'Shidi,' probably used earlier, and instead add the *nisba* 'Baloch' to their personal names.[30]

Regarding the question 'Who, then are the Baloch?', the British anthropologist Brian Spooner aptly notes: '[…] all Baluch – despite obvious differences in occupation and status – agree on what it means to be Baluch,' and he further emphasizes 'A Baluch is one who calls himself Baluch, and no one who is not Baluch will so call himself,' adding 'anyone is Baluch who fits into the Baluch political structure.'[31] Thus there is no doubt about the Balochness of people of African descent who were assimilated into Baloch society.

Drawing on Baloch nationalist discourse with its emphasis on an inclusive Baloch identity, tribal *aslī* ('true', 'pure-blooded') Baloch, with whom I discussed the subject in question, stressed that in Lyari, 'all people are the same,' 'we are all equal,' and 'also those of Black skin color belong to us.' They pointed out that the name 'Shidi' is perceived as 'nigger' in Lyari. Tellingly, the Urdu poet Noon Meem Danish,[32] who grew up in Lyari, graduated in Urdu from Karachi University, and migrated in 2000 to New York, confessed in an interview: 'I proudly say that I'm Baloch. But when someone from my community calls me a *sheedi*, they're actually calling me a "nigger".'[33] Thus, in Lyari, despite its noble origins as an honorific appellation for the descendants of Prophet Muhammad, the ethnonym 'Shidi' is almost unmentionable. Many of 'our people' living in Lyari therefore emphasize their Balochness and frequently deny their African descent, especially those of mixed ancestry. But, as Aslam Baloch from Tando Bago said: 'Everyone knows that we are descendants of Africans.' The historian and political scientist Laurent Gayer also mentioned that although 'they are now part of the larger Baloch society, [they are] well below the tribal Baloch.'[34]

The latter also designate them at times, within Lyari, as 'Shidi Baloch,' while Urdu-speaking Mohajirs disparagingly call them 'Kale Baloch' (Black Baloch).[35] Apart from this subordinate position within the Baloch social hierarchy, they are still discriminated against because of their skin color. According to an elderly Rind Baloch with whom I conversed, some younger people have only recently begun to call themselves 'Shidi' and are developing a sense of self-confidence, following the example of Sindhi-speaking Shidis settled on the outskirts of Karachi, in Seydabad and Baldia, some of whom are well-educated. These Shidis realized that, despite the discriminating experience of 'Blackness' in Pakistan, their history of migration, survival, talents, and accomplishments can also be considered a source of pride rather than shame. Hence also the people of African descent among the Baloch, whom we may call 'Afro-Baloch,' venerate their African ancestor saints and write their names on the walls of their shrines (!), such as Shidi Mukhtiar, Shidi La'l Badshah, Shidi Bilal, and Shidi Sahibo. When I became familiar with them over the years, many frankly admitted their adherence to the Shidi *jamā't*. Thus, as among people with African roots in India, the name 'Shidi' appears as a term of immense religious, historical, and cultural importance with no neat boundaries. One Afro-Baloch from Shah Baig Lane in Lyari, who plays a leading role in processions and saints' festivals, talked about *hamāra silsila* (our chain, genealogy) and praised their patron saint Bava Ghor (already briefly mentioned afore in the introduction).

Fig. 13   Imran, a young Baloch of African descent, enjoying a cup of tea; Baghdadi in Lyari, Karachi (November 2017)

Here it needs to be clarified that hyphenated terms like 'Afro-Baloch' and 'Afro-Sindhis' are artificial descriptive categories based on descent and physical features (genetic imprint). They are, of course, not intended to stigmatize; on the contrary, the prefix 'Afro' is intended to point to the fact that Baloch and Sindhis with African roots are not peoples 'without history,' but with their own perspectives, narratives, and cultures. At present our people would hardly call themselves such. Nevertheless, in conversations, local intellectuals from Lyari conceded to the use of these terms in academic contexts. Prof. Ghulam Husain Hajjisar, for instance, told me that he has no objections against the term 'Afro-Baloch' or even 'Afro-Pakistani'[36] as he is proud to be a Pakistani Muslim as well as of his African roots.

For him as well as for the chief author of this book, such umbrella terms (similarly to the newly invented 'Afropean' in Europe[37]) do not imply an artificial homogeneity but indicate plural identity. The journalist and writer Latif Baloch showed me an article written by him in Urdu entitled *Afrika ke Baloch!* Likewise, Aslam Khwaja also uses the term Afro-Baloch in his works and the musicologist Jean During writes about 'African Baloch.'[38] In reality, there is a lot of ethnic mixture and overlapping, rather than fixed ethnic boundaries between groups. Often Africanness is not emphasized and only becomes visible to a certain extent (see for instance the features of daughters born from a man from the Kolwah tribe and his wife who is a Baloch from Gwadar).[39] However, contrary to the Rind Baloch's moral statement, *aslī* Baloch and other Karachiites sometimes condescendingly just call dark-complexioned people among them 'Makrani.'

According to Khurshid Qaimkhani, in Balochistan people of African descent are known as Makranis although they themselves prefer to be called Baloch.[40] Throughout Sindh, 'Makrani' is the most widespread stereotypical name for our people imposed by others. Thus, it is an example of external labeling in which essentialising is all-pervasive. Theoretically, it could be used as a *nisba*, denoting the indigenous people of Makran in coastal Balochistan, although, of course, not all of them are descendants of former slaves.[41]

However, Makranis and Shidis are perceived by outsiders as one and the same, while the former, heavily loaded term is felt to be more degrading, carrying the connotation of being a 'Negro.'[42] For instance, when I asked several inhabitants of Sukkur, a town situated at the river Indus in the north of Sindh, about the local Makrani neighborhood, they immediately designated the 'lowly people' living there as 'fishermen, dancers, and drunkards.' Likewise, people of the Makrani neighborhood in Sehwan Sharif are called by others in town 'Makrani Baloch' and a 'mixed *nasab*' (population) to mark their difference to 'real Baloch' or 'ethnic Baloch.' These negative connotations are despite the word 'Makrani' originally merely indicating a region. 'Makrani' is in any case a heavily loaded term.

The American anthropologists Stephen and Carroll Pastner, who did fieldwork in littoral Balochistan, explained: 'The often Negroid appearance of Makrani menial classes derives from the African slave trade. Since it is this group that makes up the bulk of migrants from the area, urban Pakistanis who encounter these impoverished refugees often characterize all Makranis as *habshi*, or Blacks.'[43] Albinia adds: 'Whatever their exact genetic make-up, the Negroid Makranis who have intermarried with local tribes, taken local names and adopted local customs, prefer to forget, ignore or deny their ancestors' origins. Partly, this reflects the extent to which they have been assimilated into Baloch society. But it is also symptomatic of the stigma that Negroid features carry in this society.'[44]

In Sindh, the term 'Makrani' is indiscriminately applied to all dark-skinned people who migrated to this province from different parts of Balochistan as well as from Iran. According to oral tradition, the Makrani neighborhood of Sehwan Sharif was founded some eight generations ago, probably in the early nineteenth century, by a Rind Baloch from the village of Mand near Sarawan in the Iranian part of Balochistan. He is thought to have arrived with a group of pilgrims and set up the first huts.[45] Also in later periods, relatives of these Rind Baloch, whose physiognomy appears African, migrated from there to the Makrani neighborhood of Sehwan Sharif. This was confirmed by an old lady I spoke to, who emphasized that she was born near Sarawan and reached Sindh before Pakistan was created.

In southern Balochistan another humiliating name imposed on our people is 'Gadra' which means 'half-breed,' or in Sindhi 'Gaddo,' 'mixed.'[46] Thus, it is written in the Gazetteer of 1907 for Las Bela: 'The Gadras [...] constitute the descendants of the slave population of Las Bela. It is impossible not to recognise their African type of features and there can be no doubt that they are descended from slaves in the importation of whom the Memans [Memon; author's note, JWF] or Khojas of Sonmiáni were formerly engaged. A large portion of the Gadras were set free by their masters from time to time, and now (1906) occupy an entire village close to Béla.'[47] The population of the town of Las Bela is said to have been 4,183 in 1907, 'and consists chiefly of Gadras.'[48] Some 'Gadras' may later have called themselves 'Khaskeli' when they migrated to different parts of Sindh, although, as history and ethnography shows, such newly invented names usually do not change the social prestige of groups treated by society as the 'disreputable poor.'[49]

Baloch society developed as a function of the interaction of nomadic pastoralists and the local settled communities.[50] Within the 'feudal' social structure characteristic for Makran, there are landless people (many of African descent) doing menial jobs who are categorized as the lowest class. Those are called 'Darzada' respectively 'Darzadag' in the south and 'Nakib' in the north, sometimes also 'Ghulam' (servant, slave).[51] In Persian, *darzāda* literally means a 'sluice by which they bring water to the mill,' a 'mill-dam;' in Makran and Las Bela, however, it means a person 'born on the threshold – a term used for children born to slave women sired by "white" Baloch masters.'[52] This latter statement stands, however, in contradiction to the information that Darzadas 'are reputed to be descendants of the original inhabitants of the region.'[53] The word *naqīb*, on the other hand, derived from Arabic, means 'chief' and 'leader,' but also, and this is essential in our context, 'a servant whose business it is to proclaim the titles of his master, and to introduce those who pay their respects to him.'[54]

Carroll Pastner notes: 'The Nakib are persons with Negroid characteristics, generally believed to be descended from a population of East African slaves brought to Makran by the Arabs, although another opinion holds that they are aboriginal to Makran. Historically there have been far more Nakibs (or Darzada as they are called in Kech) in Makran than in any other district of Baluchistan'.[55] It seems that in Makran and Kharan the composition of both groups is more complex as several local divisions are mentioned; in district Kharan only one subgroup is called Habashazai indicating a clear African descent.[56] Thus, we cannot verify if all Darzadas and Nakibs in these regions of south Balochistan have African roots. In this region people of African descent are also noted to call themselves or be called by others 'Siddi.'[57] Opposite the Persian Gulf, in Oman with its significant Baloch population, people of African origin, that is (ex-) slaves, are stigmatized by designating them as *khaddām* (sg. *khādim*), 'servants'.[58]

The assumption of the mixing of people over centuries through intermarriage and subsequent assimilation into different ethnic groups in Makran, into those with African roots as well as other local communities, is also confirmed by the results of genetic studies (DNA testing) undertaken through fieldwork in this region. Thus, we learn that 'the Negroid Makrani, with a postulated origin in Africa, carry the highest frequency of haplogroup 8 chromosomes found in any Pakistani population. [...] This haplogroup is largely confined to sub-Saharan Africa, where it constitutes about half of the population [...] and can thus be regarded as a marker of African Y chromosomes. Nevertheless, it makes up only 9% of the Negroid Makrani sample, and haplogroup 28 (along with other typical Pakistani haplogroups) is present in this population. If the Y chromosomes were initially African, most have subsequently been replaced; the overall estimates of the African contribution is ~12%.'[59] Referring to another study, it is argued that 'more than 40 per cent of the maternal gene pool of the Makrani of Pakistan derived from Africa, most from Mozambique, but only 8 per cent of the paternal gene pool did so – a pattern that reflects the importance of the Indian Ocean World slave trade in females, and of concubinage.'[60]

Language Diversity

Throughout history, language and dialect have often been used to demarcate different population groups. With people of African descent, ethno-linguistic distinction first depends on the region where they live and second on their affiliation to other ethnic groups as reflected in ethnonyms and designations imposed on them by others. We must remember that languages of origin, in our case those from Africa, can be lost through migration. Today, most of our people are multilingual, sometimes growing up with two languages, for instance, when mother's language is Balochi and father's Sindhi, as in the case of the late Hajji Ghulam Akbar Shidi.

Shidis and Khaskelis living in Sindh generally speak Sindhi and usually the men, in addition, Urdu. Those with roots in Las Bela speak the Lasi dialect of Sindhi. In Karachi, however, the situation is much more complex. There Shidis, who migrated after Partition from Kathiawar, the peninsula in west Gujarat bound by the Gulf of Kachchh, and in particular from Jamnagar, the former state of Nawanagar, still speak, apart from Urdu, their native Kachchhi, a Sindhi dialect, as well as Kathiawadi, a dialect of Gujarati. In Karachi, they live mainly in Lyari in the quarter of Musa Lane. Often men wear a Muscati *kulāh*, typically worn by businessmen dealing with Oman and other regions of the Middle East, similar to people from the Kachchhi community. Shidis settled in Baldia and Syedabad speak Sindhi, Gujarati, and Urdu. Those who came from Gujarat usually converse in a mix of Gujarati and Urdu. Most of our people settled in Lyari are Afro-Baloch. They speak Balochi and, in addition, also Urdu. Their language is locally called *shahrī Balōchī* or *Kach'e jī bōlī*, a form of Balochi typical for cities like Karachi and Hyderabad, a city markedly influenced by Sindhi language.[61] It is different from the Balochi spoken in the countryside (*dehātī Balōchī*), such as the *Sulaimānī Balōchī* of the Sulaiman mountains, the *Irānī Balōchī* spoken towards the Iranian border or the *Makrānī Balōchī*, all interspersed with Persian loanwords.

The latter's pronunciation is said to be much harder than *shahrī Balōchī*. Instead of *Makrānī Balōchī*, the renowned linguist J.H. Elfenbein prefers to speak of 'coastal dialects' of Balochi, 'which is spoken from Biyābān in Iran along the coast eastwards to Čāhbahār [...] including Qasrqand, and in Pakistan Mand, Dašt, and the coastal strip from Jīwanī near the Iranian frontier eastwards to Gwādar and Karachi.'[62] The 'Gadra' from Las Bela speak a Sindhi dialect known as Jadgali, commonly spoken in the Dashtiari area of Iranian Balochistan situated to the east of the Iranian port town of Chahbahar. The Jadgal tribe migrated long ago from Sindh westwards.[63] Therefore Jadgali is said to be practically identical with Lasi.

Depending on the age of speakers and cultural context, the languages spoken by our people still contain words borrowed from Swahili (respectively Kiswahili), a Bantu language with loanwords from Arabic. It is spoken as a lingua franca not only in the coastal region of East Africa from Somalia in the north as far to the south as Mozambique and Madagascar, but also in the Central African Lake District and the Congo, as well as the Indian Ocean world called in Arabic *al-bahr al-hindī*. In addition, it should be mentioned that till the mid-twentieth century Swahili also had been the most common ethnonym adopted by freeborn Muslims of coastal East Africa. In 1851, Richard F. Burton published a vocabulary of 104 'African' words, written down 'as pronounced by one of the most intelligent Africans.'[64] Later he consulted other Shidis to ensure as much accuracy as possible.

The historian Shihan de Silva Jayasuriya carefully examined this word list (building also on Freeman-Grenville's list) which covers different domains of daily life. She identified the vocabulary spoken in the mid-nineteenth century by 'Afro-Sindhis' as having been adopted from Swahili and called it 'Afro-Sindhi.' She juxtaposed Burton's word list with the Swahili equivalents and their meaning in English as in some cases words spoken in today's Pakistan had changed their meaning.[65] Sindhi-, Gujarati-, and Kathiawadi-speaking Shidis were using and to some extent still use words in Swahili. Afro-Baloch and probably Khaskelis and people of African descent living in Makran also use Swahili words. Mixing their native language with words in Swahili can be considered an identity marker of our people. Unfortunately, my partners in conversation observed a marked loss of such words over recent decades. They emphasized that today at best some elderly women would mix their language with Swahili when at home. They would also use words in Swahili in communication with saints and spirits and in songs. Incidentally, according to my friend 'Baba,' who works as a magic healer, certain spirits themselves, i.e. a certain class of *jinn*, speak 'Sudanese' (sic!).

Identities

The various ethnonyms, ethnic labels, and languages discussed above reflect identities not only influenced by indigenization, but above all fragmented by migration and oppression. Individual and collective identities were broken and wounded several times beginning with the uprooting of individuals in Africa, cutting them off from their own societies, followed by migration to the subcontinent, a theme examined more closely in the next chapter. Continuous processes of assimilation were expected of them, yet they have not been praised for these achievements. The historian Edward Alpers tells us that, except for the Shidis, people of African descent in the Indian Ocean world 'generally do not identify themselves as African in any diasporic sense or do not feel that the social space exists for them to do so comfortably in their societies.'[66] Thus, many of them, besides their regional and local collective identity as inhabitants of Makran, Las Bela, parts of Sindh, or Karachi, identify themselves as Baloch or – in the case of Khaskelis – as Sindhis. Immigrants often try to create a new identity, and this is the case here.

The distinct language or dialect is also an expression of the common ground based on a shared lifestyle. As for the people who developed a sense of 'we-ness' with a strong attachment to the ethnonym Shidi, we observe a struggle for recognition promoted by their intellectual elite. They do not want to be viewed solely as descendants of slaves, a point strongly emphasized by Yaqoob Qambrani and other leaders of the community. They value their own history and African religious and cultural traditions, such as the veneration of African ancestor saints with its preponderance of music and dance, as particular expressions of their cultural identity. However, today the cult of these saints is only more or less preserved at shrines in Karachi (see Chapter V). In interior Sindh and Makran, this religious heritage seems to be fading slowly but steadily. Yaqoob Qambrani notes with regret the following about these traditional rites of veneration: 'In ancient times these festive days were duly remembered and participation in it unquestionable, but now everyone is confined to his own territory and sometimes only the *muggarmān* is left to reflect the tradition of Bava Ghor. The younger generation takes little interest in our sacred drum, thus, its players are becoming fewer and fewer with each passing day.'[67]

Apart from shared language and the sense of connection to a specific region in southern Pakistan, the key sites of Shidi identity construction are the awareness of having historical roots in Africa, veneration of ancestor saints in dramatic performances in which memory is grounded in the body, and – as an icon of their indigenous religious traditions – the sacred *muggarmān* drum.⁶⁸ Consequently, music and dance, but also sports, are prominent identity markers (see Chapter VI).

Endnotes

1   Ahmed 1989: 2.
2   Kenoyer & Bhan 2004: 44.
3   Baillie 1890: 2, 28-29, 88-89.
4   Kirmani 2017: 118.
5   Gazdar 2013: 21.
6   Slimbach 1996: 139.
7   Baloch 2017: 35.
8   Cf. Baloch 2017: 37; Paracha 2018: 71-72; Frembgen 2020: 154-155.
9   Bhutto 2010: 232.
10 Burton 1851: 5.
11 Baloch 2017: 83.
12 Cf. Gayer 2014: 38, 40.
13 Nizamani 2006: 25, 33.
14 Frye 1961: 45; Gabriel 1974: 158.
15 On the troubled affairs of the Makran state in the first half of the twentieth century, see the case-study presented in Axmann 2008 (pp. 240-257).
16 Sultana 1996: 30.
17 Ahmed 1989: 28.
18 Swidler 1996: 173; cf. Pastner & Pastner 1982: 67, 71 (on *hizmatkar*).
19 Fabietti 1996: 10.
20 C. Pastner 1971: 31-32; Bijarani 1974: 359-361; Pastner 1978: 440; Gazetteer Balochistan 1906: 448, 454, 464, 498-499 (mentioning, for instance, the Habashazai among the Nakibs settled in the oasis of Washuk), 560-561; Gazetteer Baluchistan: 189; Gazetteer Las Bela: 62; Masson 1843: 50.
21 Richardson 1975: 529.
22 Qambrani 2017.
23 Cf. De Silva Jayasuriya & Pankhurst 2003b: 8.
24 Cf. Albinia 2008: 60.
25 Gazetteer Sindh: 180 (tellingly Khaskeli is translated as 'an attendant slave'); Nizamani 2006: 42. According to the Talpur noble Mir Muhammad Khokhar (Karachi and Tando Allahyar), Khaskelis were labourers (*kāmdar*) for the ruling Talpurs and lived in their *qīlā*s (fortresses), from which the word -*kēlī* might be derived (conversation on 1 March 2020, Karachi). Calling them a 'mixed breed', he emphasized the importance of intermarriage.
26 Ahmed 1989: 25.
27 De Silva Jayasuriya 2009: 19, 11; De Silva Jayasuriya 2010: 9.
28 Ahmed 1989: 26; Khwaja 2013: 42.

29 Badalkhan 2008: 277. Another case in point, only briefly referred to here, are dark-skinned people originally from Central India who work as domestic servants for chiefs of the Bugti Baloch. They are the descendants of Marathas '[…] captured in war by the Mughal emperors and given to their Bugti troops as slaves in lieu of wages' (Lieven 2011: 362). For more details, see Matheson 1975, index p. 212 (Mrattas).
30 The young anthropologist Sikander Ali Nizamani states that 'there are two types of Sheedis in Sindh, one is Arab and speaks Balochi and other is African and speaks Sindhi' (2006: 40, cf. 1, 23, 43). This statement is based on a misreading of Burton's differentiation of two types of African slaves, namely those brought from Africa via Muscat and other port towns of the Arabian Peninsula and those who were (already) born locally, that is to say whose forefathers reached Sindh and Makran earlier (cf. De Silva Jayasuriya 2009: 127). Thus, no people of African descent in Pakistan are Arab. Referring to slaves in Balochistan, A.W. Hughes (1877: 45) says: 'The greater number are Sidis [sic!], or Negroes from Maskat, but they also comprise the issue of captives taken in war.'
31 Spooner 1983: 93-95.
32 Nur Muhammad Danish, commonly known as *nūn mīm dānish*, was born in 1958 in Lyari. 'Danish' is his pen-name.
33 Fatah 2005: 114; cf. Ahmed 1989: 31; Ahmed 2010: 297.
34 Gayer 2014: 129.
35 Personal communication by Yousuf Younus (22 June 2021, Munich), a friend of mine who was born and grew up in Lyari.
36 Cf. Paracha 2018: 69.
37 Pitts 2020. – In Germany, people of African descent proudly call themselves 'Afro-Deutsche' (Afro-Germans).
38 Khwaja 2016: 357; During 1997: 39.
39 Husain 2010: 56.
40 Qaimkhani 1996: 64.
41 Thus, there is for example a 'Makrani *mohalla*' and a 'Makranipada' in Mumbai, initially settled by Baloch quarrymen who migrated to the city from Makran as early as the thirteenth or fourteenth century as well as again later between the 1890s and 1930s from Karachi, mainly to escape slavery (oral communication by Vikalp Kumar, November 2014 in Karachi). When I visited the quarter of Makranipada in Matanpur Nagar/Malad, I found only a few families originally from Balochistan who still speak Balochi sometimes at home.
42 St. Pastner 1978: 250.
43 Pastner & Pastner 1977: 122; cf. St. Pastner 1978: 250.
44 Albinia 2008: 64. Cf. Baloch 1987: 41 ('The Baluch along the coastal area [Makran] are a mixture of Iranian, Assyrian and Negro stock.').
45 Personal communication by Michel Boivin, the renowned French historian and scholar on Sindh and especially Sehwan Sharif.

46 Burton 1851: 255; Qambrani 2017: 18. In addition, Feroz Ahmed (1989: 25) notes that individuals with one parent from the Shidi community are (derogatorily) called *bī-sar* (two heads).
47 Gazetteer Las Bela: 62; Gazetteer Balochistan 1906: 464 (with the same wording); cf. Gazetteer Baluchistan: 189 ('The Gadras […] who are distinctly negritic in type and generally servile dependents or freedmen [...]'); Masson 1843: 306.
48 Gazetteer Las Bela: 209.
49 Cf. Pfeffer 1970: 14-15.
50 Spooner 1983: 107, cf. 103.
51 Gazetteer Baluchistan: 153; Pastner & Pastner 1977: 122; St. Pastner 1978: 250; Spooner 1983: 103; cf. Ahmed 1989: 26; Fabietti 1996: 10,17; Badalkhan 2008: 277. Conversation with the Pakistani anthropologist Hafeez Ahmed Jamali in Karachi (29 March 2020).
52 Gazdar 2013: 21.
53 Fabietti 1996: 10.
54 Steingass 1892: 511, 1421.
55 C. Pastner 1971: 31-32.
56 Gazetteer Balochistan 1906: 498-499.
57 Frishkopf 2006: 165. For instance, also the Austrian geographer Hans Pozdena, who explored the Dashtiari region of Iranian coastal Balochistan, mentions a group called 'Shiris' [most probably an orthographic mistake; author's note, JWF] among the population of the port town of Chahbahar (1978: 51).
58 Barth 1983: 42, 46-48.
59 Qamar et al. 2002: 1119.
60 Campbell 2008: 67.
61 Sommer 1997: 104-111.
62 Elfenbein 1966: 26.
63 Gazetteer Balochistan 1906: 464; Pozdena 1978: 50, 58; cf. Pottinger 1816: 298.
64 Burton 1851: 372-374; cf. Freeman-Grenville 1971; De Silva Jayasuriya 2009: 123-127. In addition to the words listed by Burton, I collected some more words during fieldwork, such as *mákwa* (incense), *póde, póde* (slowly, slowly), *kuánjar* (good morning, good day), *kómba* (veil), *gōma* (dance), and *muggarmān* (ceremonial drum). Albinia (2008: 70) mentions the words *makoti* (bread), *magera* (money), and *hakūna* (there is none).
65 De Silva Jayasuriya 2009: 123; cf. Freeman-Grenville 1971: 12-17.
66 Alpers 2003: 32.
67 Qambrani 2017: 47.
68 Personal communication by Yaqoob Qambrani (23 November 2014, Karachi). Cf. Basu 2000: 265.

Fig. 14 Conversation over tea at Lea Market; Lyari, Karachi (November 2017)

3

Historical Perspectives: From Africa to the Coastal Belt of Makran and Sindh

Introduction

The editors of a recent volume on 'Afro-South Asia in the Global African Diaspora' aptly introduce their topic by emphasizing that 'Africans and their descendants have long migrated across the Indian Ocean world as sailors, merchants, soldiers, scholars, musicians, and explorers. Written sources and archaeological evidence point to sustained contacts between East Africans and South Asians from the Horn of Africa to Sind and Gujarat going back two millennia.'[1] Nevertheless, in this chapter on historical perspectives, we need to consider the disparate nature of text-based historical material on the migration of Africans to what is now Pakistan. Thus, it is not easy to examine the history of subaltern people of African descent in this country and to investigate the specificity of their experience. I will therefore rely on the one hand on legends and oral traditions, and on the other hand refer to the much richer sources available for India, which until 1947 also included the peripheral regions of Sindh and Makran. Here it should be noted in passing that there are other regional settlements of the African diaspora with their own histories.

Although the presence of our people in South Asia is rather marginal, they live in a vast area, from Gujarat to the western Ghats, the Deccan, Karnataka, Goa (during the Portuguese colonial period), Andhra Pradesh,

Bihar, the megacities of Delhi, Mumbai, and Kolkata as well as outside India in Sri Lanka.[2] Our focus is, of course, chiefly on the lower Indus Valley and coastal Balochistan.

We begin with notes on the legendary descent of our people as an essential part of their identity (for memories of their African past related to ancestor saints, see Chapter V) and continue with information on early peaceful commercial contacts between Africa and South Asia. We also refer to the probability of diasporic settlements along the Makran coast in the aftermath of the Zanj rebellion in the ninth century (investigated by Aliya Iqbal Naqvi and Hasan Ali Khan). Both contributors then examine the question of the assimilation of our people into the Baloch nation, before I deal with the complex narrative of slavery. Keeping in mind the theme of the present work, we will not discuss slavery in South Asia in general (as there were many slaves of non-African origin as well), but the Black slave population only. The exploitative institution of slavery marks a ruthless cultural collision supported throughout history by negative stereotypes and prejudices, unfortunately still widespread (discussed above in Chapter I). After a chronological overview of slavery in what is now south Pakistan, I refer to Africans in positions of authority and include fragments of history related to Kalhora and Talpur rule in Sindh, highlighting especially the deeds of the war commander Hosh Muhammad Shidi. Notes on oral traditions of migration in the nineteenth and twentieth centuries, highlighting especially the deeds of the educationist Muhammad Siddiq Musafir Shidi, conclude this main chapter of the present work.

Legendary Descent

In the Middle East the notion is still widespread that mankind is a family and that consequently each individual can trace back his or her origins to an ancestor in the past, finally back to Adam as the first human being. For obvious reasons, in the patrilineal societies of the Muslim world, only male ancestors are considered. Thus, when asked about his view of the history of Shidis, Yaqoob Qambrani responded that all Habshis were descendants of Ham (Hām), one of Prophet Noah's (Nūh) sons.[3] In this context, it should be added that according to legends handed down by al-Kisa'i in his *Qisas al-Anbiyā'*, based on the well-known biblical story in the book of *Genesis*, the earth was divided between Noah's three sons (Sem, Yaphet, and Ham). Ham, the youngest, received Sudan, Nubia, Ethiopia, and Zanj; in some versions of the tale Hind and Sindh are also attributed to him.[4] It is said that his children were born with Black skin color (sic!). Therefore, in Islamic legends, Ham is called 'the one who was destined to become the father of all Africans.'[5] Arab and Iranian historians and geographers explained that Noah had cursed his son Ham for having emasculated him; henceforth Ham should have Black-skinned descendants who would have to serve his two other brothers.[6] This 'Hamitic hypothesis' later served Arab Muslim traders as legitimation for the enslavement of Black Africans.

In his treatise, Yaqoob Qambrani praises important 'Black' public figures in the history of Islam, namely women such as the Nubian Fiza (Arabic: Fidda), the domestic help of Prophet Muhammad's daughter Fatima, who had learned the Qur'an by heart, and Umm Aiman al-Habishiyya, a female slave who nursed the young Muhammad and was later freed. He also praises men such as Bilal ibn Rabah (d. 641), an Abyssinian slave who became the first *mu'azzin* of Islam because of his exceptional voice.[7]

Hazrat Bilal is regarded by many as the ancestor of 'all Africans' and the national saint of Black African Islam.[8] He is said to have been born from an Abyssinian mother and an Arab father. Deeply inspired by the sermon of Prophet Muhammad, Bilal became his steadfast follower. He was tortured by the Prophet's enemies for refusing to worship the idols in Mecca, and therefore Abu Bakr, the Prophet's father-in-law, purchased Bilal and freed him. Bilal continued to stay with Abu Bakr. He followed the Messenger of God to Medina and accompanied him in the most critical battles. According to hagiographic tradition, he was responsible for the food during travelling, became treasurer in Medina because of his integrity and honesty. He was also given the honor of walking ahead of the Prophet on certain occasions, carrying the special spear known as *'anaza*. Sana'i (d. 1131), the poet of the Ghaznavid court in what is today Afghanistan, praised him by saying 'the sandal of Bilal is better than two hundred Rustams', Rustam being the greatest hero of the old Persian epic.[9]

In the self-imagining of his community Yaqoob Qambrani further mentions Qambar, the servant and close aide of the Prophet's cousin and son-in-law Ali ibn Abi Talib (d. 661), who was finally freed by him.[10] As far as the *nisba*s Qambrani and Bilali among Shidis is concerned, Feroz Ahmed mentions that 'Qambrani has become a popular surname among the educated *sheedis*. Others who do not wish to be identified with the freed slave of Ali call themselves Bilali, after the Black muezzin and companion of Prophet Muhammad.'[11]

Moreover, the mother of Muhammad ibn al-Hanafiyya, Ali's third son and Imam Husain's half-brother, is said to have been a Black-skinned slave woman of the tribe of Hanifa hailing from Sindh.[12] Likewise, the mother of Zaid ibn Ali (d. 740), son of the fourth Shi'ite Imam Ali Zain al-Abidin (d. c. 713), was reportedly a Black slave woman from Sindh.[13] In fact, Zaid established the Zaidiyya line of Twelver-Shi'ism which exists to this day in north Yemen. The mother of the ninth Imam Muhammad at-Taqi (d. 833) was a Nubian concubine.[14] Similarly, the mother of the eighth Fatimid Caliph-Imam al-Mustansir (ruled: 1036-1094) originally was a Sudanese slave who became queen mother and wielded enormous power at the court as her son ascended the throne at the tender age of seven.[15] Moreover, Prophet Moses (Mūsā) is said to have married a Cushite woman from the region of Cush, south of Ethiopia.[16]

In the history of early Arabic literature two Black poets made their mark: Antara ibn Shaddad (6th c.), the son of an Arab father and an Abyssinian mother, and Nusaib ibn Rabah, who passed away around 730 in Madina.[17] Nusaib composed verses of praise for several caliphs in Damascus and for the Umayyad ruler, Abd al-Aziz ibn Marwan, in Egypt, who purchased him as a slave. His father belonged to the Beduin tribe of Bali ibn Amr, and his mother is said to have been a Black slave. A personality held in high esteem by our people is Luqman, a legendary heroic figure of ancient Arabic paganism. He was later incorporated into Islam and praised as a wise man in sura 31 of the Qur'an which is named after him; in some later legends, shaped after the Greek slave Aesop (Aisopos), the famous writer of fables, he is depicted as an Egyptian, Nubian, or Ethiopian slave.[18]

There is another legend commonly told among Shidis and Afro-Baloch according to which the famous Chishti saint Baba Farid (d. 1265), whose shrine is in Pakpattan in the Punjab, travelled to Africa to spread Islam and brought with him a large group of followers who became the forefathers of our people in Pakistan.[19] Of crucial importance for them is their social memory of male and female African ancestor saints, that is to say of Bava Ghor and his family, expressed and performed through ritual performances in which images of the past are kept alive. This mytho-history will be explored in detail in Chapter V.

Early Contacts between Africa and South Asia

Archaeological findings and historical sources indicate that commercial links between Africa, the Arabian Peninsula, and South Asia across the Red Sea and the West Indian Ocean date back at least for two millennia. The earliest evidence for overseas contacts between northeast Africa, the Near East, and South Asia dates to c. 2500 to 1700 BC, and even as early as the third millennium BC. At this time 'Meluhha' (most probably Egypt) and ancient Mesopotamia exchanged goods with the Harappa civilization of the Indus Valley (which kept ports along the Makran coast) via Dilmun. The latter is in all likelihood the isle of Bahrain.[20] After the Ptolemians of Egypt gained maritime supremacy over the Red Sea in the third century BC, they extended their influence step-by-step and after 173 BC dominated the seafaring trade between the coast of Ethiopia and India.[21]

While in the first decades before Christ some twenty ships sailed annually from Egypt to India, utilizing one of the main monsoon winds, long-distance seaborne trade significantly increased in later periods. With the occupation of Egypt by the Roman empire in the years around the birth of Christ, according to Greek historian Strabo, 120 ships left every summer in early July for the western coasts of India which they reached in late October.[22]

In the second half of the first century CE, the so-called *Periplus Mare Erythræum* (Periplus of the Erythrean Sea) was written, a handbook for sailors written by a Greek trader and seaman in his native language.[23] The latter probably lived in Egypt and undertook the journey to India several times. The *Periplus* is the most important source on trade relations between Africa and South Asia as well as the Persian Gulf. During this time, the *mare erythræum* or *al-bahr al-habashī*, was not only thought to consist of both sides of the Red Sea but to extend as far as China including the Indian Ocean, significantly contributing to the flourishing of great civilizations. It supported the long-distance trade routes to India and its remains are now being excavated in Yemen, Oman, and the Gulf, in Sudan, Ethiopia and in Eritrea.[24] Of special relevance was the contact between the kingdom of Aksum (in today's Ethiopia) and Indian empires in the first centuries of the Common Era evidenced by Aksumite coins. Apart from various material goods exchanged through maritime trade routes between Africa and India, such as textiles, gold, and ivory, the *Periplus* already mentioned that slaves were exported from northeast and east Africa especially to the rulers of Barygasa (modern Bharuch in Gujarat) on the western Indian littoral. However, they are explicitly not included in the trade goods reaching the delta of the river Indus.[25]

The eastward movement of Africans to the Indian subcontinent and other parts of Asia occurred over several centuries, possibly long before the advent of Islam. During the pre-Islamic period, dark-skinned African traders and merchants were already present along the coastal belt.[26] Referring to the first centuries of Islam, the historian Edward Alpers notes: 'It is without question that Africans, whether from the Red Sea and Gulf of Aden coasts, the

Benadir coast of southern Somalia, or the Swahili coast, were aboard many, if not most, of the sailing vessels that plied this trade.'[27] The subcontinent was already closely connected with the Arab Near East, the Persian Middle East, and the Turkic world of Central Asia.

Most of my interlocutors said that it is a well-known oral tradition among our people that 'their forefathers, the first Shidis,' reached Sindh in the year 711 CE (93/94 in the Islamic Hijra calendar) as soldiers in the army of the young Arab commander Muhammad ibn al-Qasim. Marching from Shiraz through Panjgur and Makran with camel riders and footsoldiers, his campaign was part of the military expansion of the Umayyad Caliphate.[28] However, according to Feroz Ahmed, '[...] it appears quite unlikely that the present-day *sheedi* community descended from the Africans who may have arrived in Sindh prior to the advent of the Talpur rule.'[29] There is, in fact, only historical evidence of a single African warrior (although it may be assumed there were many more!) mentioned in the *Chachnāmah*, 'the history of the Hindu ruler Chach' or Rai Sahasi, the critical source for early Islam in the Indus Valley. It is a Persian account from the early thirteenth century translated from an eighth century Arabic manuscript written on the Umayyad campaigns in Sindh.[30] In it, it is reported that a man by the name Shuja Habshi (d. 93 H) fought against Chach's son Rai Dahar. According to the *Chachnāmah*, 'his bravery was unbounded, and in the field of battle he had already worked miracles. He now came before Muhammad Kásim, and solemnly swore: "I shall not eat or drink till I have faced Dáhar and wounded his elephant. As long as my soul is in my body I shall fight on till I become a martyr." It was on Thursday, the 10th of the sacred month of Ramazán 93, that Dáhar came forth seated on a white elephant and ready for battle. The Abyssinian, on a black horse, then advanced to engage in combat. Rái Dáhar was informed that the man was coming to challenge him, and Rái Dáhar turned towards him and drove his elephant at him. The Abyssinian too spurred his horse and brought it before the elephant. But the animal, frightened at the sight of the elephant, tried to turn aside. The Abyssinian then immediately took off his turban, tied the horse's eyes with it. Rushing on the elephant, he wounded its trunk with a single blow. Rái Dáhar placed a bifurcated arrow in the shape of scissors on his bow string, and with his usual firmness and skill discharged it at the Abyssinian. The arrow sheared the man's head from his neck, his body still remaining on the horse. Dáhar then shouted out: "I have smitten the Abyssinian and killed him".' Afterwards, the fierce battle between Muhammad ibn al-Qasim's soldiers and the local Hindu ruler's army continued; it is reported that Rai Dahar died on the evening of the very same day.

As for the presence of people from 'Black African' sub-Saharan origin living on the subcontinent during this period, Alpers notes, 'there was almost certainly a diaspora of African sailors (whether free or enslaved) around the Indian Ocean,' and 'no doubt some settled in the ports of the littoral and married or cohabited with local women.'[31] Thus, although migration was no doubt forced and connected with slavery, it also happened voluntarily to escape persecution, as described below, or to pursue commercial interests.[32]

The Zanj Rebellion
(by Aliya Iqbal Naqvi and Hasan Ali Khan)

Although physically removed from the Makran littoral, the magnitude and scale of the Zanj rebellion (868-883)[33] in coastal Iraq as well as neighboring Khuzistan is likely to have contributed to the dispersion of African-descended communities connected to it, particularly after the Abbasid Caliphate suppressed this well-organised revolt.

Sindh had been a popular destination from the seventh century onwards for dissidents escaping the long arm of the Caliphal state. Earlier stereotypical analysis by a number of western scholars presents the Zanj revolt as a chaotic mutiny of 'Black savages' and also justifies the modern era European slave trade by claiming that the Muslims started it first.[34] More recent scholarship has provided a much-needed corrective to such views and also cites inadequacies in orientalist scholarship in dealing with Classical Arabic, and what the word *zanj* meant in the hands of Abbasid writers. Indeed, the historian Ghada Hashem Talhami clearly states that '[…] primary Arabic sources do not indicate that the Zanj were the major segment of the rebels, nor that any other group was numerically predominant.'[35]

Indeed, it would seem it was primarily a slave revolt against the ruthless exploitation of human labor in draining the huge salt marshes in the delta around Basra, the main port of the Abbasid Empire, in which all kinds of slaves were involved. The majority of those who revolted may have been Black, but they were not just east Africans or Zanj in which the population had already been mixed to a significant degree. This acculturation and mixture of people with African and non-African ancestry is also reflected in the development of the Baloch of African descent and the wider South Asian Shidi communities.

The entire recorded history of the Zanj, based in modern-day Basra in Iraq, and all their surviving writings are in Arabic, indicating the substantial assimilation of a supposedly foreign slave class. The reverse of a Zanj coin, referring to their leader Ali ibn Muhammad al-Zanji, reads: 'Ali, Muhammad

– the messenger of God. The *mahdī* (the expected Rightly Guided whose appearance is eagerly awaited), Ali the son of Muhammad.'³⁶ Al-Tabari states that Ali ibn Muhammad's paternal grandfather was said to have been a member of Abd al-Qais lineage (he was a slave), and his paternal grandmother a Sindhi slave woman,³⁷ which in the context of this book provides a link to our own region of concern. Later commentators have presumed him to have been of Persian rather than Arab origin.³⁸ He claimed an Alid descent and initially began his revolt espousing a Shi'a cause, gaining a huge following in Bahrain where taxes were collected in his name. Seeds of this may have contributed to the slightly later proto-Isma'ili Qarmati rebellion there which propagated the idea of the return of the *mahdī*. Later in Basra, he realigned his doctrine with the Kharijites, a militant religious movement against the oppressive state, so as not to alienate his Zanj followers with elite Shi'a eclecticism.³⁹

No matter what his religious origins were, his (at least partly) African ancestry and that of the rebels that he led gives us a clue to the regional situation, challenging the traditionalist orientalist view of 'rarefied' Black slavery in the Muslim world, akin to European plantation slavery.

Nigel D. Furlonge stated that '[…] some Arabs and (free) Africans probably believed that once the enslaved converted to Islam, it was their obligation to free the *Zanj* from slavery.'⁴⁰ He goes on to say: 'The victorious 'Abbasid general Muwaffaq (the caliph's brother) dismissed all claims of masters who sought the return of their *Zanj* slaves. Instead, Muwaffaq incorporated thousands of Zanj into his own government forces.'⁴¹

Considering this it would be natural to ascribe the beginnings of the African diaspora communities on the Makran coast, in the eyes of an historian, to the Zanj – with the most obvious clue being geography. The Zanj anti-regime movement lasted for nearly fifteen years and spread to the heart of Iraq from the coast. However, after it was crushed, not all managed to join Muwaffaq's forces and one wonders where the survivors went. Eastward migration must be the only natural possibility since to the west and to the south lay the deserts of Syria and the Hijaz, inhospitable for any escapees to venture into or to settle in. Both areas were under the control of the Abbasids in any case. To the north lay the heartlands of the Abbasid caliphate that defeated the Zanj. Finbarr Barry Flood has described '[…] the remote frontier areas of the Indus Valley and Sistan (Baluchistan) as the resort of heterodox Muslims.'⁴²

This would include many of the Zanj, who at first espoused a Shi'a cause, and then adopted one akin to that of the Kharijites. Much like the Umayyad army that conquered Sindh the century before, and like the Baloch themselves, who according to their traditions of Semitic origin, traversed the Makran coast as well as the Sistan region on their migration from northern Syria to Balochistan, probably over a period of many centuries until about the thirteenth century.[43] It would appear that many of the free men and women from the Zanj migrated eastwards and settled along the Makran coast. They might have mingled with the original inhabitants of the region which seem to have been Meds (fishermen) and Sindhi-speaking Jats, who practice irrigated agriculture.[44] Interestingly, the small African settlements found in Iranian Balochistan and Kerman province are connected with the ethnonym Zanj and thus point to the historic Zanj rebellion as well as to Bantu-speaking regions in East Africa.[45] This is not to argue that subsequent slavery did not swell the numbers of the African diaspora already present in the region, but it was by no means its beginning – a case usually argued by historians of early modern era slavery in the Persian Gulf.

The Baloch Confederacies and the Assimilation of People of African descent into the Baloch Nation
(by Aliya Iqbal Naqvi and Hasan Ali Khan)

The nomadic, semi-pastoral, and sedentary Baloch have had several loosely defined confederacies which have given shape to their tribal structure and their idea of nationhood. This tribal system has defined the groups known today as the Pakistani and Irani Baloch, which in turn explains why certain Baloch groups in Pakistan have Iranian nationality.

According to Baloch ballads and oral traditions, a legendary character in the twelfth century, Mir Jalal Khan, had four sons and one daughter, named Rind, Lashar, Korai, Hot, and Jato Bibi, who went on to become the founders of the five major tribes of the Baloch. This formation has been termed the First Baloch Confederacy.[46] Amidst the five sons, Rind Khan and Lashar Khan were prominent and gave rise to two of the major Baloch denominations, the Rind and the Lashar. It should be noted that Lashar is a district in Iranian Balochistan. The major division of this confederacy is said to have been established by the Rind Baloch in Makran.[47]

In the early sixteenth century, a decades-long intertribal war took place between the powerful factions of the Rind, headed by Mir Chakar Rind, and the Lashar, headed by Mir Gwaharam.[48] It resulted in the disintegration of the confederacy and the expulsion of Mir Chakar Rind to India in 1511. He then aided the Mughal emperor Humayun (ruled: 1530-1556) in his reconquest of India, who was also helped by the Safavid Shah Tahmasp. As a result, many of Chakar's clansmen settled in what is today the Indus Valley. After the fall of the First Baloch Confederacy, the region was divided into three political entities: Makran state, the Dodai Confederacy of Derajat, and the Kalat Confederacy or the Khanate of Balochistan.[49] The Lashar on their part, even though they are present in Pakistan, can be seen roughly along with other tribes as Iranian Baloch. Although there is no rule of thumb for this definition, the Lashar of Pakistan are more likely to have family ties in Iran. The Lashar settled in the Indus Valley under Nader Shah Afshar (ruled: 1736-1747) on his conquest of India and served in Afshar's army. Both Rind and Lashar have assimilated people of African ancestry particularly along the coast into Iran, but much less so inland.

Mir Nasir Khan the Great (d. 1795) of Kalat was the most powerful ruler of the Khanate of Balochistan. In 1758, he declared his independence and signed a treaty of non-interference with the Afghan ruler. He also put together for the first time a full confederate structure and a parliament for all the Baloch tribes under his rule, irrespective of their division.[50] He also began the incorporation of the Brahui and other ethnic groups into the Baloch fold. In doing this, he may also have begun the conscious incorporation of the African-descended inhabitants along the coast into the Baloch fold – something that is very prominent today. Nasir's actions define the concept of the Baloch nation. His actions were also responsible for the eventual assimilation of the few Kurdish clans who were settled in the area by the Qajar rulers of Iran.

The Baloch nation that Nasir Khan constructed is largely divided into the Makrani, i.e. the population along the Makran coast, and the Sulaimani who live in the mountains. The two are separated by the Brahui-speaking tribes who inhabit the central Balochistan plateau, but these too are regarded as a part of the Baloch nation, so successful was Nasir Khan's social experiment at building nationhood. With respect to the assimilation of the people of African descent into the Baloch fold, it is instructive to read a passage from a colonial gazetteer which shows that tribes – whether Baloch or Brahui – have no coherent genealogy, but rather are based on political allegiance to the chief (*sardār*) in question: '[…] a Bráhui tribe is based primarily not upon agnatic kinship like an Afghán tribe, but upon common good and ill; in other words, it is cemented together by the obligations arising from the blood-feud, and heterogeneity, rather than homogeneity, is the striking feature of its composition. Round a nucleus, several groups of diverse origin, including Afghán, Baloch, Jat, and even sometimes freed slaves, gathered together in times of emergency and became consolidated into a tribe.'[51]

Thus tribes have porous boundaries which allow the assimilation of unrelated groups. The French ethnomusicologist Jean During states: 'During their migration from West to East, the Baluchis absorbed numerous ethnic groups. The most exogenous elements in this assimilation process were the Africans who live today in large numbers notably in Karachi. These Africans are so well integrated that the Baluch often deny their foreign origins. The Baluchis state that at one point in time, Baluch groups settled in Zanzibar and in Tanzania (having emigrated from Muscat and Oman), and their descendants returned to their country of origin physically and culturally affected by this sojourn. They brought back with them customs, chants, and exotic dances, and spoke only Swahili. Such explications attest to the Baluch' ability to integrate ethnic groups of all origins (Brahu'is, Sindi, Makrani, Jatt, etc.) without racial distinctions, while adopting elements of their culture. There is a tendency at times to forget that there are indeed slave descendants among the Baluch, although the African origin of certain traditions notably evident in the zâr and lewa musical rites are not forgotten.'[52]

African ancestry is visibly present amongst the Baloch communities settled along the Makran coast, crossing over into Iranian Balochistan, and stretching all the way to Hormuzgan province and its capital Bandar Abbas. This is also the case in Karachi which was part of the Kalat Khanate that Nasir ruled over.[53] African physical characteristics become less and less evident as one moves inland in either country, suggesting that its inception with the arrival of the Zanj, as well as later immigrants (with slaves among them as outlined in the next chapter), is indeed almost entirely a coastal affair.

Slavery

Introduction

With the remarkable exception of Australia, slavery as an institutionalized oppression in milder as well as more cruel forms had been widespread across the world from antiquity to the colonial period. We find it in different guises, for instance, in the ancient Greek and Roman empires, Mesopotamia, Persia, India, Central Asia, and China as well as in Central Europe, Polynesia, and Africa. As far as the Muslim world is concerned, slavery is a 'severely understudied issue.'[54] Unfortunately, systems of human bondage and forced labor still exist in the present time of global capitalism.

In her book *African Identity in Asia*, noted historian Shihan de Silva Jayasuriya emphasizes right from the beginning: 'While slavery and the slave trade have underpinned African migration, they tend to obscure the

African contributions, most notably in military services and music.'55 She explains that, unlike in the Atlantic world, where 'the slave was a chattel who labored in plantations and mines, in the Indian Ocean world, slaves performed a variety of tasks, for example, as sailors, soldiers, musicians, water carriers, road builders, seamstresses, concubines, palace guards, body guards, harem guards, and pearl fishers.'56

It has been estimated that between the eighth century and the end of the nineteenth century 'between 4.7 million and 11 million Africans were sold into slavery in Arabia, Iran, and India' with the East African coast being the trading center and the isle of Zanzibar and Muscat in Oman as main entrepôts.57 Tellingly, in the pre-colonial period, Tuareg and North African Arabs used to call Sub-Saharan Africa *dar al-abid*, the 'land of slaves'. In comparison, approximately 12 million people were enslaved and shipped from Africa across the Atlantic to the Americas between 1519 and 1867 where they were often treated 'like animals.'58

Slaves and Soldiers in India

Slavery was widespread in India where from the time of the Delhi sultanate (13th to 14th c.) slave markets continued to exist well into the Mughal period. Among the military slaves and court officials employed in north India were above all ethnic Turks, but also Habshis (from Christian Abyssinia/Ethiopia), as they were referred to in contemporary sources.59 We learn that 'in the pecking order for African slaves, Abyssinians were the most desired, probably because of their lighter skin color.'60 In the Deccan, the presence of Africans in royal households is attested for the Bahmani sultanate (1347-1489); some of them rose to high ranks.61 Likewise, the Bahmani rulers as well as those of its successor-states Golconda, Bijapur, and Ahmadnagar recruited African soldiers via the Persian Gulf (see also below the subchapter on 'Africans in Positions of Authority'). The Indian historian and anthropologist Purnima Mehta Bhatt aptly explains: 'Most African slaves were not brought to India for their labor, since the existing feudal system and caste structure provided ample cheap labor. They were symbols of status and prestige, mainly for elite consumption.'62

This trade in slaves as a prestige commodity increased considerably from the late fifteenth century until the early twentieth century.63 In the nineteenth century, there was a royal guard, known as the Sidi Risala ('African Guards') consisting of Habshi slave soldiers at the court of the Nizam of Hyderabad in the Deccan. As part of the army's Irregular Forces they had a secure lifetime job and thus a position which 'was perceived as quite privileged by the other less privileged Hyderabadis.'⁶⁴ These Habshis were purchased in the 1840s in Muscat, the main trans-shipment centre for slaves between Africa, the Persian Gulf, and India. From here they were taken to Hyderabad for sale by Arab dealers from Hadramaut, a region in present-day southeast Yemen. This trade was carried out in collaboration with Deccani Habshis engaged in the slave trade.⁶⁵ About the army of Raja Rameshwar Rao I (ruled: 1845-1866) of Wanaparthy, a feudatory of the Nizam of Hyderabad, we learn that 'he supplied himself in part by buying slaves that Arab traders brought from Somaliland and sold in the market in Bombay. Along with them he bought women for their wives. These men were trained like soldiers and companions in arms; they were not treated like slaves, and apparently they did not consider themselves as such.'⁶⁶ Some of these slaves later formed the African Cavalry which later became the African Guard of the Nizam. As for the life of these soldiers, Omar Khalidi adds: 'Most Africans reached Hyderabad as young unattached males. African women rarely accompanied them to the Deccan. Consequently they married local women. Soon a community of Deccan-born Habshi grew up.'⁶⁷ After abolition of the Hyderabad state in 1948 and the disbanding of the Nizam's Irregular Forces in 1950, Habshi soldiers lost their work and were forced into unskilled low-paid jobs.

Unlike the Habshis, who appear in Indian history above all in military-administrative functions, Shidis are chiefly the descendants of former slaves derived from East African populations who labor in the domestic and agricultural sectors.

Slavery in Makran and Sindh

We can assume that there were several migratory waves to the coastal belt of Makran and Sindh, with a dramatic rise by immigrants in the nineteenth and even in the early twentieth century. The trade in African slaves was dominated by Arab brokers and shippers, although since the sixteenth century the Portuguese as well as Swahili and Kutchi merchants also competed in this profitable protocapitalist business.⁶⁸ We learn that 'as early as the third century, Omani Arabs settled on the Makran coast and became the principal slave dealers and middlemen, feeding the South Asian demand,' which means the Indian Ocean labor market.⁶⁹ Their 'human cargo' was shipped on Arab *dhow*s and bartered for manufactured Indian goods including cloth, spices, pottery and beads, and in later periods also for goat hair from Balochistan and cotton brought by caravans from Central Asia.⁷⁰ There is evidence that by the end of the twelfth century slaves were traded from northeast Africa via Zanzibar and the Pemba Islands to the port of Tiz at the Makran coast (today in Iranian Balochistan).⁷¹ For centuries Makran was a 'transitory zone for slaves destined for different South Asian markets.'⁷²

Consequently, we find 'Black ex-slave communities' in south Iran in places like Jiroft, Zanjiabad, and smaller towns and villages around the principal port city Bandar Abbas as well as on Qeshm and neighboring islands in the straits of Hormuz. Mainly they were imported to the Persian Gulf via Muscat.⁷³ Many were purchased by the Qajar nobility (and employed as eunuchs and entertainers in the palace or assigned for the army) as well as by tribal chiefs.⁷⁴ Along the Makran littoral and in the Khanate of Kalat where slavery was formally abolished as late as 1926, Baloch and Brahui tribal chiefs kept slaves brought from Muscat.⁷⁵ At present the descendants of the latter vehemently deny that their forefathers had been slaves and had come from Africa, although various customs and in particular music point to their origin in Africa.⁷⁶

There is historical evidence that interregional contact in the Persian Gulf between Makran and Oman intensified after Mir Nasir Khan the Great, Khan of Kalat, donated Gwadar to an exiled prince of the Sultanate of Muscat reportedly as a gesture of hospitality.⁷⁷ In consequence, since the end of the eighteenth century, the Sultan of Oman controlled ports and islands along the coast from Bandar Abbas to Gwadar and brought the region under his sovereignty.⁷⁸ Omani Arabs recruited mercenary troops from Baloch tribes for their extensive slave trade in East Africa via Zanzibar, the key entrepôt between Africa and India.⁷⁹

The Norwegian anthropologist Fredrik Barth (1928-2016), who did fieldwork in the Omani town of Sohar, notes: 'There can be no doubt that Omanis were major agents of the slave trade in the Indian Ocean, and that the prosperity of Oman's coastal towns in the seventeenth through nineteenth centuries depended on this trade as well as trade in spices and other Eastern and tropical African products. Africans were shipped from Zanzibar and the East African coast, and brought via Oman for sale to eastern Arabia, to the Ottoman Empire via Basrah, to Iran and Central Asia, and to India.'⁸⁰

Feroz Ahmed adds in detail: 'The African slaves, who were used in maritime activities in the Persian Gulf [gaining a reputation not only as stokers and firemen, but also as pearl fishers; author's note, JWF]⁸¹, most likely sailed to Gwadar and other ports in what is now Pakistan. Besides, Makrani landlords [namely Rind Baloch; author's note, JWF]⁸² acquired slaves from the traders who brought their cargoes from the port of Muscat across the Gulf of Oman. [...] In the late 19th and early 20th century, severe famines and slave rebellions in the coastal areas of Iran resulted in the freeing of many slaves and the fleeing of a large slave and non-slave population towards the East. Some of them settled in eastern Makran. Most went on to Karachi and inhabited the Lyari Quarters of the old town where former slaves of Sindhi merchants already lived.'[83]

That enslaved Africans were treated differently along the Makran Coast, we learn from an incident reported by the Pakistani anthropologist Hafeez Jamali: 'In May 1876, three slaves belonging to one Dad Mahomed of Rind tribe and others escaped from their masters' houses along the Makran-Persia border and took refuge in Gwadar Town. The Omani Wali or Governor of Gwadar was bound by the treaty of 1873 with the British not to return any slave to their masters against their will.'[84] Thus, slaves were given shelter among other freedmen in a British-protected territory, although Dad Mahomed (Muhammad) retaliated by cutting the British telegraph line, burnt the Telegraph Line Guards' house, kidnapped an employee, and stole property. Drawing on the Gazetteer of the Persian Gulf, the author continues: 'These troubles renewed in 1892 when the Rind tribesmen demanded the return of some 70 runaway slaves who they alleged had absconded to Gwadar.'[85]

Insightful for our overall theme is a comment given on the background of these conflicts by Nasir Sohrabi, a local social and political activist, as quoted by Jamali: 'The families of runaway slaves came to Gwadar to take refuge from the cruelty of their masters in Persian Balochistan. Our people had their own slaves and servants, but we didn't treat them harshly like the Rinds did, so they didn't have a reason to run away and take refuge with other people. These Baloch slaves settled in Toobag Ward and a few families are still there. But they don't like to talk about their past or accept that they are descendants of former slaves. They claim that they belong to Rind and Hoth tribes but, of course, people know better. We called them *koheeg* or mountain folks, because they spoke Balochi in a thick accent and their masters from Rind and Hoth tribes lived in mountains in Persian Mekran.'[86]

From Distant Lands to the Indian Ocean World

Africans were kidnapped during slave raids and sold (many of them were, in fact, captives of internal wars), without any chance to decide for themselves about their future destination and the kind of labor they were forced to do.[87] They had lost their families, tribal roots and original homeland, had to learn new languages, and to adapt to local societies through a process of learning and socialization in an entirely unknown world. As pointed out by the historian Beatrice Nicolini, 'the slave trade practised along the East African shores had certain principal characteristics: the slaves did not come from areas of Swahili cultural influence, and were called *mshenzi* (pl. *washenzi*) meaning barbarians or uncivilised. They were not Muslims, [unlike] all free Swahili within the domains of Omani Arabs, and were the property of their owners [...]. The slaves formed a separate caste. There were *watumwa wajinga*, not yet assimilated into the coastal populations, the *wakulia*, transported as children to Zanzibar, and, in this category, also the *wazalia* (pl. of *mzalia*), those generations born on the coast and fully acculturated into coastal Islamic culture.'[88] Slaves were thus of diverse origins and mostly adherents of pagan religions or Christians (such as many Habshis who belonged to the Ethiopian Orthodox Church).

The Africans may have converted to Islam quite soon after they were captured in Africa and brought on board the ships sailing to Middle Eastern and South Asian ports (mainly in Gujarat). Inevitably they gave up their original names in favor of Muslim ones. Edward Alpers rightly comments: 'This was unfortunate from the historical point of view, for it destroyed the possibility of identifying the slaves' places of origin from their personal or family names'.[89]

After having become Muslim, mostly of the Sunni sect, they were, unlike slaves in Christian lands, protected by the laws of Islam; although, and this must be stressed, slavery was not prohibited in Islam and was always part of the *sharī'a*, hence also a legitimate part of Muslim society.[90] However, Islamic teachings reminded the masters to treat their Muslim slaves as if they were their brothers.[91] In the Qur'an, slaves are referred to in eleven suras, altogether nineteen times; in it the pious are frequently recommended to set free a believing slave. Therefore Islam remained the common denominator among forced migrants.

Once they became Muslims, they were formally liberated from slavery and had a prospect of emancipation[92] – in principle at least, because the circumstances in which they had to live, being landless and having lost their kinship ties, usually made them dependent on local rulers and noblemen who had them purchased as a commodity. Often, contrary to the laws of Islam, Muslim slaves were bought and sold by Muslim traders (mostly Arab) and buyers.

Nevertheless, it should be emphasized that in practice, during this period to be a 'slave' in the Indian Ocean world meant the juridical status of being a serf. However, this did not necessarily imply being poor, having a low social status, or being without political influence.[93] This holds especially true for slave soldiers owned by rulers, unlike domestic slaves owned by private persons. After domestic slaves were officially freed, they usually remained in slave-like conditions. On the Indian subcontinent, there was 'an urban, market-oriented system where slaves were like chattel, being brought and sold', as well as 'a traditional system of domestic slavery which was limited to a local supply.'[94]

Male African slaves were sometimes castrated and made eunuchs to serve in the female quarters of royal palaces.[95] Female slaves were often purchased as maids, wet nurses, cooks, or concubines. In fact, slave-based concubinage was an important facet of slavery not only in South Asia, but also elsewhere. According to the laws of Islam, concubines could not be sold by their master when they gave birth to a child; a boy born from such a liaison could even become the master's legitimate heir if his rightful women had no sons.[96] Often the master himself married a concubine. It is reported that in the nineteenth century 'men and women under the age of 20 were the most sought after. Ethiopian females were prized in the Middle East for their renowned beauty, while males were in greater demand in South Asia as soldiers. Ethiopians were generally preferred over Nubians or Bantu, who are darker in colour, across the Indian Ocean world.'[97]

As noted by Barth with respect to the coastal town of Sohar in Oman, when slaves were purchased '[…] they were counted as members of their owners' tribes. Thereby they also acquired an indirect ethnic identity: there were Arab slaves, Baluch slaves, and Ajam slaves [originally from Sindh; author's note, JWF] according to the ethnic identity of their owners.'[98] This statement is also insightful for the conditions in Balochistan.

Slaves in Karachi

An established slave trade already existed in Karachi in the late eighteenth century. The total revenue of Karachi port was then 8.1 million rupees and most of it came from buying and selling African slaves.[99] As mentioned by Alexander F. Baillie, in the late 1830s 'from 600 to 700 slaves were annually imported of whom about three-fourths were females,' by 1840 the number rose to 1,500.[100] Baillie's report, quoted here at length, provides several interesting details. He wrote: 'Not only were many slaves kept in the town, but Kurrachee [sic] was a great depot for supplying the up-country districts. […] Muscat was the port with which the trade was carried on. From that place boats were sent down the coast of Africa, with cargoes of coarse cloths and dates, calling at certain spots, where the dealers would be awaiting them. In exchange for its cargo of cloths, the Muscat crew got a living one, consisting of Africans or *Siddees*, as they are called, mostly quite young children, these being considered preferable to grown up persons, who were more likely to run away. The price at Muscat was from 15 to 30 *dollars* per head, and at Kurrachee they sold at from Rs. 60 to Rs. 100 each, according to their strength and appearance. The Siddee boys were extremely intelligent and sharp at learning any trade, and the Kurrachee fishermen, who owned a good many, found that they made active and bold sailors.'[101]

Richard F. Burton added that most of the Africans brought from the Swahili coast came from district Kitomondo as well as from Lamu.[102] Apart from the 'human cargo' brought from East Africa, Baillie mentioned 'Black slaves' transported to Karachi from today's Ethiopia: 'Another class of slaves were the *Hubshees* or Abyssinians; they were brought down in much smaller numbers, not more than 30 to 40 in each year, and these were generally females of more mature age. Their cost was high, from Rs. 170 to Rs. 250, according to their good looks, and they were purchased for the households of men of rank, so much as Rs. 500 being sometimes paid for a great beauty. The price of a Hubshee boy was about Rs. 100, but they were only brought down on commission, and were seldom for sale. Then again there were certain classes of slaves not imported, but born in the town and its neighbourhood, as for instance, Guddos, the offspring of a Sindee Moslem and a Siddee woman, whose child would be a slave equally with herself, and the child of a Guddo and a Sindee father was called a Kambrani.'[103]

The female Abyssinian slaves, mentioned by Baillie, could have been Oromo from south Ethiopia as they were most sought after because of being tall, bronze-colored, and having Europid facial traits.[104] As we know from nineteenth century Mecca, their sexual attractiveness was highly praised.[105] From Karachi they were even sold to Kabul.[106] The Oromo were subjugated by the ruling Amhara and became their serfs; many of them followed their indigenous religion, others converted to Christianity or Islam. According to Baillie, slave trade flourished in the latter years of the Talpur's rule, before the British occupied Sindh, thus 'not less than 1,500 slaves arrived at Kurrachee from Muscat and the African coast in the year 1837.'[107]

The Abolishment of Slavery

After the British had captured Karachi in 1843, they formally abolished the slave trade and slavery in Sindh. In fact, after the Abolition Movement started in England in the late eighteenth century driven by humanitarian pressure, the British Parliament had already issued a respective Act in 1807, but officially trade was abolished only in 1843.[108] Although British '[…] naval ships began to patrol the Indian Ocean to capture and confiscate dhows transporting African slaves to India,'[109] in many regions of what is now

Pakistan, bonded labor continued. Most slaves remained tied in servitude to their masters whose assistance was required for the British to administer the colonies.

Feroz Ahmed notes for example: 'Even though the ruler of Kalat, under the pressure of the government of British India, had legally abolished slavery in 1914, ownership of domestic slaves was not uncommon until the late 1950s. Even today some landlords and mullahs have Black servants who can be defined as slaves, for they do not have the freedom to leave their masters and they are given only the barest of food, shelter and clothing while they remain at the beck and call of their masters for 24 hours a day.'[110] Likewise, the British traveler and archaeologist Sylvia A. Matheson, who lived among the Bugti-Baloch, says that the abolition officially declared by the Khan of Kalat was largely ignored in the countryside.[111]

The Misery of Slaves

Although in principle 'the comparatively privileged social and legal position of slaves in Islam laid the foundation for a less physically abusive type of human bondage,'[112] slaves often had to live under miserable conditions. In this context, I quote the sad example of a boy from a place called Kahnu near Jiroft in southeast Iran. The author reported an encounter in the 1870s with 'a slave of almost pure African blood. He was so fearfully emaciated that he could hardly stand; yet he had no appearance of disease. He said he was dying of starvation, and I really believe he was. His story was that he had belonged to Ahmed Khan, a relation to Chiragh Khan. Ahmed Khan had come to Kahnu to hunt with Chiragh Khan, bringing this boy as his groom. The boy fell ill, and failing in some feat of activity which seriously affected Ahmed Khan's chance in the hunt, he had been beaten so much that he could not stand. When he could walk again, he found Ahmed Khan gone. He was perfectly destitute. No one would employ him, for he was still Ahmed Khan's slave, and no one would give him food without work.'[113]

The same situation prevailed in Sindh as reported by Siddiq Musafir: 'A slave who ran away was considered a criminal and until he had a handwritten note of freedom from his master with him no one was permitted to give him protection or to feed him.'[114]

In Retrospect

Nevertheless, it must be emphasized once again that not all our people were enslaved, some migrated voluntarily to the east, for instance in the context of the Zanj rebellion, and many of those who reached the coastal belt as slaves were freed sooner or later. At least, as far as the medieval Deccan is concerned, we learn that 'the transition from a master-slave to a patron-client relationship appears to have been so smooth that, on the death of the patron, a former slave emerged as a de facto freedman, with or without a letter of formal manumission [the voluntary freeing of slaves; author's note, JWF].'[115] The situation was similar in Gujarat throughout the nineteenth and early twentieth centuries, where in urban areas Sidis, after migration from East Africa, often worked as servants in the homes of Parsi traders.[116]

As for Makran and Sindh, Burton noted in the mid-nineteenth century that manumission was rare,[117] although, with respect to Las Bela, government records published in an early twentieth century report that although people of African descent 'are freed men, but a certain undefined bond of connection still ties them to the particular group to which their former master belonged.'[118] In fact, domestic slaves or servants were often, following the rules of Islam, treated like members of the family. In Sonmiani, a little coastal town and fishing port in Makran, it is said that there is 'scarcely a family without one or more' of them.[119] However, the explorer Charles Masson, who had been in the service of the East India Company, reported from east Balochistan, that sometimes 'their masters, from inability to clothe and feed them, dismiss them to provide for themselves in other lands.'[120]

Those who were thus freed or freed themselves from the economic dependency on feudal lords and moved to cities and smaller towns, usually ended at the bottom of the social hierarchy, remaining the object of racial stereotyping and treated with contempt. Slavery in south Balochistan was only de facto abolished in the 1920s.[121] Through processes of individual acculturation by the slaves, they influenced and enriched local Baloch and Sindhi cultures, bringing their own musical and spiritual traditions.

Africans in Positions of Authority

Sindh

Some almost forgotten fragments of history refer to three Shidis in the military service of Kalhora and Talpur rulers of Sindh, namely Shalmin Shidi, Yaqut Shidi, and Hosh Muhammad Shidi, who were able to reach the higher echelons of power.[122] Yaqoob Qambrani points out that under the reign of Mian Yar Muhammad Kalhoro (d. 1719), son of Mian Nasir Muhammad and ruler of the Kalhora dynasty of Sindh from 1700 to 1718, Shidis served as soldiers in his army.[123] This can probably be explained by the fact that the Kalhoras were migrants from Kech in Makran, a region with a sizeable population of people with African roots.[124] Qambrani further emphasizes that the Kalhoras invited Shalmin Shidi from Jodhpur in Rajasthan and installed him as a military commander, adding that 'many Shidis were brought in from outside especially from Jodhpur state.'[125] Historical and visual sources verify that under the Kalhora's reign, Africans were in the service of Rajput kings.[126]

When the army of the Baloch Talpurs, who gained influence and power in the 1770s, attacked Hyderabad, Shalmin Shidi and Yaqut Shidi bravely defended the fort for two years. This heroic defense dates to the late eighteenth century. Shalmin afterwards returned to Jodhpur.

After overthrowing the Kalhora dynasty in 1783, Talpur chiefs ruled Sindh. In 1839, they were threatened by the Sikhs as well as the British, who had installed Shah Shuja on the Afghan throne in 1836. Both Sindh and Afghanistan became part of the Great Game pursued by the imperial powers of Russia and British India.[127] The confrontation between the Talpurs and the British under their Resident and General Sir Charles Napier escalated in 1843. On 17 February 1843, the Talpur Mirs, who had greater military strength, fought against a modest contingent of British invaders near Miyani, not far from Hyderabad.

In his comprehensive book on the history of Sindh, the architect-cum-historian Suhail Zaheer Lari (d. 2020) explains: '5,000 men of the Talpur army and 256 men including 19 officers of the British force were killed in the battle. The Mirs took refuge in the Hyderabad Fort, and the British occupied the camps left by the Talpurs. The following day the Mirs surrendered to Napier. Mir Sher Muhammad, the Lion of Mirpur [who belonged to the Mirpur branch of the Talpur rulers; author's note, JWF], who was too late to take part in the battle of Miani, arrived with his army of 20,000, along with stragglers from the Battle of Miani. He sent an envoy to Napier with an offer of safe conduct to leave Sindh. Napier's response was to march out and defeat him on 24 March 1843 at Dabbo (Do-aba), six miles from Hyderabad. His African slave soldier Hosh Muhammad Shidi (born in 1782 CE probably in Zanzibar), often simply called Hoshu Shidi (Fig. 15), advised Mir Sher Muhammad to escape. He took upon himself the charge of Mir's artillery, raised the cry "We will die, we will die, but we will not give up Sindh" [in Sindhi: *marson, marson, Sindh na deson*; author's note, JWF; Fig. 16] He fought on like a man possessed till he was bayonetted by the Irishmen of the 22nd Regiment.'[128]

Here it should be mentioned that Hoshu Shidi had been first in the service of Mir Sobdar Khan, son of Mir Fateh Ali Khan, and only later joined the service of Mir Sher Muhammad from Mirpur Khas.[129]

The historian H.T. Lambrick (1904-1982) pointed out that there are no detailed reports on the battle from the perspective of the Baloch. However, the few indigenous sources such as letters, memoirs, and poems do mention that certain Baloch tribes fought bravely and others were considered to have been disgraced. It is also emphasized that among the non-Baloch tribes taking part, 'the small body of the Mir's paid troops, the Khatian Pathans, fought stoutly, as did many of their khizmatgars [servants; author's note, JWF], particularly Hosh Muhammad Kambrani.'[130]

Fig. 15   Tomb of Hosh Muhammad Shidi, hero of the battle against the British in 1843 near Hyderabad, Sindh (February 2016)

Fig. 16 Hosh Muhammad Shidi's famous slogan and promise 'We will die, we will die, but we will not give up Sindh!', raised at the battle of Dabbo near Hyderabad (February 2016).

The latter's bravery and military skills not only made him famous among our people, but were also acknowledged by General Napier, commander of the British-Indian troops. About the carefully planned campaign by the Talpur princes from northern Sindh, W.F.P. Napier writes that it 'was arranged with a skill and intelligence far beyond the Ameer's capacity – having nothing barbarous in the conception. Subsequent intelligence made known that it was the work of the purchased Abyssinian and Arab slaves of the Ameers, called "*Seedees*," probably the same as *Sidi* the Arab word for Lord. Amongst these Hoche Seedee, a Black [...] was conspicuous for his ability, greatness of mind, and heroic courage.'[131]

Khurshid Qaimkhani notes that, according to some informants, these Shidis had chained themselves together so that no one would be able to lose heart and run away.[132] Referring to the battles of both Miyani and Dabbo, it is said that Hosh Muhammad Shidi 'ruled the operations of the Belooch army,' that 'his vigorous exhortations had urged the Ameers to war; his genius had principally directed the operations at Meeanee,' and 'the dark hero displayed a military skill worthy of a European General (!).'[133]

In his manuscript, Yaqoob Qambrani devotes a whole chapter to this courageous warrior.[134] He first draws on the detailed narrative of the military conflict between the Talpur and the British, reported by Qaimkhani in his book *Bhataktī Naslaiñ*. In this book, Hosh Muhammad Shidi is depicted as an energetic soldier who sent a group of young Shidi soldiers to Mirpurkhas to inform Mir Sher Muhammad that Hyderabad had been plundered and urgent military support should be called for.[135] Referring to the battle on 24 March (according to other sources on 23 March!) 1843,[136] at Dabbo north of Hyderabad, Qambrani mentions an article written in Urdu about 'the day when Hosh Muhammad Shidi was martyred' which includes a revealing detail when the Shidi commander in vain called another contingent of Baloch soldiers for help after Mir Sher Muhammad had already left the battleground. 'Hosh Muhammad Shidi asked them to attack, but they felt it humiliating to obey the orders of a Shidi [sic!]; so they didn't move forward and when the Shidi was martyred, the British targeted them as well and saw them fleeing.'[137]

In his treatise, Yaqoob Qambrani aims to demonstrate that this Shidi hero was a soldier from the very beginning and not a slave; thus he criticizes 'fabricated stories to deprive Hoshu Shidi of the place in history that he deserves' and the historians' 'reluctance in presenting the true facts.'[138] He consequently dismisses Qaimkhani's and G. Allana's statements that Hosh Muhammad Shidi was neither a General nor a regular soldier in the army, but born and raised in the royal household of the Talpur Mirs. However, Qaimkhani's and G. Allana's statements are also supported by Lambrick's and Burton's accounts, with the latter referring to Hoshu Shidi as 'the favourite attendant of the Ameer Sher Mohammed.'[139]

According to Feroz Ahmed, 'to accord respect to such slaves, the Talpurs gave them the family name of Qambrani, derived from Qambar' (in fact, this argument sounds more convincing than the explanation about this name proposed by Baillie given in the previous section).[140] We do not know if Hosh Muhammad Shidi was paid for his fighting, received any non-monetary remuneration or simply had to obey his Talpur master. Notwithstanding his actual status as a slave soldier in the Talpur army, his military achievements and farsightedness made him an outstanding personality. Yaqoob Qambrani emphasizes that the Shidis of Sindh commemorate the anniversary of Hosh Muhammad Shidi's death every year on 26 March with great zeal. However, the role played by Africans in the military during this period has thus far not been sufficiently recognized.

India in Comparison

As the above-mentioned examples of Shalmin Shidi and Yaqut Shidi under the Kalhoras and Hosh Muhammad Shidi under the Talpurs show, African slave soldiers were not merely part of the military ranks, but were also able to occupy positions of leadership, gaining recognition in battle. Unfortunately, our knowledge about the actual situation of Shidi soldiers in Sindh is scarce. In seats of Muslim power in the Deccan between 1400 and 1650, Habshis were sold via Middle Eastern slave markets and recruited especially because of their soldiering abilities.[141] Probably the situation was similar in later periods in Sindh. Below some examples of individual African elite slaves in India are spotlighted:

Particularly between the fifteenth and seventeenth centuries, Africans were able to rise to positions of great authority, acquiring military power and holding high administrative posts in the Sultanates of Bengal, Jaunpur, Khandesh, and Gujarat, as well as in the city-states situated on the South Indian Deccan plateau.[142] Thus, Habshis usurped power in Bengal and ruled for seven years, Malik Sarwar established the Sharqi dynasty of Jaunpur in what is now eastern Uttar Pradesh, and Habshis played important roles especially in the political history of the Deccan. Already in the late fifteenth century, Habshis ruled as ministers, key governors, and keepers of the royal seal in two of the four provinces of the Bahmani sultanate. After the fall of the Deccani kingdom, Habshis continued to hold high positions throughout the sixteenth century in the newly emerging states of Ahmadnagar, Bijapur, and Golconda.

In Ahmadnagar, the ex-slave Malik Ambar (1548-1626), originally named Sambano (and nicknamed Chapu), became the *pēshwa* (prime minister) and finally, after the fort fell into the hands of the Mughal, virtually ruled the reconstituted and revived Nizam Shahi state from 1600 to 1626.[143] As a charismatic commander highly respected by people in the Deccan, he became the great adversary of the Mughal emperor Jahangir (ruled: 1605-1627); the Mughals, by the way, had a Habshi navy based at the port of Surat used to escort pilgrims to Mecca.[144] With his outstanding military skills Malik Ambar even managed to expel the Mughals from Ahmadnagar fort. The renowned Islamic Studies scholar Richard M. Eaton notes that he was probably born in southern Ethiopia and '[…] as a youth had fallen into the hands of slave dealers operating between the Ethiopian highlands and the coasts of eastern Africa. He might have been captured in war, or he might have been sold into slavery by his impoverished parents. After being brought to a slave market in Yemen, he was sold and resold several times before being 're-exported to the Deccan plateau to meet that region's insatiable demand for slaves'.[145] Finally, he was bought by Chengiz Khan, then *pēshwa* of Ahmadnagar who was a Habshi slave himself.

In Bijapur, a group of ex-slaves known as the Abyssinian Party dominated politics under their leader Dilawar Khan. He is 'said to have dismissed almost six thousand soldiers who followed the Shia sect of Islam, replacing them with Africans of the Sunni persuasion.'[146] He was finally superseded by the Habshi Ikhlas Khan (1627-1656) who oversaw general administration and was commander-in-chief of the army, built mosques and wielded great power in Bijapur; Ikhlas Khan is depicted in portraits more often than any other Africans. Later, in the seventeenth century, the Habshi noble Khavas Khan led the sultanate's defence and became *wazīr* (regent minister).

Also in Golconda, Africans played important roles; the sultan's slave Malik Khushnud became a well-known poet in the Deccani dialect of Urdu. Additionally, the rulers of the Deccan established a navel power dominated by Habshis along the Konkan coast which continued to exist until the first half of the nineteenth century. The command of the island fort at Janjira (situated about 100 km south of Bombay), which belonged to Ahmadnagar, was given to the Habshi noble Sidi Yaqut Khan because of his successful military exploits as a courageous seaman. Ruled by Sidis, the small state of Janjira existed from 1618 to 1948. The Janjira Sidis position themselves as a royal lineage.[147] In a conversation, the granddaughter of Sir Sidi Ahmed Khan, who was knighted by the British government, stated that her ancestors were said to have been expert seafarers. 'The Moghul Emperor's daughter Zaibunissa was taken for Haj on a ship we built and that is how we received the title Khan. As the children of Khan we are known as Khanzadas.'[148] In 1791, a member of the Janjira family founded the small state of Sachin in Gujarat. In the latter province, Habshis had served as soldiers and sailors since the fifteenth century.

For detailed information on African elites in India, the reader is referred to Kenneth X. Robbins' and John McLeod's well-researched work (2006). In it, ample use is made of paintings in which African nobles, administrators, and palace guards are depicted as well as numismatic and architectural remains related to Indians of African descent.

Oral Traditions of Migration

Introduction

The reader is reminded that history, whether written or oral, is never objective. What we have at hand are constructs of the past contingent on interpretations of the present and anticipations of the future. History can be authenticated to a certain extent when culled from primary sources, but too often it is literalized into what is thought to be concrete facts, turned into fictive reconstruction, and not seldom also subjected to nationalist claims. Written knowledge is thus not immutable. Keeping in mind these reservations about textual manifestations of traditions and questions of historical accuracy, one needs to emphasize that history is not only the domain of the archive as also oral tradition, much like the written word, offers meaningful perspectives about societies. Orally transmitted folk traditions play an important, even indispensable part in the reconstruction of the past. As the Belgian ethno-historian Jan Vansina (d. 2017) aptly remarked, 'they correct other perspectives just as much as other perspectives correct them.'[149]

Oral source material for people's history has its limitations and, in many cases, may not be as reliable as written historical records, but this is no reason to neglect or to denigrate it. Unwritten messages were and are essential for largely oral societies such as those of Africans in Pakistan. Memory is thus of crucial importance, also in the realm of religion (see Chapter V). As the historian Kerwin Lee Klein argues, memory has become a 'metahistorical category' that subsumes folk, myth, and popular or oral history.[150]

Destiny

The fragments of oral traditions narrated to me chiefly refer to memories about the past preserved in families only over the last two or three generations. Many elderly males with whom I had the chance to converse, told me that their forefathers reached the coast of what is now Pakistan via Mombasa, Zanzibar (pronounced Zinjibar), and Omani port towns, such as Muscat, Sur, and Sohar.

According to the famous Shidi educationist and benefactor Muhammad Siddiq Musafir (see below in more detail) who recorded memories among his people in interior Sindh, most slaves were kidnapped from East Africa by Arab traders, allegedly with the help of 'Pathan' donkey drivers, and later shipped to the subcontinent for sale. These donkey-drivers were most probably Baloch from Makran and hardly Pathan, as Baloch soldiers and bodyguards accompanied Arab slave traders and safeguarded the trade routes to the interior.[151] As described by Siddiq Musafir, the method of capturing was as follows: 'Groups of traders and donkey-driver thugs would go into villages in the jungles and give out sweets, jaggery, sweet-and-savory snacks and chickpeas to young children. Once the children trusted them, they would tell them that there were ships anchored on the coasts stuffed with these kinds of foods and if they came with them they could eat as much as they wanted. In this way innocent little boys and girls would be tricked into coming to the ships and when there were enough children, the ships would raise their anchors and then sell the children in slave markets.'[152] The favourite method was to have armed groups 'surround isolated villages at night when the villagers were asleep and set fire to them. When the villagers would run to try to save their lives, the armed groups would attack them and capture the men, women and children and then take them to the anchored ships.'[153]

Siddiq Musafir also collected other harrowing tales, such as reported by two slaves from Tando Bago (near Badin in Lower Sindh), one of them by the name of Nasibo, who were said to have escaped mutilation, forced cannibalism, and death in Muscat in the late nineteenth century. They described a particularly horrific incident: 'In one corner of the premises, huge cauldrons were being heated filled with boiling water or oil. The slaves were hung in the giant pots like kebabs and fat from their bodies would begin to drop off into these cauldrons. The Arab traders would use this human fat to make a wax or concoction for increasing sexual power from which they made a lot of profit and which sold at the same price as gold. What remained of the flesh of these unfortunate slaves was fed to the other slaves.'[154] 'The two men from Tando Bago were saved from death when a guard took pity on them, feeding them a handful of salt to bring on sickness. Instead of being killed, they were sold to a trader from the Indus.'[155] Of course, the reader is reminded that Siddiq Musafir's account, which echoes caricature-like stories from colonial Africa, stands for itself and has not been verified by other sources.

Origins

Today Pakistanis of African descent have practically no idea where in Africa their ancestors came from, if the latter were forcibly taken as slaves (which mostly seems to have been the case), or if they migrated voluntarily. As for their ethnic or regional origins in Africa, Burton compiled a list of twenty-two 'tribal names,' today no longer remembered by their descendants in Sindh. The African ethnonyms he mentioned were: 'Dengereko, Dondere, Gindo, Kamang, Makonde, Makua, Matumbi, Mkami, Msagar, Mudoe, Mukodongo, Murima, Murima-phani, Muwhere, Myas, Myasenda, Mzigra, Nizizimiza, Nyamuezi, Temaluye, Zalama, Zinzigari.'[156] These names refer to Bantu-speaking groups and to some villages in today's Tanzania which, with the exception of only three names, could all be identified.[157] Apart from the entire East African coast and its immediate hinterland, slaves were also captured from the Great Lake region, east Sudan and all along the Nile Valley.[158] They were forced first to march in long caravans to the coast to be sold on markets in Kilwa, Zanzibar, Pemba, Mombasa, and other port towns before being boarded on armed slave *dhows* and finally shipped via markets in Arabia and Oman to ports on the coastal belt between Iran and India.[159] These people were bound together by common destiny, of course not by common descent. According to the historian G.S.P. Freeman-Grenville (d. 2005), the majority of the Shidis Burton encountered in Sindh were relatively recent immigrants.[160]

Arrival

In Karachi our people are said to have settled first, as aforementioned, in the Shidi Goth (Shidi village) close to the old fortified city. According to Hajji Ghulam Akbar Shidi, in the nineteenth century a man by the name of Arif Shidi founded the quarter called Baghdadi and built the *Arabī Shīdī masjid*. Baghdadi and other parts of Lyari were mainly settled in the late nineteenth century and the first half of the twentieth century by laborers who had escaped slave-like working conditions under feudal lords in the countryside, but also because of the effects of severe droughts in Makran.[161] Haris Gazdar adds: 'Karachi became a destination for former slaves of African origin who had previously worked in the houses and orchards of Baloch landowners. It also became the place where the former slaves began to be recognized as Baloch and not merely as Ghulam or Darzada.'[162]

Thus, for instance, Hajji Ghulam Akbar Shidi's paternal uncle migrated from Turbat in Makran to Karachi. Others know that their grandfather came from Las Bela or Kalat to settle in Sindh. Their forefathers became domestic servants in the households of landowners, merchants, tribal chiefs, and officials, but were also farmhands and engaged in other professions. Burton noted that in Sindh 'African slaves were generally employed as horse-keepers, grass cutters, day labourers, and apprentices to the different trades, as carpenters, blacksmiths, and others.'[163] In Karachi freed slaves were manual laborers and, for instance, water-carriers.[164]

As far as their level of living is concerned, it was in any case different from the cruel fate of slaves shipped across the Atlantic. Thus, with respect to India, Eaton remarked: 'Once sold to a state official, the lives of these men [who were captured in Ethiopia; author's note, JWF] took a dramatic turn from what they had known in Africa. Their buyers fed them, housed them, taught them in the ways of household life and duties, and in all respects protected them, receiving in return an absolute and unswerving loyalty.'[165]

Eaton admittedly refers to the institution of elite slavery in the Deccan and not to common slavery. Therefore we might assume that the living conditions of slaves in Sindh and Makran in terms of maintenance and protection were not as comfortable to say the least, although, according to Burton, in Sindh slaves 'were treated as inmates of the family' and 'received an allowance of food and clothes.'[166] This short general statement, however, does not provide a nuanced picture of the actual treatment of slaves which often was much worse. The case of the ill-treated slave near Jiroft in Iran quoted above is just one telling example.

Another case was told to Siddiq Musafir by an old Shidi woman near Tando Bago. She narrated: 'I was the slave of a rich man who had a camel which he loved very much. When it was time to give the camel its feed, the command for me was to carry about 20 kg of fodder on my head (in a trough) and let the camel feed whilst I stood in front of it. This was because if the grass feed was put on the floor it would be more difficult for the camel to eat as it would have to lower its neck. I would have to stand for hours with this heavy load on my head as the camel fed and the slave owner had no idea how hard it was for my neck. In short, whether it was the burning heat of summer or the freezing night of winter I would stand and have to go through this torture for hours every day.'[167]

Siddiq Musafir

We have at least some detailed information on Shidis in Tando Bago and their memories 'from distant lands.' They explained that their forefathers had been in the service of Talpur rulers of the Mankani section in Mirpurkhas and 'eaten their salt,' with these words emphasizing loyalty to their masters. About two or three generations from now, many of them migrated to the town accompanying Mir Ghulam Ali Khan Talpur (1909-1963). Their most prominent scion was Muhammad Siddiq 'Musafir' Shidi (1879-1961), a devout Sunni Muslim and great educator who also significantly contributed to Sindhi literature, poetry, music, history, and journalism.[168] His parents had been slaves in Tando Bago, the town where he was born.

Musafir's father was most probably born in 1793. At the age of seven, his entire family was killed by a rival tribe and he alone sold into slavery. He remembered being taken down to the sea by the attackers and being brought to the slave market in Zanzibar. The slave ship finally docked at Muscat on the coast of Oman, where a trader, Shaikh Hasan, bought the whole human cargo. The Shaikh, instead of selling him than all the other slaves, kept him and re-named him Bilawal. We can assume that this marked the young boy's conversion to Islam. Two years later, Shaikh Hasan sold Bilawal to a trader from Sindh, who took him by boat along the coast and up the Indus to Thatta. There he was bought by one Ghulam Ali, a stonemason, who had been commissioned to build a large stronghold for a member of the ruling Talpur clan in Tando Bago.

Drawing on Siddiq Musafir's Collected Works, Qaimkhani describes a crucial incident in Bilawal's life: 'One day the stonemason Ghulam Ali had fresh fish sent home from the bazaar to be cooked. His wife asked Bilawal to go to the nearby stream to clean the fish. While Bilawal was sitting at the bank of the stream cleaning the fish, it suddenly slipped from his childish hands and fell into the rivulet and drifted away. At dinner time, when Ghulam Ali came home and did not find the fish on the dining table he flew into a rage at his wife. When his wife told him about the incident of the fish at the hands of Bilawal, he first beat him soundly and then, dragging him by the hair, went to the bazaar. On the way, he met a local notable, Sayyid Makhdum Hur Ali, who asked Ghulam Ali why he was beating this child like that and where he was taking him. When he discovered that he was taking the child to be sold, Makhdum Ali bought Bilawal.'[169] Bilawal, now renamed Gulab Khan, worked as a domestic help in the home of the childless Hur Ali. The latter's wife educated Gulab and taught him how to fast and pray. Gulab showed great faithfulness in his service. When he became a grown man, Hur Ali purchased a Shidi girl to be his wife. When the British banned slavery in 1843, Hur Ali freed his slave, but as he was very fond of him, he built him a house at the bottom of his garden and asked him to stay. At the age of fifty, Gulab became the elected leader of the local Shidi *panchāyat*, the community's decision-making body, with seven nearby villages under his charge. Unfortunately, all the eighteen children born from his wife died in infancy. Soon afterwards, his wife died too. At the age of sixty, Gulab married again, and his second wife gave birth to twelve children. Of these only the youngest, Siddiq, survived.

After completing his education, Siddiq became a teacher in 1901 at the Hyderabad Training School. He also began to learn Arabic and Persian. Later this school became a training college where Siddiq Musafir worked as a teacher and researcher until 1921. In 1919, together with Mir Ghulam Muhammad Khan Talpur (whom he already befriended as a child) he helped to establish a primary school in Tando Bago which eventually became the Lawrence Madrassa (completed in 1924). Siddiq Musafir served there as a principal for about twelve years. He also promoted female education. With support of the Talpur ruler he could open a girls' primary school, now run as a girls' high school. Later he taught at the Teachers' Training Center in Hyderabad. Khurshid Qaimkhani acknowledged Siddiq Musafir's soft-heartedness, honesty, and humility, but added that this remarkable learned dignitary lived in great poverty from birth to his final days: 'He would often sell his literary drafts for a few pennies in order to be able to eat two meals a day.'[170]

Qaimkhani ends his chapter entitled 'Musafir Africanus' with the words: 'Life is a long and painful journey. From the jungles of Africa to the deserts of Sindh, a never-ending sequence full of grief. And who was more aware of this journey than Musafir?'[171]

Reconnecting with Africa

Distant Africa still evokes strong feelings of belonging among our people, particularly among those who migrated in comparatively recent times to Pakistan. Some of them even renewed contact to their places of origin, for instance to the Great Lake region bordering the Congo, Uganda, Kenya, and Tanzania (created by the union of Tanganyika and Zanzibar in 1964).[172] About the politician Tanzeela Qambrani, it is said that 'her ancestors came to Sindh a century ago from what is now Tanzania. Her family has maintained ties with their ancestral homeland, with one sister currently living in Tanzania after marrying a local. Another of her sisters has a husband from Ghana.'[173]

Through these trans-regional marriages, Africa remains a significant genealogical horizon for her family. 'No matter how small such a step may be, it is of historic importance,' commented Khurshid Qaimkhani, devoting a chapter on Tanzeela Qambrani's sister Shahida and her marriage in his book.[174] Shahida matriculated from Matli, taught children in a school in Baghdadi, Lyari/Karachi, and finally received a BSc degree from Sindh University. The sisters' mother was a school teacher and their father, Abdul Bari Shidi, a lawyer and amongst the most promising students of Siddiq Musafir.

Likewise, some Sidi families settled in the neighboring Indian province of Gujarat only two or three generations ago, migrating from East Africa as late as the early twentieth century.[175] After Partition, some of them migrated to Karachi. Most of them reached the city by ship and still maintain ties with their relatives in India.

Endnotes

1   Ali et al. 2020: 11.
2   Cf. Lodhi 1992: 83; Alpers 2004: 29 ff; De Silva Jayasuriya 2009: 30.
3   Personal communication by Yaqoob Qambrani (6 November 2013, Seydabad/Baldia in Karachi). Cf. Qambrani 2017: 5.
4   Wensinck & Kramers 1976: 160, 590. The term 'hamitic' is problematic and has ideological undercurrents (Stöhr 1972: 154-155). It was first used in 1880 in linguistics to differentiate certain African languages from 'semitic' languages; later it was also used in physical anthropology and became a

multi-layered and blurred expression. Since the mid-twentieth century the term has become obsolete.

5   Knappert 1985: 45.
6   Southgate 1984: 13-14; Basu 2003: 230; N'Diaye 2010: 56.
7   On Hazrat Bilal, see: Wensinck & Kramers 1976: 80-81; al-Akkad 1978; Ali 2011: 13. On Fiza and Umm Aiman, see also Forkl 1993: 299.
8   Cf. Basu 1995: 92; Basu 2000: 249; Forkl 1993: 299.
9   Schimmel 1981: 19.
10   Qambrani 2017: 3-4, 6, 49-58.
11   Ahmed 1989: 26.
12   Hollister 1953: 55, 195 (I owe this bibliographical reference to Aliya Iqbal Naqvi and Hasan Ali Khan; e-mail dated 15 March 2021); Momen 1985: 34-36, 47.
13   Jafri 2000: 251 (I owe this bibliographical reference to Aliya Iqbal Naqvi and Hasan Ali Khan; e-mail dated 15 March 2021).
14   Momen 1985: 42.
15   Hollister 1953: 235 ff. (I owe this bibliographical reference to Aliya Iqbal Naqvi and Hasan Ali Khan; e-mail dated 15 March 2021); Daftary 2007: 193-195.
16   Hays 2003: 71 (referring to Numeri 12, 1).
17   For further information, see Rotter 1967 and Khannous 2022.
18   Wensinck & Kramers 1976: 366.
19   This legend was told to me, for instance, by Hajji Ghulam Akbar Shidi and 'Nawab,' both persons of memory among our people living in Lyari (cf. also Rashdi 1992: 142).
20   Jansen 1986: 163-164; Nissen 1987: 45-49; cf. Alpers 2004: 27; Kenoyer & Bhan 2004: 44.
21   Brentjes 1973: 37-38.
22   Raunig 1971: 122-123.
23   For a detailed discussion, see Baptiste 2008: 126-132. Cf. Bhatt 2020: 29.
24   Raunig 1971: 122; Raunig 1997: 5.
25   Raunig 1971: 125; Pankhurst 2003: 189; Kenoyer & Bhan 2004: 44-46.
26   Kenoyer & Bhan 2004: 43.
27   Alpers 2004: 27; cf. Brentjes 1973: 63.
28   Albinia 2008: 56; Bhutto 2010: 228-230; Paracha 2018: 70; cf. Awan 1985: 18.
29   Ahmed 1989: 23.
30   On the textual history of the *Chachnāmah* see Edwards 2015 (p. 15, endnote 32).
31   Alpers 2004: 27-28; cf. Harris 1971: 5-10.; Campbell 2008: 44.
32   Cf. Campbell 2008: 43; De Silva Jayasuriya 2010: 2-4.
33   Furlonge 1999: 1.
34   Talhami 1977: 444-448.
35   Talhami 1977: 452.

36   Walker 1933: 652.
37   al-Tabari 1964: 1742-1743; cf. Waines 1992.
38   Talhami 1977: 453.
39   Talhami 1977: 454-455.
40   Furlonge 1999: 11.
41   Furlonge 1999: 12.
42   Flood 2011: 43.
43   Janmahmad 1982: 2-15; Awan 1985: 22-23; Baloch 1987: 34, 39-43, 90-95; Quddus 1990: 13-18.
44   Gazetteer Balochistan 1906, Vol. I: 580; Baloch 1987: 95, 118.
45   De Silva Jayasuriya 2009: 25-26.
46   Baloch 1987: 95-96; Badalkhan 2013: 20.
47   Baloch 1987: 95.
48   Awan 1985: 25; Asimov & Bosworth 1992: 305.
49   Baloch 1987: 97-105; Swidler 1996: 173-176; Axmann 2008: 22-25.
50   Hughes 1877: 186-189; Gazetteer Balochistan 1906, Vol. I: 581; Awan 1985: 31-33; Baloch 1987: 104-124; Axmann 2008: 22-23.
51   Gazetteer Balochistan 1906, Vol. II: 391-392; cf. Axmann 2008: 38, endnote 1; Swidler 1996: 176.
52   During 1997: 39.
53   According to noted writer and expert on Karachi, Arif Hasan (personal communication), Karachi only became part of Sindh in 1759 with the Kalhora takeover and was part of Balochistan. See also, Aitken 1907: 118 ('In 1795 the Talpurs recovered Karáchi, which had been ceded to the Khan of Kalat by the Kalhoras as the price of the blood of the Khan's brother, whom they had slain in battle.'). And Hamida Khuhro confirms: 'Until the eighteenth century, the Karachi area was controlled by the chieftains who ruled the coast and hilly region of the Sindh and Makran coast' (1997: 7).
54   Hopkins 2008: 630, 670.
55   De Silva Jayasuriya 2009: XI.
56   De Silva Jayasuriya 2009: 2; cf. De Silva Jayasuriya 2010: 2.
57   Harris 1971: 5-7; Robbins & McLeod 2006a: 19.
58   For more information on slavery, see for instance Davis 2014.
59   Basu 1995: 43-47; Alpers 2003; Alpers 2004: 31; Eaton 2006: 51; Robbins & McLeod 2006a: 125; N'Diaye 2010: 44-45; Bhatt 2020.
60   De Silva Jayasuriya 2009: 10.
61   Robbins & McLeod 2006a: 31.
62   Bhatt 2020: 28.
63   De Silva Jayasuriya 2009: 4.
64   Khalidi 2006: 250.
65   Khalidi 2006: 247-248.
66   Harris 1971: 102-106; Lynton & Rajan 1987: 178-179, see also 183.
67   Khalidi 2006: 250; cf. Eaton 2006: 61.

68	N'Diaye 2010; cf. Eaton 2006: 51; Nicolini 2006: 354. Basu 2008b: 229; De Silva Jayasuriya 2009: 6, 46-47, 57-58; Prasad & Bradbury 2020: 58.
69	Harris 1971: 5-6; De Silva Jayasuriya 2009: 28; cf. Masson 1843: 50.
70	Ahmed 2011: 23.
71	Alpers 2004: 28; cf. Alpers 2003: 33.
72	Badalkhan 2008: 276.
73	Harris 1971: 77-78; Pozdena 1978: 57-58; Bashiri 1983: 2-3; De Silva Jayasuriya 2010: 9; Ali 2011: 16-18; Ehsaei 2015; cf. Campbell 2008: 52.
74	Nicolini 2006: 356; Khosronejad 2017.
75	Masson 1843: 50, 306: Jamali 2020: 172.
76	Fartacek 2014: 580.
77	Baloch 1987: 34.
78	Cf. Jamali 2020: 166-167, 169; Prasad & Bradbury 2020: 54-56.
79	Nicolini 2006: 350; cf. Basu 2005: 171, 174, 177.
80	Barth 1983: 46.
81	Campbell 2008: 50.
82	Cf. Nicolini 2006: 365. Janmahmad (1982) notes: 'Slavery was very general throughout Balochistan' (72); and specifies that 'all the slaves belonged either to the indigenous population of Negroes brought into Balochistan by way of trade and commerce or by the conquering Arab armies. There were also slaves of Maratha and Hazara origin' (72).
83	Ahmed 1989: 26-27.
84	Jamali 2020: 169.
85	Jamali 2020: 169-170, cf. 173.
86	Jamali 2020: 170.
87	De Silva Jayasuriya 2009: 7; cf. Bitterli 1986: 37.
88	Nicolini 2006: 355.
89	Alpers 2003: 190.
90	For more details, see Bürgel 1991: 90-93. Cf. Nicolini 2006: 350.
91	Hopkins 2008: 636.
92	Ahmed 1989: 24; De Silva Jayasuriya 2009: 6-7, 10.
93	Basu 1995: 43.
94	De Silva Jayasuriya 2009: 14.
95	Robbins & McLeod 2006a: 22-23, 26.
96	Cf. Patai 1962: 41-42.
97	Ali 2011: 4.
98	Barth 1983: 47.
99	Qaimkhani 1996: 65.
100	Baillie 1890: 35; cf. Harris 1971: 70.
101	Baillie 1890: 35; cf. Burton 1851: 253; Basu 1995: 44.
102	Burton 1851: 253.
103	Baillie 1890: 35.
104	Cf. Basu 2003: 226; De Silva Jayasuriya 2009: 39.
105	Snouck Hurgronje 1931: 106-107.

106 Hopkins 2008: 652-654.
107 Baillie 1890: 36.
108 De Silva Jayasuriya & Pankhurst 2003b: 12; Prasad & Bradbury 2020: 53.
109 Bhatt 2020: 37.
110 Ahmed 1989: 28.
111 Matheson 1975: 42.
112 Hopkins 2008: 635.
113 Floyer 1882: 259.
114 in Qaimkhani 1996: 71-72.
115 Eaton 2006: 62.
116 Basu 1995: 145; cf. Basu 2015: 35.
117 Burton 1851: 254.
118 Gazetter Balochistan 1906: 464.
119 Masson 1843: 306.
120 Masson 1843: 50.
121 St. Pastner 1971: 182.
122 Recently, the editors of the volume 'African Diasporan Communities across South Asia' called expressly in their introduction to pay scholarly attention to Hoshu Shidi (Ali et al. 2020: 17).
123 Personal communication by Yaqoob Qambrani (6 November 2013, Seydabad/Baldia in Karachi). Cf. Qaimkhani 1996: 80; Qambrani 2017: 12, 15; Ahmed 1989: 2.
124 Lari 2002: 173.
125 Qambrani 2017: 12, 15, 27. It should be remembered that under Kalhora rule relations between Sindh and Kachchh were not always peaceful (cf. Kalhoro 2017: 237-247).
126 Robbins & McLeod 2006b: 165, 169 ('Although Africans are not generally associated with the kingdoms of Rajasthan, they do sometimes appear in Rajasthani paintings.').
127 Lari 2002: 199-200.
128 Lari 2002: 203-204. See also the detailed report on the battle fought at Miani by Lambrick (2005).
129 Qaimkhani 1996: 80-81.
130 Lambrick 2005: 184.
131 Napier 1845: 220, cf. 322, 384.
132 Qaimkhani 1996: 82.
133 Napier 1845: 379, cf. 385, 393.
134 On the following, see Khalique 2009: 43-49; Ahmed 2010: 298; Qambrani 2017: 21-28.
135 Qaimkhani 1996: 79-83.
136 Qambrani 2017: 23, 28; cf. Qaimkhani 1996: 79.
137 Qambrani 2017: 25.
138 Qambrani 2017: 25, 28; cf. Albinia 2008: 54.

139 Burton 1851: 254; Ahmed 1989: 24 (partly based on an article by G. Allana about Hoshu Shidi originally published in the 1950s); Khalique 2010: 44-45.
140 Ahmed 1989: 24; Khalique 2009: 47.
141 Eaton 2006: 45.
142 On the following, see Alpers 2003: 191-215; Alpers 2004: 32; Robbins & McLeod 2006a; De Silva Jayasuriya 2009: 14, 67-71; Khalique 2009: 18-24.
143 Harris 1971: 91-98; Qaimkhani 1996: 73; Eaton 2006: 58.
144 De Silva Jayasuriya 2009: 70.
145 Eaton 2006: 45, cf. 57.
146 Baptiste & McLeod & Robbins 2006: 33.
147 Shroff 2007: 316-318; cf. Harris 1971: 80-87 (on the Sidis of Janjira); Qaimkhani 1996: 72-73.
148 Shroff 2007: 318.
149 Vansina 1985: 199.
150 Klein 2000: 128.
151 Nicolini 2006: 358, 360, 362, 365.
152 in Qaimkhani 1996: 65-66. Siddiq Musafir's account on 'Dreadful Scenes from Slavery and Freedom', originally written in Sindhi in 1952, was recently translated into Urdu by Aslam Khwaja (Siddiq Musafir 2021).
153 Qaimkhani 1996: 66.
154 in Qaimkhani 1996: 69.
155 Albinia 2008: 74-75.
156 Burton 1851: 254; cf. Freeman-Grenville 1971: 8-11; Qaimkhani 1996: 66. This insightful information on the historical background of our people is corroborated by Eaton's estimation concerning the 'scattered communities of "Sidis" that survive in western India today.' They 'appear to be descended not from elite Habshi slaves of the fifteenth through seventeenth centuries, but from male and female domestic slaves brought from East Africa by European or Arab dealers in the eighteenth and nineteenth centuries' (Eaton 2006: 60-61).
157 Freeman-Grenville 1971: 11.
158 Harris 1971: 11; Nicolini 2006: 351.
159 Harris 1971: 27-39.
160 Freeman-Grenville 1971: 6.
161 Personal communication by Aslam Khwaja (7 February 2015, Karachi); cf. Baloch 2017: 53.
162 Gazdar 2013: 21.
163 Burton 1851: 254.
164 Burton 1877: 40, 47.
165 Eaton 2006: 52.
166 Burton 1851: 254; cf. Pottinger 1816: 64.
167 in Qaimkhani 1996: 70.
168 On the following oral history, see Qaimkhani 1996: 84-86 (based on Siddiq Musafir's Kulliyat); Qambrani 2017: 29-31 (based on Qaimkhani's writings).

The books written by Siddiq Musafir in Sindhi language (1952, 1965; see bibliography) are nowadays difficult to access (see Albinia 2008: 72-74). In Albinia's text are many misspelled names due to a false reading of Siddiq Musafir's Sindhi text.

169 Qaimkhani 1996: 84-85.
170 Qaimkhani 1996: 86.
171 Qaimkhani 1996: 87.
172 Paracha 2018: 76-77.
173 Ahmed 2018: 2.
174 Qaimkhani 1996: 92, cf. 87-91.
175 Cf. Basu 1995: 46; 2015: 35.

Socio-economic Life: Subsistence and Social Organization

Introduction

Social, economic, and political issues are usually closely connected. With regard to Africans in Pakistan, these domains are shaped by sheer poverty, economic exploitation, and powerlessness. Most of our people still live on the fringes of society, often dependent on landlords and former masters. As their original family ties were cut off and their traditional social structure destroyed through predominantly forced migration, they no longer live in close-knit communities, but in extended families scattered over Sindh and Balochistan.

This chapter first analyses the basic social institution of the family and then describes ways of earning a livelihood, thereby providing a glimpse of the standard of living especially in impoverished neighborhoods of Karachi, but also in underdeveloped rural towns and villages. In short, it examines different socio-economic conditions. In general, the lifestyle of our people is shaped by what Pierre Bourdieu has called a 'taste of necessity.'[1] Some information will then be given on social and political activities and on institutions working to uplift Shidi communities. Finally, a few religious congregations will be mentioned briefly to build a bridge to the following chapter on religion.

Fig. 17   Dressed for a wedding in Lyari, Karachi (November 2010)

Family and Kin

In Pakistan as elsewhere family constitutes the elementary unit of social groups. It provides stability, stands for mutual moral prescriptions, and is a model for socialization. It also creates an important network, in addition to neighborhood and personal friendships, providing support for all involved. For the poor and underprivileged the family is the only social security net. Survival is their main concern.

Among our people, households often consist of joint families in which siblings cooperate and live and eat together. It is remarkable that patrilinear descent is not as pronounced as in other ethnic groups, such as among tribal Baloch, and women live in a less segregated environment. Kinship among Shidis, Afro-Baloch, and Afro-Sindhis rather emphasizes the complementary relation of siblings based on the ideal ancestral brother-sister pair of Bava Ghor and Mai Mishra, the main African saints they venerate.[2] Thus the relation between genders seems to be more balanced than within the stricter patriarchal households typical for other ethnic groups. Children can even opt to take their mother's family name, and in general maternal kinship is highly valued.[3]

Women often enjoy more freedom and do not observe the stringent urban forms of *pardah* (seclusion) to the extent expected from women of other ethnic groups. This also holds true as far as female labor outside the home is concerned. In general, the position of women is more like that of traditional African societies where women act more assertively. Intermarriage between Shidis, Afro-Baloch, and Afro-Sindhis from different regions (Makran, Las Bela, interior Sindh) is rather common, especially in the megacity of Karachi (Figs. 18-19). For instance, a male Afro-Baloch from Makran can marry a Shidi female from Sindh. Shidis from different sections, such as Qambrani and Kathiawadi (originally from Gujarat) as well as Sunnis and Shiʿas, do intermarry, although endogamy within the respective group is preferred.[4] Furthermore, in Sindh and Makran, our people marry with other impoverished castes, such as Mallahs (fishermen), Katris (dyers), Koris (cloth-makers), as well as other 'Makranis' and 'Darzadas.'[5] Tribal Baloch families are often outraged when such mixed marriages are arranged – out of poverty, as a second marriage, or to hush up a previous relationship. Their offspring hide or deny their 'Black ancestry' as best they can.

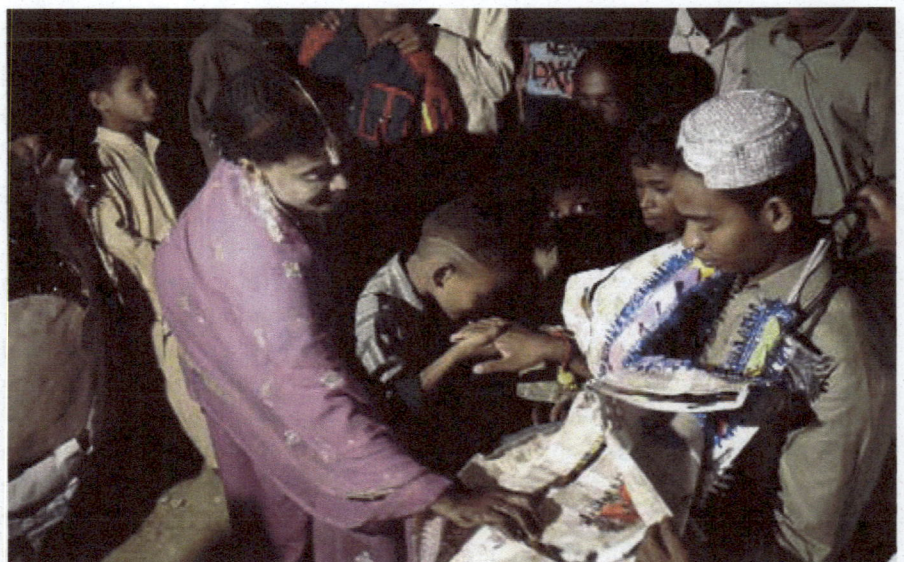

Fig. 18   Honoring the young bridegroom; Lyari, Karachi (November 2010)

Fig. 19   Wedding guests; Lyari, Karachi (November 2010)

Chapter 4

Beyond the nuclear or extended family living in one home, ideally the place of utmost security, unanimity, and expression of most intense identity consciousness, there is a cohesive group of maternal and paternal relatives, that is to say lineages, to whom an individual should behave with solidarity.

Subsistence and Poverty

In view of the situation of Habshi soldiers after the abolition of Hyderabad state in the Deccan, it is insightful to read what happened to them in the mid-twentieth century. Thus, an old Indian with African roots living in a slum of that city narrated: 'Our prestige died with the Nizam. My boys are now pulling rickshaws, some are in petty security jobs, some are hawking. Our widows are sick and they don't have money to buy medicines. […] There is no allotment of land for us, there is no colony for us, there is no reservation for our children in schools. I want my children to be educated but how can I pay Rs. 30 per month in fees when my pension of Rs. 100 a month has to feed a dozen mouths?'[6]

Fig. 20   Rooftop-school in Lyari, Karachi (July 2010)

Social conditions of our people in urban and rural Pakistan only vary insofar as in cities and towns they work mostly as manual laborers in the informal economy, whereas in the countryside as menial workers and laborers they still depend on landlords and tribal chiefs. Poverty is widespread among people of African descent and most income is spent on food.

In Karachi, men perform day labor for cash or are employed in various low-paid menial jobs. Manual labor is commonly called *mazdūrī kām* in Urdu. During my fieldwork in Lyari, known as 'a locality of hard workers and laborers,'[7] I observed that male Shidis, Afro-Baloch, and Afro-Sindhis are often semi-skilled factory workers, for instance in metal and steel factories as well as in flour mills. Moreover, they work as mechanics, repairmen, carpenters, masons, railway firemen, and seamen, as well as at the port where they load and unload ships. The latter work is known as *tālī-yard*, a word derived from English *trolley*, whereby cargo is divided in *tālī*s (loads). They also carry loads in the bazaar, for example in the paper market, or heave luggage on the top of buses at Lea Market.

Fig. 21   Janu Jerman, the famous *biryani-wala* from Shidi Goth near Lea Market; Lyari, Karachi (November 2015)

Chapter 4

Fig. 22   Working in a metal factory; Karachi (April 2005)

Fig. 23   Tinning cooking vessels on the roadside; Karachi (July 2010)

In this field of hired hands, called *hawā'ī rōzī* (literally 'windy daily work') with uncertain or unpredictable earnings, there are no government regulations, no social security, no health benefits, no paid holidays or bonuses from employers. Others drive rickshaws, work as cleaners, errand boys, handymen in shops, ticket touts at cinemas, sell wicker baskets, mats, dates, and fruit or do odd jobs, such as overseeing a public toilet, selling lime for a few coins to *naswār*-makers,[8] or selling *gutka* (stimulant made of a dark-red paste and lime). But there are other professions as well: an old gentleman from the old Shidi Goth told me that he earned his living since his youth as an ironer. In Kharadar, the oldest part of Karachi, I met a middle-aged man who worked as a courier delivering mail. Others are government clerks or tailor masters.

It is also instructive to look briefly at the biography of the late Hajji Ghulam Akbar Shidi (Fig. 2). Born in 1943 in Baghdadi, he first visited the small Mulla Hajji Adina School in his locality, then Abdulla Haroon School. As his father worked in the department of civil engineering at Karachi Port Trust, he managed to get an office job there at the age of fifteen to help organize the loading and unloading of ships. Later he became an active member of the dock workers' union. In 1976, he left office work and earned his living by painting signboards, managing housing construction, and doing a bit of export-import business. Additionally, he was active in various social and political organizations (see below).

Since the 1970s, spurred by the oil boom and construction work, men also found employment as unskilled or semi-skilled laborers in the Gulf states. Many migrated to Oman to join the local police force.[9] Others, however, because of unemployment and poverty, strayed from the honest path and descended into crime, some joining thuggish street gangs. However, our people are in no way more crime-prone than others. In the words of Laurent Gayer, who extensively investigated Karachi's conflicts and criminal violence, 'the biggest criminals in the city are its most privileged residents,' for instance those engaging in land-grabbing or illicit trade in water.[10]

As the women of our people generally do not observe strict *pardah* in the sense of being confined to their homes or to the narrow inner lanes of congested urban quarters, many of them work outside traditionally female gendered spaces to contribute to the family income. On the oasis of Panjgur in Makran, women not only work as domestic servants in homes of the upper class, but also as midwives and peddlers selling things to other women, for

instance embroidery.[11] Thus, women of the Shidi, Afro-Baloch, and Afro-Sindhi communities are less controlled by men than women of other ethnic groups, although admittedly their work is concerned with the non-public, female sphere of social life. In Karachi, they find employment in fisheries or as assembly line workers at packaging units. Often they work as housemaids (*māsī*, literally 'mother's sister').[12]

Rumana Husain, who portrayed two maids in her formidable book on Karachi, first tells about an elderly Makrani lady living with her family in Lasi Pada at Mohajir Camp (Baldia Town): 'In the mornings, Allah Bachai works as a *maasi* in a few houses in Juna Market. She washes clothes and utensils. She is usually exhausted by the time she returns home late in the afternoon. More than two decades ago she worked as a cook in a Karachi Municipal Corporation (KMC) hospital. All her daughters-in-law work as *maasis* in different houses in the old city area.'[13] About Zarina, a Shidi lady, around forty years old, living with her family at Agra Taj Colony, we learn: 'She has been working as a housemaid for the past eight years in a house in DHA [Defence Housing Authority; author's note, JWF], and is determined to provide a college education for her two children. Prior to this job, she sewed bed sheets. Later she worked in a garment factory sewing children's plastic knickers.'[14]

Over the last decades, many of our people acquired higher education and became medical doctors, professors, lawyers, and engineers. An outstanding example for a career in teaching and education is Professor Ghulam Husain Hajjisar from Baghdadi.[15] Born in 1965 in a poor family, his father worked as a fish-cutter at a local market and his mother sold deep-fried pastries at the roadside. Studying first at the local Baloch Free Education Centre and later teaching himself at a secondary school, he made his way up by graduating from Federal Urdu College (MA in Political Science) and Karachi University (MA in Sindhi Literature) and learning English at the Pak-American Cultural Centre. In 1994, he became a lecturer at Sindhi Muslim Government College, taught at Lyari Girls College (2001-2010), and since then is teaching as a professor at Abdullah Haroon College in Lyari.

Nevertheless, most of our people living in smaller towns in Sindh, such as Sehwan, Kotri, Tando Bago, Badin, or Sujawal, are poor and the men work as hired hands. They do what is commonly called 'donkey work,' for instance carrying loads and doing construction work. Others sell fish, juice, or ice cream. Many are day laborers, wash cars, and do whatever is needed. Some work as carpenters. Of course, there are also people belonging to the lower middle-class, such as my friend M.B. Baloch (already mentioned in the introduction to this book) from Sehwan who works as an accountant (*munshī*) partly with a construction company and partly with an ice factory. In Sujawal's Shidi neighborhood of Haqqabad, I met a retired lecturer at the Degree College in Thatta, and in Tando Bago a young Shidi whose father was a PIA Station Manager. His mother teaches at the Girls' Higher Secondary School, one sister works in a bank and the other is studying medicine in Beijing. He himself owns a little land and keeps five buffaloes whose milk he sells in the bazaar.

In the countryside of Sindh, many of our people work as share-croppers, farm servants, and manual laborers for the landowning elite, growing wheat, rice, and vegetables.[16] Usually, they have been attached to feudal families for generations. In return for their work, patrons are responsible for their welfare. As peasants in labor-intensive irrigated agriculture, they are on the same level as their fellow villagers who belong to other ethnic or occupational groups, such as Kolhis, Mallahs, or Kumhars. Often many of them are indebted. Taking the example of village Rajo Nizamani near Tando Muhammad Khan in Lower Sindh, it is said that Shidis also run a few shops, work as cooks when their service is needed in the course of life cycle rites and on other occasions, and a few have small government jobs.[17] In Makran and Las Bela, men work on date-farms, as fishermen, sailors, and porters, as well as shoemakers, tanners, potters, and weavers.[18] Women work as maids in the households of wealthy people, help their menfolk in the fields, participate in salting and drying fish, act as midwives, and prepare pickles for sale.[19]

In Karachi as well as interior Sindh, men traditionally also act as *mujāwir*s (caretakers, attendants) at saints' shrines (see Chapter V). Moreover, it is an important source of income for both men and women to sing and dance as commercial entertainers at wedding parties and on other joyful occasions (see Chapter VI).

Social and Political Organization

As our people were uprooted from their African kin, most of them enslaved and living as servants of feudal lords, they lost any given social structure such as kin groups, clans, tribes as well as their original ethnicity. After they were freed by their masters, some continued to stay with them. Others, as Feroz Ahmed rightly points out, 'went out into an unfamiliar world to start a new life as free citizens, without the security of feudal patronage. However, they managed to establish their own residential communities in villages and towns, and developed their own social organization. Mutual help and solidarity have been the key to their survival until today.'[20]

In rural areas, they borrowed the organizational structure of *panchāyat* (lit. 'five member' leadership group of men) from other local communities. A *panchāyat* is, in principle, a village council of notables and respected elders who act as arbitrators in social and political conflicts. Among Shidis it usually consists of all adult male members of the local community. The council, in which all matters of the community are discussed and decided, exists in parallel with state jurisprudence. Punishments can be in the form of fines in cash or kind or of public reprimand. Such comparatively informal councils function successfully in small communities where everyone knows everyone else, but not in cities. *Panchāyat*s mainly work as welfare committees and guard Islamic values and morals.

It is interesting to note that in some cases in the countryside a differentiation between groups developed among our people in which modes of subsistence also played a role. Thus, Nizamani reports from Rajo Nizamani that there are four divisions in the Shidi neighborhood, namely people descended from the war hero Hosh Muhammad Shidi, from a local Maulvi, from a group whose women work as *dā'ī* (midwives), and from a group whose members are said to be mostly bald.[21] At the village level, there are also women, men, and youth groups.

As briefly mentioned above, Shidis perceive themselves as a *jamā't* (community, brotherhood, congregation, association). In the Hindu-context in India, *jamā't* is perceived as a caste, *zāt* or *jatī*, based on common descent and henceforward integrated into the existing caste hierarchy. Sidis are thus categorized in Gujarat as a caste of low status endowed with *faqīrī*, i.e. it possesses the charisma of ascetic fakirs who mediate with the world of spirits.[22] Although the ritual dimension of caste is weaker among Muslims and allows easier merging with other communities, in south Pakistan Shidis, Khaskelis, and other groups with African roots also find themselves at the bottom of the hierarchy of usually landless Muslim *zāt* (occupational groups).[23]

Since Pakistan came into being in 1947, several local organizations were founded in Sindh to represent the interests of the Shidi community following a quest for emancipation and progress. Being victims of social and institutional neglect, most of our people still live in poverty and are economically exploited. Their literacy rate is very low, in rural Sindh sometimes only 1.5 per cent.[24] Consequently, these organizations and clubs chiefly dedicate themselves to social welfare and uplift, trying to improve health, education, and job opportunities, but they also constitute a political forum with the functions of a union. These organizations are often quite small with only a few dozen members. Their structure consists in a minimum of a chairman or president, a vice-president, a secretary, a treasurer, and an executive committee. Usually, there are at least two monthly meetings, and they charge a small monthly fee. Some larger organizations which maintain their own offices also have a youth wing and a women's wing.

To name a few organizations known in Sindh over recent decades: Yaqoob Qambrani had been chairman of the Muslim Sheedi Habshi Jamaat and now leads the Pakistan Sheedi Ittehad (PSI). In addition, there is the Sheedi National Party (SNP) and the Al-Habash Sheedi Jamaat. The latter, focussed on education, was founded in 1954 by Muhammad Siddiq Musafir Shidi. In interior Sindh there are several smaller local organizations, for instance, in Tando Bago, Sujawal, and Mirpurkhas, but especially active is the Young Sheedi Welfare Organization in Badin founded in 1987 by the advocate Faiz Mohammad Bilali.[25] In addition to seminars and lectures, it also arranges vocational training for women in embroidering and sewing.

In the working-class town of Lyari, our people generally vote for the Pakistan People's Party (PPP). Its founder Zulfiqar Ali Bhutto became President on 20 December 1971, and Prime Minister on 14 August 1973; he remained in power until July 1977. In those years, when the charismatic socialist ruler inspired the masses with his slogan '*rōtī, kaprā aur makān*' (bread, clothes, and housing), he ensured in a populist strategic move that the inner-city working class of Lyari finally obtained membership rights for their homes, mostly single-story stone houses often without access to sewerage and water. First people were reluctant to make their way out of Lyari to the Karachi Municipal Office (KMC) to obtain their lease orders, but when an office was especially opened for this purpose at Lea Market, they submitted their forms.[26]

For the last fifteen years, our people have sometimes also voted for the Baloch National Party which tries to reach out to the middle class. As far as renowned Afro-Baloch politicans are concerned, one must mention Allah Bakhsh Gabol (1895-1972). In pre-Partition times, he was one of the founding fathers of the nationalist Baloch League and later became mayor of Karachi. His mother was of African descent, and he himself married a colored woman.[27] His son Abdul Sattar, a lawyer, was elected to the National Assembly both in 1970 and 1977 and served as a minister in the cabinet of Prime Minister Zulfiqar Ali Bhutto. Allah Bakhsh's grandson Nabil Gabol also became a member of the National Assembly from Lyari.[28]

The late Rahim Baloch was a member of the National Assembly; like Rahim Bakhsh Azad (d. 2019), he was active in leftist politics. Recently, in August 2018, the PPP nominated the then 39-year-old Tanzeela Qambrani from Matli in district Badin, daughter of a lawyer and a headmistress, to a women's reserved seat in the provincial Sindh Assembly. She became the first female MPA from the Shidi community. In an interview with the news' platform *Cutacut*, she emphasized: 'Our community has been left far behind in education. The government should ensure that we have opportunities in education. Give us the net, we will catch the fish ourselves.'[29]

Social organizations of another kind are the various local community associations and clubs called *anjuman*s (assemblies or congregations) among the male population of Lyari. Our people are also members of these local Baloch-dominated associations dedicated to social welfare founded around the time of Partition. They pursue various community-oriented interests, ranging from cultural activities and settling 'family-related disputes to the provision of civic amenities.'[30] Their members help, for instance, in the organization of weddings and funerals. For this, they usually block a road in the neighborhood, spread out mats and cloth to sit on, set up a *shamiāna* (awning) for the women, and do the cooking. In times past, when funerals were held they would also dig the grave. If water becomes short in the neighborhood, they organize provision with water tankers.

Additionally, there are *anjuman*s pursuing specific interests in sports or dedicated to the veneration of saints. Thus, in Baghdadi, Saifi Club (Seypi Club) is basically a sports' club focusing on football and boxing, others are associations of pilgrims annually visiting shrines of Sufi saints, performing rituals, and taking out processions. By the way, every *anjuman* has its own patron-saint. Apart from this practised solidarity with its positive approach to life, being a member of an *anjuman* also means meeting frequently, sometimes daily, to chat and gossip. The men I talked to about these organizations admitted that for some decades now, membership has been decreasing because people have to work more to make ends meet, and, in addition, families would now be more likely to watch TV. In the chaotic years of the first decade of the twenty-first century, when Lyari became a centre of gang war, the social activities of these associations were also severely curtailed by gang violence which made life miserable and insecure in Lyari.[31]

A few organizations known in Lyari over recent decades include Anjuman Qasarkandi (named after Qasr-e Qand, a region in Iranian Balochistan), Yak Musht (meaning 'one fist,' i.e. union), as well as Anjuman Dashtiari (named

after a region in Iranian Balochistan), Anjuman Mustafai (named after the late Hajji Ghulam Mustafa, see the subchapter on the Rifa'i Sufi order in Chapter V), and Baba Farid Anjuman. The three latter organizations focus on saints' festivals and are connected with Sufi orders.

Finally, in the context of group relations, the social and religious 'houses' (*makān*) of the Shidis in Karachi should be at least mentioned briefly here; they will be followed up in the next chapter. In Sindhi Sufi culture, *makān* means a place 'which is sacred because a Sufi saint stayed there for a while.'[32] Traditionally, there are four 'houses,' namely Kharadar *makān*, Hyderabadi *makān*, Lasi *makān*, and Belara *makān*. All of our people living in Karachi, who venerate their African ancestor saints, belong to these associations and jointly perform rites of veneration at shrines. It also includes a network of kinship relations extending to interior Sindh and Makran. The oldest 'house' is the Kharadar *makān*, in which probably the first people from Africa were organized. Today it comprises people of African descent who speak Sindhi, Balochi, and Gujarati. The other 'houses' are named after regions in Sindh and Balochistan from where our people migrated to the city. Thus, the members of Hyderabadi *makān* came from the city of Hyderabad and from Upper Sindh, the members of Lasi *makān* from south Balochistan, and those of Belara *makān* from Las Bela and surrounding areas.[33] The premises of the Belara *makān*, which were located on Musa Chaudhary Road in the neighborhood of Juna-Baghdadi, no longer exist. Their members joined the Lasi *makān*.

A male and a female master head each 'house'. In the 1970s, Hajji Ghulam Akbar Shidi became the representative of these four Combined Shidi *jamā't* in Karachi which mainly organize the annual festival at the shrine of Mangho Pir. In addition to these four *makān*, there is the sacred space of the Kachchhi Shidis and Jamnagarwale in Musa Lane, i.e. of Shidi latecomers to the city, also called *Ghōrwāle kī makān*. Today, this 'house' is sometimes considered the fifth *jamā't* of the Shidis, all of whom follow the tradition of Bava Ghor.[34]

Endnotes

1   Bourdieu 1982: 298.
2   Basu 1995: 92-93.
3   Ahmed 1989: 30; Albinia 2008: 67.
4   Cf. Basu 1995: 76, 91-92 (on marriage among Indian Sidis in general: 98-106); Basu 2003: 224; Basu 2008 b: 230; Husain 2010: 20.

5 Albinia 2008: 69; cf. De Silva Jayasuriya 2008: 429.
6 Khalidi 2006: 252 (quote from a newspaper article by M.R. Sameeran entitled 'A Dark Future' in the *Illustrated Weekly of India*, 5 December 1982, p. 25).
7 Baloch 2017: 76.
8 *Naswār* is a mouth-tobacco (not 'chewing tobacco' as the substance is in principle not chewed!) of brownish or greenish color, especially common among Pakhtun/Pashtun/Pathan in Pakistan and Afghanistan, consisting of a mixture of tobacco, the ash of various plants, as well as lime (for detailed information, see Frembgen 1989).
9 Paracha 2018: 76.
10 in Hussain 2016: 103.
11 C. Pastner 1978: 440.
12 Baloch 1917: 44.
13 Husain 2010: 16.
14 Husain 2010: 20.
15 On the following, personal communication by Ghulam Husain Hajjisar (6 March 2020, Baghdadi in Karachi).
16 Apart from my own observations in different parts of Sindh, see, for example, Gazetteer Balochistan 1906: 561; C. Pastner 1971: 32.
17 Nizamani 2006: 53.
18 Gazetteer Balochistan 1906: 561; Gazetteer Las Bela: 126; Ahmed 1989: 28.
19 Nizamani 2006: 56.
20 Ahmed 1989: 25.
21 Nizamani 2006: 40.
22 Basu 1995: 9, 27-29, 33, 35-36; Basu 2000: 243; Basu 2003: 224.
23 Ahmed 1989: 25.
24 Nizamani 2006: 33.
25 Cf. Albinia 2008: 65-66; Khalique 2009: 48.
26 Personal communication by Aslam Khwaja (2 March 2020, Karachi).
27 On the following, see Ahmed 1989: 27.
28 Gayer 2014: 131.
29 Interview conducted by Zehra Husain on 5 June 2020 (see: https://cutacut.com/2020/06/05pakistan-s-first-sheedi-woman-mpa-talks-about-george-floyd-and-racism/).
30 Slimbach 1996: 154-156; Kirmani 2017: 127.
31 Kirmani 2017: 126-129.
32 Boivin 2015: 205.
33 Rashdi 1992: 141.
34 Qambrani 2017: 4, cf. 42.

5

Religious Traditions: Saints, Shrines, Rituals, and Sufi Orders

Introduction

To my knowledge, almost all Afro-Baloch as well as most Afro-Sindhis are Sunni Muslims following the Hanafi legal school, whereas among Shidis the percentage of Sunnis is estimated at around 70-80 per cent. The rest are Twelver Shi'as. Since the sixteenth century, a number of our people also became adherents of the small Zikri or Mahdawi sect founded in North Indian Jaunpur by Sayyid Mahmud (1443-1505), reverently called Nur Pak (Pure Light). His disciples, but probably not their *mahdī* (based on the idea of the Islamic messiah) himself, performed the missionary work in Makran.[1] This sect is part of the wider spectrum of Sufi Islam. Nowadays, Zikris (in Makran pronounced *zigrī*) face considerable religious discrimination by Sunni Muslims.

In Baghdadi, the heart of Lyari, men say their prayers in various Sunni mosques. Most of the latter are affiliated with the Deobandi school (such as *Madnī masjid, 'Arabī Shīdī masjid, Jama' masjid Seypīlēn*), one also with the Barelwi school, namely *Jama' masjid Baghdādī*. A number of our people, in Karachi and in interior Sindh, became members of the Tablighi Jama't. Otherwise they follow other purist forms of scriptural Sunni Islam, much in line with the growing influence of reformist discourse in Pakistani society over recent decades. For them, Africanness is rather a source of shame, not of pride.

Fig. 24　Hyderabadi *makan*; Lyari, Karachi (November 2014)

Yet, as everywhere, the roots of culture are in religion. Therefore, in what follows, my focus is entirely on the indigenous religious traditions and everyday religiosity of Shidis and of those among our people who venerate Bava Ghor and other African saints. Today, according to my own observations, only a smaller part of the male population of the African diaspora participates in ancient religious rituals that reflect memories of the mythological past significant for the present. Their pivots are culturally hybrid African-Islamic practices impregnated by lived Sufi Islam, such as the belief in saints and their miracles as well as ritual practices of spirit possession. The latter are often articulated in a distinct 'African idiom' of music. Shidis wholeheartedly identify with their ritual music-dance culture, which also includes the dance called *laywa* (see Chapter VI) and gives ample space for female religiosity. In my view, this devotional milieu marks a higher cultural 'intensity' in comparison to groups with less prominent African cultural traits.

After introducing the pantheon of gendered Shidi saints buried near Ratanpur in the former Rajput kingdom of Rajpipla (Indian Gujarat) – particularly Bava Ghor, the towering figure of the Shidi tradition, I describe and examine major shrines of the Shidi community in Karachi. I then share my observations on smaller Shidi shrines (including private ones which are part of the domestic domain) and sacred places in interior Sindh. Usually, we find larger and smaller memorial shrines or 'proxy shrines' known as *astāna*s (in Indian Gujarat named *chillā*); in contrast, shrines with real tombs and mausoleums are called *dargāh*s. The sacredness of these spaces emerged through the investment of meaning by telling narratives about the African saints in question as well as the performance of rituals. Above all, it is the saints' *barakat* or healing power which is disseminated through these sacred sites. In this way, through texts and rituals, shrines constitute spaces of remembrance or 'memoryscapes' connected to the history of the Shidis. To use an apt formulation by the historian and Islamic Studies scholar Nile Green, they mediate between the Shidis' past and their present geographies of belonging.[2]

Notes on various sacred sites are followed by a subchapter written together with Yaqoob Qambrani on the Shidi *mēlā* (festival) at the shrine of Mangho Pir, situated in the northern part of Karachi. Another topic is the diversity of ritual performances through which Africans in Pakistan remember their benevolent saints and ward off malevolent spirits. The belief in spirits coexists with Islam and related ritual practices do not negate an Islamic mode of life. Instead they tend to reflect people's experience of everyday life.[3] This chapter on religious traditions and practices will be concluded by notes on the relation of people of African descent to mystical or charismatic Islam. Many of them are affiliated with the Sufi orders of the Qadiriyya, Qalandariyya, and especially the Rifa'iyya. The latter case is investigated in detail by Aliya Iqbal Naqvi and Hasan Ali Khan who did ethnographic fieldwork on the subject.

Bava Ghor and the Pantheon of African Saints

According to Shidi hagiography, their patron saint Bava Ghor (also called Ghori Shah in Karachi and Gori Pir in Gujarat) is considered the descendant of the Abyssinian Bilal, the first reciter of the call to prayer in Islam.[4] His real name was Sidi Mubarak Nobi – the *nisba* Nobi suggesting an origin from Nubia, the Nile region in the Sudan. It is said that he remained at the tomb of Prophet Muhammad in Mecca for many years.[5] Different strands and variations of legends represent him on the one hand as a successful warrior and on the other as a wandering fakir who became an agate trader.

It is narrated that through a dream the Prophet sent him on a campaign to Gujarat in India to break the power of the dangerous female demon Makhan Devi (a local deity from the Hindu pantheon) who used to devour human beings daily. In fact, this legend echoes the deeds of Habshi warriors in India. According to one version, on the way he became the disciple of the Sufi saint Ahmad ar-Rifa'i (d. 1182/83) who renamed him Bava Ghor thus giving him a new Sufi identity. Ghor or Ghur means 'deep pit' or 'grave,' so Bava Ghor could be translated as 'the entombed saint.' In Pakistan this name is usually pronounced with the Persian-Arabic *gh*, but in India it lost this fricative and became Bava Gor.[6]

Another version suggests that the saint belonged to the army of Sultan Ghiyath ud-Din Muhammad (d. 1202) of Ghor in today's Afghanistan who dispatched a contingent of soldiers with him;[7] although it is more likely that he arrived in India in the fourteenth or fifteenth century.[8] Legend has it that when he and his army reached Ratanpur, situated in a forest region of Gujarat, he played chess with Makhan Devi on the condition that if she lost, she would have to embrace Islam, otherwise he would become her servant. The game lasted for a long time and after one year Bava Ghor's younger brother Bava Habash, who lived in Abyssinia, became furious because the demon was still alive. He therefore rushed to Ratanpur by sea with his own followers to kill her. Bava Ghor, however, ordered him to calm down as she was a female.

His sister Mai Mishra, who stayed in Egypt, also became furious and quickly sailed to Gujarat on board a large ship accompanied by her sisters.

Makhan Devi offered a cup of poisoned buttermilk to her and her followers, but Mai Mishra refused and finally killed the demon by striking her with her wooden sandal whereby Makhan Devi sank into the ground.[9]

Afterwards, Bava Ghor decided to stay in Ratanpur to lead the life of a religious mendicant (*faqīr*), but, according to yet another version of legends, the saint already reached Gujarat as a wandering ascetic. When he prayed for help to feed his people, God miraculously created semi-precious stones and henceforward the holy man became a successful trader in agate beads. An oral tradition widely understood as historical says that the African saint came to Gujarat sometime during the fifteenth century or earlier and started agate mining and bead manufacture.[10] The already well-established agate bead industry in the area surrounding his shrine flourished again and beads were traded through the port towns of Bharuch and later through Khambat to inland towns as well as to Arabia and Africa. Agate was also used in the manufacture of weapons, for instance in the case of agate-tipped arrows and spears. Bava Ghor's shrine in Ratanpur is a centre of pilgrimage not only for Sidis, but also for the local indigenous Bhil population and members of other lower Hindu castes.[11] As the three African saints in this mythical tale represent the good and strongly oppose the evil, they are also considered Sufi saints.

Shidis venerate Bava Ghor as a powerful miracle-working saint who possesses enormous 'blessing power' (*barakat*) and rules over malevolent spirits.[12] Thus, he is thought to cure people possessed by spirits. Legends about Bava Ghor provide a meaningful context for the religious beliefs and practices of the Shidi communities in both Sindh and Gujarat. They render this holy man an anchor for the collective memories of migration from Africa to South Asia. It is from him and his family that Shidis derive their special religious identity and close association with Sufi Islam. The ancestor-saints represent ideals of moral behavior – as devout Muslims, powerful leaders, and successful merchants as well as modest women, dutiful wives, and good mothers.

The name Bava Ghor carries the connotation of a pantheon of African saints. In addition to this chief patron-saint, who introduced the affiliation with Sufi Islam, it includes his younger brother, the virile warrior Bava Habash, and his sister Mai Mishra (Mother Egypt, often addressed as Mai Sahiba), both said to be his 'real' natural siblings.[13] More than being a conqueror of evil spirits, Mai Mishra assumes a mother-goddess-like role believed to foster progeny and protect childbearing. She embodies the whole spectrum of the feminine – bestowing life, birth, nurturance, and beauty. Mai Mishra never married and remained 'pure.' We follow Helene Basu's characterization of this extraordinary female holy figure who stands for the presence and power of African women in South Asia: 'She represents several ideals at once: an exemplary sister aiding her brother to obey a command of the Prophet; a good Muslim woman keeping *purdah*; one with healing powers who heals female infertility; one who is stronger than evil spirits and expels them from the bodies of the afflicted; one who takes possession of those she loves, removing their sufferings and bestowing knowledge upon them; one who speaks through their mouths; and finally the ancestress of all Sidis.'[14]

Besides these three major saints, there are many subordinate male and female saints, said to be Bava Ghor's 'ritual' brothers and sisters. The Indian Sidis know, for instance, eleven brothers and seven sisters although the number of siblings is in principle infinite (see below).[15] With the exception of the commander of Bava Ghor's army, the names of all other male and female 'Black' saints venerated throughout Gujarat are mostly unknown in Pakistan.

With the veneration of their African ancestor saints, our people in Karachi also lay special emphasis on Bava Ghor's younger brother Shidi La'l, said to live in the wilderness. Shidi La'l is also called Shidi Badshah ('king of the Shidis'), and in Gujarat he is known as Bava Habash. Another name for Shidi La'l is Shidi Mukhtiar (also pronounced Mukhtar or Mukta); a *mukhtiārkar* means 'head of administrative unit' in Urdu. Sometimes people also call him Dada Maqbul. He is considered the *sipāh sālar* (commander-in-chief) of Bava Ghor's army and his first *khalīfa* (deputy).[16] While Shidi Habastan is not Bava Ghor's proper brother, Shidis refer to him as brother. Other 'brother saints' are said to be Shidi Sahibo and Shidi Bilal. Several small memorial shrines are dedicated to these major male Shidi saints.

According to 'Apa,' who is a renowned female ritual leader, Darya Shah is also considered a member of the Ghoriya *silsila*. This benevolent god of the river Indus, primarily worshipped by high Hindu castes, is a prominent saintly figure or deity of 'syncretistic cults' widespread not only in Sindh, but across neighboring Gujarat, especially in coastal areas. He is also called Darya Pir and identified with Khwaja Khizr or Zinda Pir and Uderolal.[17] Dominique-Sila Khan rightfully calls this water deity 'a great reconciler of religious differences' whose message symbolizes 'rather the philosophical and tolerant spirit of Sufism as opposed to a more legalistic and rigid form of Islam.'[18]

The major female saint is Bava Ghor's sister Mai Mishra. According to local Shidi tradition, there are seven sisters in total. Apart from Mai Mishra, several names are listed which differ somewhat from one informant to another. I collected the names of Mai Goma, Mai Ratani, Mai Nuri, Mai Garhi (said to be a contemporary of Shah Abdul Latif Bhitai, d. 1753)[19], Mai Bhagi, Mai Mastani, Mai Garochi, Mai Khelni, and Mai Aipala. Basu mentions the names of the following seven female saints: Mai Mishra, Mai Goma, Mai Ratani, Mai Dukhri, Mai Khelni, Mai Miriam, and Mai Ghumli.[20] These female saints represent the dimension of the Divine Feminine firmly integrated into the individual and collective spiritual consciousness of the Shidis.

There exists the concept of 'hot' and 'cold' qualities in beings, spirits, actions, emotions, and substances, widespread in the Indo-Persian world and based on Galen's classical Greek medicine as well as among Hindus on Ayurvedic medicine. The ascetic Bava Ghor with his loving-kindness is classified as *thandā* (cool), whereas his brother Shidi La'l, who can easily become furious, is described as *garam* (hot-tempered).[21] The latter term characterizes the awe-inspiring state of *jalāl* representing the frightening power of God. Their sister Mai Mishra, on the other hand, is considered both *thandā* and *garam*. In general, a vital balance between the two extremes is sought: 'heat' should be surrounded and balanced by 'cold' to avoid destruction, but both qualities do not imply moral differences. According to their respective temperament, African saints prefer special drinks and food. The benevolent Bava Ghor is said to consume white and sweet milk, whereas the hot-tempered Shidi La'l/ Bava Habash drinks hot, black tea with ginger.[22] Their sister, on the contrary, eats a dish (*kichādī*, Urdu *khichrī*) made from black lentils and white rice cooked in milk, sugar, and *ghī*.

During ritual performances, the qualities of these African saints are also visualized through different colors. Male saints wear Arabic cloaks in various colors: Bava Ghor is dressed in green or white, but never in black (!), Shidi La'l in blue, Shidi Mukhtiar in white, Shidi Sahibo in black or white, and Shidi Bilal and Darya Shah in white.[23] Mai Mishra's and her sisters' costume is of bright colors, so women follow this habit out of veneration not only in rituals, but also in everyday life (although they predominantly wear Baloch dress). This association with specific colors and personal characteristics, combined with examples of devotees becoming 'possessed' by these saints in rituals, suggests that an original cult of African spirits may have been later superimposed upon by Sufism and the popular veneration of saints.

Among Shidis, male *faqīr*s and female *faqirānī*s act as ritual specialists and shrine attendants on behalf of their community (see below). According to Basu, 'although Shidi *faqīr*s are not renouncers, they do tend to be oriented

towards some kind of other-worldliness. This other-worldliness exists more in the form of an imagined space, as a threshold between the living and the dead, as a symbolic space inhabited and circumscribed by the ancestor saint.'[24] In the memory of their ancestor saint Bava Ghor, some of them wear a finger ring with the special eye-agate known as *bābāghorī*. Some *faqirānī*s, who stand out because of their religious knowledge and successful mediation with the saints, become charismatic personalities and ritual leaders whose reputation helps them acquire a wider following.

Major Shidi Shrines in Karachi

As already mentioned, there are four social and religious 'houses' (*makān*) of the Shidis in Karachi, each headed by an *ustād* (master) respectively *jama'dār* (headman) and an *ustāda* (female master). In Basu's words, such shrines 'are sites of memory where a sense of genealogical continuity with African forefathers persists.'[25] Various rites of veneration such as *'urs* are routinely organized and performed at these holy places 'to remember the saints' (*bāvā kī yād*). The latter are also visited regularly on Thursday evenings after *maghrib* prayers.

The oldest 'house' is the Kharadar *makān*. This shrine, with its ornamented portal, small courtyard, and an old tree, is located behind Kharadar's police station in the Zeri neighborhood, named after a Baloch tribe. It is said that in former times the shrine was hardly a hundred meters away from the sea. This sacred place represents an interesting amalgam of two different religious traditions, on the one side the veneration of a highly respected, learned descendant of Prophet Muhammad, namely Sayyid Ahmad Shah Bukhari, whose tomb is situated in the main room of the building, and on the other side of African saints. The shrine is an important *astāna* for the Shidis: there is a triangular-shaped niche for burning oil-lamps dedicated to Bava Ghor, built in a corner close to the tomb of the Bukhari Sayyid, as well as two ceremonial drums (*muggarmān*) placed in another corner. The adjacent room contains four tombs: the first on the left belongs to Mubarak Faqir Ali, a descendant of Bava Ghor, and the remaining three to Bukhari Sayyids. The standard in the courtyard is dedicated to Shidi La'l and the fireplace to Ali, the Prophet's cousin and fourth Sunni caliph. In this Kharadar *makān*, Shidis, Afro-Baloch, and Afro-Sindhis celebrate the *'urs* of Shidi La'l on the thirteenth of the Islamic month of Sha'ban.

Next in importance are two 'houses' situated close to Lea Market in the old Shidi Goth of Lyari. 'Hyderabadi *makān*' (Fig. 24), in the center of the Hyderabadi neighborhood only a few meters off Shidi Village Road, is a compound consisting of a rather rectangular courtyard in between multi-storied residential buildings and three little memorial shrines. Almost in its center, there is a rather horizontally grown trunk, the meagre rest of what once must have been a taller tree, sometimes found wrapped with ceremonial green tomb covers or flower garlands.[26] On one of the long sides of this spacious courtyard is a row of three small shrine rooms, each with a separate door in the front. The little *astāna* on the right is dedicated to the Sufi saint Baba Farid (d. 1265), an eminent master of the Chishti order buried in Pakpattan in the Pakistani Punjab. He is particularly venerated by Shidis as he is supposed 'to have brought Islam to Africa.'

On the right side of the door, the façade is painted with a landscape showing mausoleums with cupolas and a minaret, palm trees, and a river with a boat. This scenery invokes the famous miracle in which Abdul Qadir Jilani (d. 1166), the great saint of Baghdad, widely known as Hazrat Ghaus Pak, lifts a boat and saves the lives of innocent people on the river Euphrates.[27] On the left of the door, there are three simple graphic depictions of *faqīrī* or dervishdom, namely begging bowl, ascetic staff (serving as a support for the forehead, chin, arm, or hand) with prayer beads, and dervish horn. Inside this pink room, in front of the green *mihrāb*-shaped niche and simple calligraphies invoking Allah and Prophet Muhammad, there is the *takht* or 'throne' of the 'absent-present' saint, a flat cushion for sitting, decorated either with flowers or a folded tomb-cover.

On its right side is a lampstand and on its left a *muggarmān*. Adjacent to this memorial shrine is the *astāna* dedicated to Shidi La'l and Shidi Mukhtiar. On the back wall of this likewise pink room is a rectangular pedestal, painted in green with a niche for oil-lamps underneath, crowned by a *gumbad*, i.e. a little cupola-shaped structure, covered with cloth. Additionally, there are three oil-lamp stands dedicated to Shidi La'l, Ghaus Pak, and a smaller one to Rashal Baba. The third *astāna*, on the left in the row of rooms, belongs to Bava Ghor's sister Mai Mishra. It is reserved for women, while men are not allowed to enter as the saint is said to keep *pardah*.

Lasi *makān* is located inside the old Shidi Goth behind Lea Market close to the main road. It consists of a larger compound with a courtyard and a flat central building painted in green. This building, shaded by a large tree, has a small veranda with two entrances, the left for men and women, the right for women only. The main entrance on the left first leads to a little room dedicated to Baba Farid with a small memorial tomb in the centre; right behind, in the second room, is the elongated tomb of Sayyid Qasim Ali Shah Ashabi. The door on the right of the veranda carries a signboard with the inscription *Māʾī Sahiba Ratanpur-walī* and leads to a little room dedicated to Mai Mishra. In the latter, twenty-one clay pots (*matkā*), covered with red cotton cloths, are stored in a corner, the pots symbolizing 'weight' or the female womb; they are carried by women during ritual processions.[28]

On the left of the shrine is a small *gumbad* dedicated to the Sufi saint Pir Mehr Ali Shah (d. 1937) whose mausoleum is situated in Golra Sharif near Islamabad. At the back of the main building are several small *astāna*s each marked by the typical memorial structure of a square pedestal with an oil-lamp niche underneath and the *gumbad* on top. Such *gumbad*s, also found in other parts of Sindh, in shape somewhat resemble a Hindu *samādhī* as well as a Buddhist *stūpā*. On Thursday evenings, they are ritually given a bath (*ghusl*) with rosewater. The *gumbad*-type *astāna*s of Lasi *makān* are dedicated to Shidi Laʿl (his honor especially marked by a turban on top of the cupola, Fig. 25), Shidi Mukhtiar, Ghaus Pak (Abdul Qadir Jilani, the great saint from Baghdad), and Shidi Habestan. Additionally, there are three standards to the memory of Ghazi Abbas Alamdar, the Shiʿa martyr who carried the standard in the battle of Karbala.

The last major Shidi shrine in Karachi to be described here is Shidi Jamnagarwale *astāna* or Ghorwale *makān* which does not belong to the traditional four 'houses,' but is connected with Kachchhi Shidis from Indian Gujarat who arrived after Partition in 1947. This shrine is in a neighborhood of Musa Lane in Lyari behind the Kakri football stadium inhabited by about seventy Kachchhi- and Kathiawadi-speaking families. The whole shrine compound appears rather new with marble tiles on the floor and the lower walls. It is dedicated to Bava Ghor whose *'urs* is celebrated here on the sixteenth and seventeenth of the month of Rajab, as well as to his brother Shidi Laʿl, to Nagarchi Baba (a younger brother of Bava Ghor venerated in Gujarat as the first drummer in his army),[29] and to Ghaus Pak. Furthermore, there is an *astāna* dedicated to Mai Mishra and the tomb of the Bukhari Sayyid Hafiz Shams ud-Din, a Sufi of the Qadiri-Chishti order. Another small domed building in the same compound is called *Qalandrī masjid*, evoking the famous Sufi saint Laʿl Shahbaz Qalandar. As usual, an *'alam* (standard), a ritual item borrowed from the Shiʿa faith, is placed in a corner.

Chapter 5

Fig. 25 Small memorial shrine of the *gumbad*-type for Shidi La l at Lasi *makan*; Lyari, Karachi (January 2014)

Secondary Shidi Shrines in Karachi

Unlike Shidi *faqīr*s at the shrine of Bava Ghor near Ratanpur, who lived until the mid-twentieth century in Gujarat as peripatetic dervishes walking in groups collecting alms,[30] today *faqīr*s of the Shidi community in Sindh are resident and work as *mujāwir*s (custodians, attendants) or *khidmatgār*s (servants) of saints' shrines, above all at smaller ancillary cult places. The role of custodian does not depend on age, although mostly older or middle-aged men attend to a shrine. Sacred places dedicated to female saints are in any case taken care of by female *mujāwir*s. Often these *faqīr*s (ritual specialists), Babas (trance healers) and other religious men and women have their own *astāna* at home, almost always equipped with a *muggarmān*. Some notes on public and domestic shrines in Karachi will exemplify this topic.

On the outskirts of Budni Goth, a dreary outlying area of Mauripur in the northwest of the city stands the shrine of Shidi Bilal. It consists of a rectangular cube-shaped mausoleum, crowned by four miniature-minarets on its corners, set on a raised walled platform, all painted in green.[31] Small flags in green, red, and yellow decorate the wall. Close to the platform is a pole (*'alam*) with a green flag. '*yā Hazrat Bilāl – Hazrat Bilālī Bābā – Ghulām Sa'īd Hazrat 'Abdullāh Shāh 'Ashābī – Shīdī Badshāh zindahbād*' is written on a marble plate beside the pole. Although I was not able to speak to the shrine's caretaker Faqir Mohammad Bilal (d. 2015), who was absent during my visit, it appears from this inscription, and from an *'urs* placard I studied in Budni Goth, that the shrine is dedicated to Bilal, the first *mu'azzin* of Islam, and to one Bilali Baba who served the saint Abdullah Shah Ashabi in Makli.

In the Lyari quarter of Singo Lane, right on the main Bakra Piri Road, there is the shrine of Sayyid Gharib Shah Bukhari with several large fresco folk paintings depicting various Sufi shrines in the courtyard. For more than thirty years, its *mujāwir* has been an Afro-Baloch. On Thursday evenings, people of African descent get together at this shrine.

A local Afro-Baloch and his family run a small neighborhood shrine dedicated to Baba Farid in the quarter of Shah Baig Lane. Inside, there is a *gumbad* with a niche for burning oil-lamps (*chirāgh*), a *muggarmān*, portraits of Baba Farid, and a fresco painting of the shrine of La'l Shahbaz Qalandar and Muin ud-Din Chishti, as well as other Islamic posters, calligraphies, and paraphernalia including a begging bowl. Its deceased long-term keeper was Muhammad Yaqub *urf* Ustad Balu Mistri.[32]

Across Lea Market lies the little *astāna* of Mai Sati or Shah Pari, said to be a fairy whose main shrine is found on Makli hill near Thatta. The *astāna* is visited above all by women afflicted by *jinn*. The *mujāwir*s, who work in shifts, are all Shidis. Before this holy place was demolished due to construction work, then rebuilt, and considerably reduced in size in late 2018, it consisted of a proper pavilion housing a rather impressive cube-shaped pedestal with a niche for oil-lamps underneath and a *gumbad* on the top, all clad in tile-work. It was a peaceful place to sit and get together, tucked away from the noisy market and main road in a hidden corner with shops on the front side. This setting fell prey to commercial interests.

During my search for Shidi shrines, I also found a tiny and very modest *astāna* in a lane in Nayabad inhabited by some Afro-Sindhi and Shidi families. This memorial shrine is dedicated to Shidi La'l, here simply addressed as Shidi Baba. Inside the small cubicle is a *gumbad* with an oil-lamp niche; the cubicle itself is painted green, the name of the saint in red and the simple graphic depictions of a dervish's staff and begging bowl in black. In early 2019, this *astāna* situated on the roadside was demolished to make way for the construction of a new residential building; it was rebuilt some meters away. Opposite is the house of 'Apa,' a renowned female ritual expert of the community. On the ground floor, a tube-like corridor leads to another tiny domestic *astāna* consisting of two little *gumbad*s, one dedicated to Bava Ghor and the other to his *khalīfa* Shidi Mukhtiar.

In Baldia's Habshi Colony, I visited a Bava Ghor *astāna* in the home of M. Husain. His sister is a medium of female Shidi saints (*Bāvā Ghōr kī bahen*) and has a special spiritual connection (*rūhānī*) to Mai Mishra; thus, she is respected as the ritual daughter of her African ancestress.[33] The power (*karāmat*) to communicate with them had been transferred to her by her mother. This domestic memorial shrine consists of a two-stepped 'altar' in tile-work for Bava Ghor, on which three sacred objects are placed: the saint's wooden staff (*muktā, dāndā*) in the centre, a fly whisk with peacock feathers (*mōr-pīchī*) dedicated to his *khalīfa*, and a rattle (*misrā*) symbolizing his sister Mai Mishra consisting of two hollowed coconuts with rattling stones in it. Both are covered in red and yellow cloth. Right above these ritual items, like a sort of canopy, three green headgears are fixed on a metal board in front of the red embroidered cloth covering the wall. The central one for Bava Ghor is decorated with a turban and crown-like diadem, the one on the right for his *khalīfa* with a smaller diadem, and the one on the left for his sister has no additional ornament. On the right side of this 'altar' stands a *muggarmān* covered with a red brocade.

Fig. 26   Domestic shrine dedicated to Mai Mishra in Daryabad; Lyari, Karachi (November 2016)

Another very beautiful domestic shrine belongs to one Faqir Bilal who, for some time, was the attendant of the Kharadar *makān*. His *astāna*, dedicated to Mai Mishra, is located in his home in Daryabad, a quarter of Lyari, and was taken over from a deceased relative (Fig. 26). It is set into a corner of a room allowing enough space for maybe ten or fifteen people to sit. The form and decoration of this miniature shrine is unique in the sense that it shows a kind of vernacular Mughal architecture on a tiny base of hardly more than one-and-a-half square meters. The little rectangular 'building' has an ornamented veranda with four arches, three on the front and one on the narrow side, and three red and silver painted cupolas on the roof. A red curtain covers the left side of this shrine, containing ritual paraphernalia, and on the corner of the right side is a tiny *chirāgh-khānā* or 'oil-lamp house', again in the shape of a domed miniature mausoleum. When receiving patients, the officiating magic healer would sit in the front of this 'building.' At the time of my visit in October 2016, this shrine was no longer used by its new owners.

A somewhat simpler, but still impressive private shrine is found in the home of 'Baba' in Baghdadi. One side of a small cube-shaped room of not more than four to five square meters also has a sort of rectangular 'building' with built-in cabinets in tile-work. On the left, there is an alcove covered by an embroidered red curtain containing, besides ritual paraphernalia (incense-holders, etc.), a *kashkōl* attributed to Bava Ghor. In the centre a glass-case is used for keeping ritual substances and right below a green-painted and arch-shaped niche for oil-lamps. This niche represents, in fact, the heart of the *astāna*. It contains five *chirāgh*s: the biggest one for Mai Garhi and the other four for Ghaus Pak (Abdul Qadir Jilani), Bava Ghor, Sayyid Yusuf Shah Modi (a Ghazi saint whose shrine is on Manora island), and Mai Mishra. Finally, on the right side, there is another tiny structure in the shape of a mausoleum with one oil-lamp burning for Yusuf Shah Modi and a second one used for personal wishes (*mannat*). There are three standards (*'alam*, *jandhā*): the longer symbolizing the Shi'a martyr Ghazi Abbas Alamdar (to whom the Baba attributes special powers to attack demons), the middle-sized for Yusuf Shah Modi, and the shorter for Shidi Sahibo. Each standard is wrapped with cloth, scented by a bundle of basil, with its 'foot' sitting in a little bowl filled with flour. Additionally, there is an iron dervish staff covered with a sash said to belong to Yusuf Shah Modi.

Finally, in another private home in Baghdadi, I saw a shrine consisting of a small chamber in which a turban symbolized the great saint Abdul Qadir Jilani (Ghaus Pak) and three oil-lamps burned in honour of Bava Ghor, Shidi La'l, and Baba Farid.

Shidi Shrines and Abodes of Sufi Saints in Interior Sindh

As far as sacred sites of the Shidi community within the colorful religious landscape of south Pakistan is concerned, I am only able to share a few stray notes about places in interior Sindh with the reader. Further field research in this respect needs to be done, also in Makran and other parts of Balochistan.

In Sukkur, a major town in Upper Sindh, I visited the tomb of Shidi La'l Badshah near the fish market of Qasimabad. It is not a mausoleum, but simply a decorated tomb in the midst of a courtyard. It has a wooden railing and is shaded by a canopy. It is said that this Shidi La'l Badshah was the servant of the saint Juman Sahibo Jati or Shiñ Badshah who lived well before the Mughal period and is buried in Sukkur. According to legend, he used to ride a lion (in Sindhi *shiñ*), a miracle motif also known from other Sufi saints in South Asia. There is also a memorial shrine dedicated to him in Shikarpur.

Further south, in Lower Sindh, there are *astāna*s of Zumurrud Faqir in Matli (located in the Nizamani neighborhood), of Sabago Faqir in Tando Muhammad Khan, and of Nango Faqir (Yaqub Faqir) in Kotri. According to legend, the latter was able to metamorphose into a snake while dancing ecstatically. In Tando Bago, there is the tomb of the highly respected educationist Muhammad Siddiq Musafir Shidi (discussed in the chapter on history), whose *'urs* is celebrated by Shidis from all over Sindh.

Frequently elder Shidis serve as attendants of local shrines, for instance at the mausoleum of Nazarmun Shah Jilani in Tando Bago where the local Shidi community also used to keep their *muggarmān*s. At the large *dargāh* of the Sufi saint Sayyid Abdul Karim (d. 1620), commonly known as Shah Karim, in Bulri, Shidis traditionally act as *mujāwir*s. In February 2012, I met Fazal Din Qambrani, the keeper of the key to the shrine (*chābīdār*). Like attendants of shrines in Karachi, he also performed the ritual practice of bestowing blessings on pilgrims. Fazal Din shared his duty with his son. Many of our people, also from Karachi, attend the annual festival in which the death of this saint is commemorated.

The Shidi mēlā at Mangho Pir
(by Sheedi Yaqoob Qambrani and Jürgen Wasim Frembgen)

Mangho Pir also known as Pir Mangho, whose name is sometimes given as Maggar Pir (derived from Sanskrit *makara* for 'crocodile'), was an ascetic Sufi saint said to have reached Sindh in the late thirteenth century. Some authors write that he came from Khorasan, others claim Arabia as his place of origin;[34] Shidis, however, preserve a different oral tradition (see below). They also emphasize that they are connected to this saint because their ancestor Bava Ghor, on his way from Ethiopia via Arabia and Makran to Gujarat, stayed for some time at Mangho Pir's shrine.[35] Shidis are the latter's traditional devotees and constitute the majority of pilgrims at the annual festival celebrating the *'urs*, meaning the mystic nuptial of the saint's soul with God, in the month of Dhu'l Hijjah. Mangho Pir appears as a great miracle-worker and healer, first because of the crocodiles living in the swamps and date-groves nearby, making his shrine an outstanding one in the whole of South Asia, and second because of the springs of hot and cold water. In the nineteenth century, this sacred place was the main Sufi centre of Karachi.[36]

The shrine, visited by both Muslims and Hindus (who venerate him as Lala Jasraj),[37] is located on a low hill in a rocky desert-like area on the northern outskirts of Karachi (Fig. 27).[38] The medium-sized compound has a shaded sitting space as well as a veranda for pilgrims around its main, green-domed sanctuary. Mangho Pir's cenotaph is sheltered by a wooden canopy with multi-cusped arches and typical screen-panels (*jālī*) painted in white, pink, green, and blue in the style of typical Sindhi folk art. Around

Chapter 5

Fig. 27 The shrine of Mangho Pir, Karachi (July 2007)

the *dargāh*, there is an old historic graveyard, also containing tombs of the Chaukhandi type, and at the foot of the hill there are stalls selling sweets, flowers, toys, cheap jewelry, household goods, and knick-knacks. Not far from the shrine are the famous healing springs to which a building is attached with separate bath compartments for men and women. Nearby is the small *mazār* or *ziyārat* (saint's tomb) of Pir Sher Shah Badshah and Pir Ahmad Shah, both belonging to the Qalandariyya, as well as right opposite a green-painted *astāna* dedicated to La'l Shahbaz Qalandar.

In 1843, Lieutenant Carless visited this area and gave a vivid description quoted here at length: 'We came suddenly upon one of the most singular scenes I ever witnessed. The accounts of my companions had prepared me for something extraordinary, but the reality far surpassed their description. Before us lay a small swamp enclosed by a belt of lofty trees, which had evidently been formed by the superfluous waters of the spring close by flowing into a low hollow in the ground. It was not a single sheet of water, but was full of small islets, so much so that it appeared as if an immense number of narrow channels had been cut, so as to cross each other in every direction.

These channels were literally swarming with crocodiles, and the islets and banks were also covered with them. The swamp is not more than 150 yards long, by about 80 yards broad; and in this confined space I counted above 200 large ones, from eight to fifteen feet long, while those of a smaller size were innumerable [...]. In a small pool, apart from the swamp, there was a very large one, which the people have designated the "chief," because he lives by himself in a kind of state, and will not allow any of the common herd to intrude upon his favourite haunt.'[39]

Since the nineteenth century, several travelers described their visit to the shrine and especially the biggest and oldest crocodile, called Mor Sahib, literally Mister Peacock. Dead crocodiles are properly buried in special graves as they are considered the disciples of the saint. It is possible that the reverence for the crocodiles serves as a site of memory for African ancestor worship as there are many cases known in Africa where people venerate these reptiles as incarnations of clan ancestors.[40]

People who pay their respects to Mangho Pir at his shrine also visit the nearby thermal springs. According to a legend, these springs are attributed to a miracle performed by La'l Shahbaz Qalandar who, it is said, 'caused a hot spring to issue from a rock and a grove of date palms to spring from the ground, in order to make the valley liveable for the Mugger Peer.'[41] The latter is venerated as a healer of all kinds of skin diseases including leprosy and rheumatism.[42] Therefore, receiving a healing treatment by taking a bath and drinking the water at this place has been popular for a long time. In 1896, Hindu, Muslim, and Parsi philanthropists set up a leper asylum at the Mangho Pir springs. Patients from Afghanistan to various parts of British India all the way to Bengal arrived and founded a leper colony nearby, called Basti Yaqub Shah, inhabited by people from diverse religions who lived together peacefully.[43]

Later, in 1960, the leprosarium was extended by the German medical doctor Ruth Pfau. Although leprosy is incurable, patients experience relief from these waters. In summer 1963, the temperature of the hot water was found to be 48° C. and that of the cold 32° C. Although the spring waters were often described as 'sulphur springs,' chemists did not find sulphurated hydrogen in these waters, but instead the presence of calcium, magnesium, sodium, potassium, silicon, iron, as well as arsenic sulphate. The scientists who performed the chemical analysis concluded that 'whatever curative power is attributed to these waters may be due to the extremely small amounts of arsenic present.'[44] Arsenic in small doses is known to have curative effects for skin diseases.

There is hardly any historical information available on Mangho Pir, but we have a particularly rich hagiography. Shidi elders narrate that the saint did not come from Khorasan or Arabia, but was a Hindu robber by the name of Mangha Ram.[45] As the legend goes, there was a path, close to where the shrine stands, used by pilgrims on their way to Mecca. These caravans were looted by Mangho (or Mangha) every now and then. One such convoy passing through comprised four famous saints, namely Baba Farid, La'l Shahbaz Qalandar, Baha ud-Din Zakariya, and Bava Ghor. As the saints reached the spot, Mangho confronted them in order to rob them, but the bandit could not bear their penetrating gaze. He repented his sinful life, gave up his wayward habits, and converted to Islam. When the saints returned from their pilgrimage, his destiny changed altogether.

Mangho had them teach him and finally he requested some gifts from them. Thus, La'l Shahbaz Qalandar granted him the springs of hot and cold water. Baba Farid flicked his cloak and lice fell from it which turned into the crocodiles which are considered the living miracle (*zindā karāmat*) of the saint.[46] Baha ud-Din Zakariya prayed for Mangho's *walāya* (sainthood) and delegated some of his followers to his service. *Walāya* also means the spiritual territory over which the saint wields power and authority. Bava Ghor promised to serve Mangho Pir with his whole community after the saint's final union with God.

According to another well-known version of this legend, it was not a group of four saints passing through the area, but Baba Farid alone who made the robber Mangho change his life after he had looted the caravan of the noble Chishti saint and had not found anything of value during the raid. Years later, Baba Farid was pleased by Mangho's character and conferred the respectful title Sakhi Sultan on him.[47] The story of the conversion of the Hindu bandit to Islam and his subsequent name-change is also told in a version in which the saint, after he had been robbed, presented sugar to Mangho so that the latter's wife could prepare some tea.[48] But, when the sugar miraculously turned into salt, Mangho complained to Baba Farid about the bitter taste. Thereupon the saint admonished him to stop looting travelers and to trust in God and then he should try again to make tea. So Mangho did and the tea became sweet and tasty. Mangho was deeply impressed, repented, and became Muslim.

In legends told by non-Shidi Muslims, however, Mangho Pir's original name is either given as Sayyid Khwaja Hasan Sakhi Sultan, said to have inadvertently brought crocodiles from Arabia to the subcontinent in the shape of head lice, or Kamal ud-Din, a Chishti saint coming from Balkh or the area of Badakhshan in modern-day Afghanistan.[49] When the saint reached the place, where his shrine stands today, he let loose the lice into the water who were reborn as crocodiles. According to another folk belief, it was La'l Shahbaz Qalandar who 'gifted the lice of a saint to Mangho Pir, and then, after instructions to put them in a pond, he miraculously turned them into crocodiles.'[50]

Rites of veneration are performed at the shrine of Mangho Pir. Shidis celebrate their *mēlā* or festival which is different from the saint's *'urs* (!), with fervour and devotion (Figs. 28-45).[51] Its focus is on the oldest and largest crocodile, the Mor Sahib, considered to be sacred and to be a saint. There are two essential ritual components here, namely *amrī* and *tikko*. *Amrī* (tamarind tree) is the term for an old tradition of gathering in the evenings after work in the shade of a tamarind tree to chat and dance (*dhamāl*). Although people also know the Swahili word *gōma* for dance, it is only used by members of the Ghorwale *makān* from Gujarat. At Mangho Pir, *amrī* designates an open space behind the shrine. *Tikko* is a term derived from the Hindi word *tīkā* which means an ornamental mark of vermilion dabbed on the forehead (Figs. 35-36). When meat is offered to Mor Sahib, the crocodile's forehead is thus marked and garlanded with flowers. This is done out of respect for Mangho Pir and in the hope of having personal wishes fulfilled.

The *mēlā* is jointly organized by the four 'houses,', Kharadar *makān*, Hyderabadi *makān*, Lasi *makān*, and Belara *makān*. Dignitaries of these congregations draw up the schedule of the rites and decide on the final dates following ancient Shidi tradition, meaning that the *mēlā* will start on a Friday and conclude on the next Thursday evening. The festival is usually between May and June. The sequence of rites is as follows:

1. Friday: laying a *chādar* (cover) on the tomb of Mangho Pir by members of the four *makān*
2. Saturday: *amrī* by Kharadar *makān*
3. Sunday: first *tikko* by Kharadar *makān* and *amrī* by Lasi *makān*
4. Monday: second *tikko* by Lasi *makān* and *amrī* by Hyderabadi *makān*
5. Tuesday: third *tikko* by Hyderabadi *makān* and *amrī* by Belara *makān*
6. Wednesday: fourth *tikko* by Belara *makān*
7. Thursday: between *'asr* and *maghrib* prayers laying a *chādar* on the tomb of Mangho Pir by members of the four *makān*

Chapter 5

Fig. 28   Shidi pilgrims arriving at Mangho Pir (August 2014)

Fig. 29   Young spectators at the Shidi mela, Mangho Pir (August 2014)

Fig. 30   Drummer with a barrel-shaped *duhl*; the late Hajji Ghulam Akbar Shidi is sitting on the right; Mangho Pir (July 2007)

Fig. 31   Ritual paraphernalia: bowl of milk, wooden stick (symbol for Bava Ghor), incense-holder, and coconut; Karachi (November 2010)

Fig. 32   Beating the sacred *muggarman*, perceived as the 'voice of Bava Ghor'; Mangho Pir (July 2010)

Fig. 33   Group of women at the Shidi *mela*; the white-dressed woman raises coconut rattles dedicated to the female saint Mai Mishra; Mangho Pir (March 2018)

Africans in Pakistan

Fig. 34 Bundles of peacock feathers are used to convey blessings; Mangho Pir (August 2014)

Fig. 35 *Tikko* ceremony: Mor Sahib, the oldest crocodile, gets an ornamental mark of vermillion; Mangho Pir (March 2018)

Chapter 5

Fig. 36　Mor Sahib, the sacred crocodile; Mangho Pir (September 2016)

Fig. 37　Drums are blessed with sacrificial blood before being played; Karachi (November 2010)

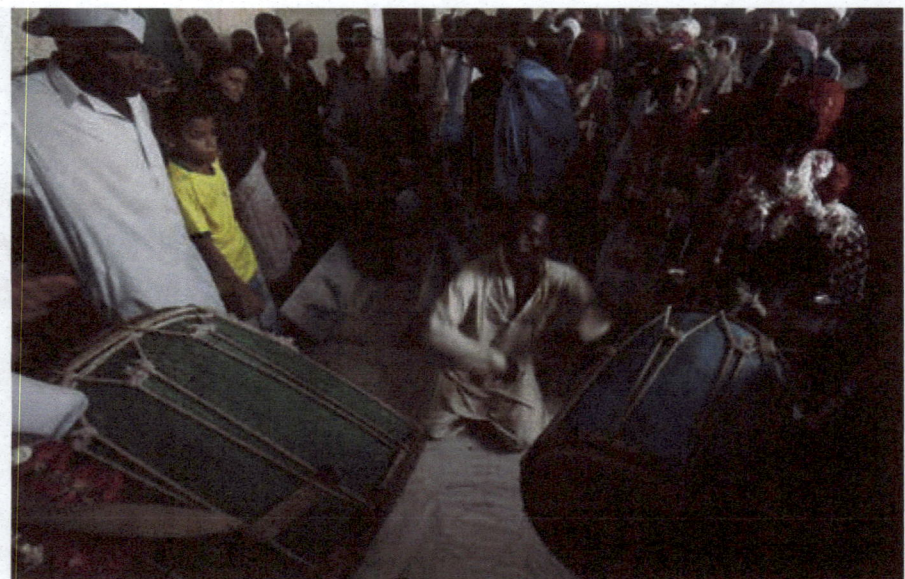

Fig. 38   Going into ecstasy at the *mela*; Mangho Pir (August 2014)

Fig. 39   Frankincense, the aroma of sacredness; Karachi (November 2010)

Chapter 5

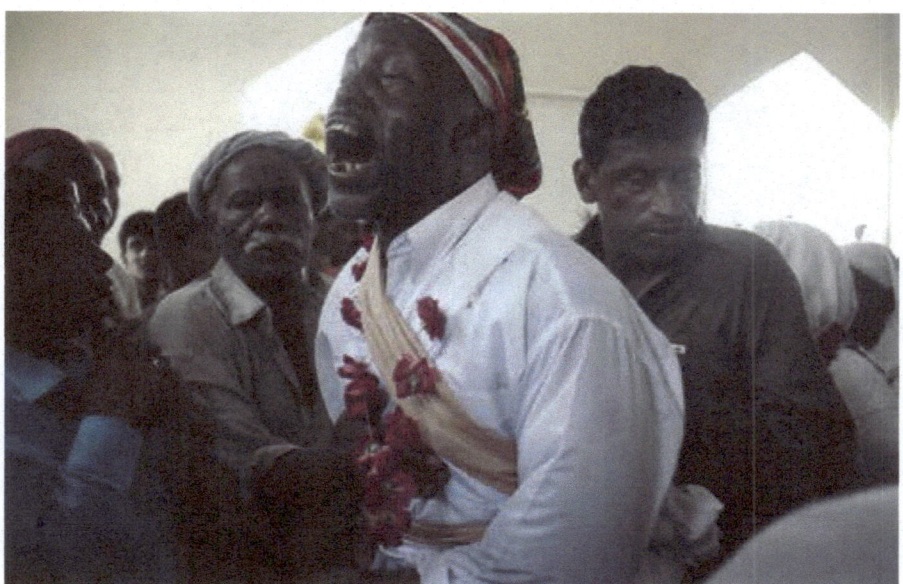

Fig. 40 Bava Ghor, the Shidis' patron saint, incarnates himself in men during ecstasy; Karachi (November 2011)

Fig. 41 Young Shidi woman in trance; Mangho Pir (July 2010)

Fig. 42   Mai Mishra, the Shidis' main female saint, incarnates herself in women; Mangho Pir (July 2010)

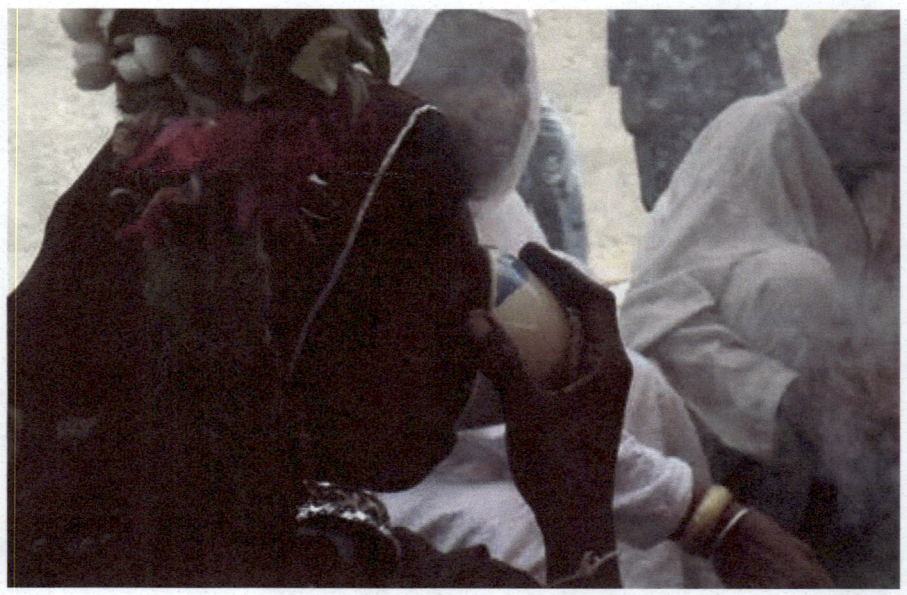

Fig. 43   A moment of relaxation during a ritual; Karachi (November 2010)

Chapter 5

Fig. 44   Aesthetic dimensions of ritual; Mangho Pir (August 2014)

Fig. 45   Carrying votive offerings to a shrine; Karachi (January 2017)

As the days of the *mēlā* approach, people become more excited. They buy new clothes for their children and new footwear. Women purchase clothes and cosmetics for themselves. The headmen of the four congregations and the elders arrange for goats and other items later to be sacrificed at the shrine of Mangho Pir. Damaged drums (*muggarmān*) will be repaired and sometimes replaced by new ones. About two months before the *mēlā*, the final dates will be announced to give everyone sufficient time to prepare. Once these dates are announced, they cannot be changed even if a dignitary or religious functionary dies. The *kotwāl* (guard)[52] of each *makān* or *jamā't* is bound to inform Shidis of other cities and regions about the dates of the festival. The festival is attended by thousands of people. According to the late Hajji Ghulam Akbar Shidi, in the 1990s there were about eight thousand participants.[53] Afterwards the numbers decreased, not only because people could not take time off from work, but mainly for security reasons as Taliban had occupied the area around the shrine.[54]

People start going to Mangho Pir seven days prior to the *mēlā*. The drums are brought there five days before in a spectacular caravan. They are first collected at Lasi *makān* near Lea Market in Lyari. Four or five of standard size are transported by vehicles, but the biggest *muggarmān* is carried by young Shidis on their shoulders in a procession all the way from Lea Market to the north of Karachi. Families take *biryānī* (rice and meat dish) and other food supplies with them.[55] Near the shrine our people set up a temporary camp called *juggī-bastī* or live in their own houses. Rumana Husain mentions that 'the land around the Manghopir shrine was allotted to the Sheedi community by the government in 1996, and is known as the Sheedi Village.'[56]

The festival starts by ceremoniously laying a *chādar* on the tomb of Mangho Pir. In the *chādar* procession, drums are beaten, and people sing praise songs for God, Prophet Muhammad, and the saints.[57] Preparations for the second day's *amrī* begins between *'asr* and *maghrib*. On Sunday early morning after *fajr* prayers, women start collecting flour and sugar from every house to prepare a special sweet bread called *rōt* in Sindhi which dancers and performers are fed. At the same time, men slaughter goats and prepare pieces from the neck to be fed to the crocodiles. Then *dhamāl* begins with the beating of *muggarmān* and other smaller drums.[58] The movement of dancers is slow in comparison to the ecstatic form of *dhamāl* performed at Sehwan and other shrines.[59] The dancers hold short wooden and multi-colored sticks (*'asā, muktā*) which are highly revered symbols for Bava Ghor; a few of these sticks even have silver handles. Some women hold bundles of peacock feathers. Dancers who intend to enter a trance veil their heads – women with a scarf (*chunrī* or *dopattā*; Figs. 41-42) and men with a large handkerchief (*rumāl*).

During this ecstatic dance participants experience a sort of positive possession or a merger between a human and a non-human spiritual being: Bava Ghor incarnates himself in male Shidi dancers while Mai Mishra incarnates herself in women (Figs. 40-42). Dancers become possessed by powerful *jinn*. In the meantime, some people start preparing a *faqīrī* drink called *tádal kā pyālā* (bowl of *tádal*) consisting of water, fennel, poppy seeds, almonds, cloves, cardamom, sugar, and licorice. According to Shidi hagiography, this spiritual drink was consumed by their ancestor Shidi Mukhtiar.[60] During the seven *zikr*s of the dance, performers are in trance and elders sit in a circle in front of the headman of the *makān*. When the dance is resumed, the latter offers each participant the bowl to drink with a piece of coconut.

Afterwards the procession called *rasm-e kuttī* starts in order to feed the crocodiles, especially Mor Sahib. It begins around nine o'clock in the morning and takes some three hours to cover a distance of just one kilometre.[61] All participants must be bare-foot. First, meat is put on a big platter topped with flowers and carried by small girls on their heads, while they repeat the chant: 'Come out in the battlefield *shamshīr* (sword)! Come out in the battlefield *shamshīr*!' The procession then slowly moves to the shrine and everyone in the crowd chants: *chāl chalenge marhaba, chāl chalenge marhaba* (Leave the uncertainty! Good morning). Afterwards they recite: *uth, kamar bandh, chalo maidān wasa hai* (Get up, put on the girdle, let's go to the battlefield, it is wide). – *auliyā' am'biyā yād kare haiñ* (Do remember the saints and the prophets!) – *Bābā mērē sang chalo* (Baba, come along with me!) – *kul auliyā' pukaraiñ* (Take hold of all the saints!) – *Makka Madina sachchā hai* (Mecca and Medina are true/pure!) – *Ghōrī badshāh nawāze* (Ghor, [our] king, is kind!) – *aei Allāh aei musalle* (Come [oh] God, come [oh] righteous [who offer their prayers]!) – *Shīdī Sahibo nawāze* (Shidi Sahibo is kind!) – *aei Allāhe aei musalle* (Come [oh] God, come [oh] righteous [who offer their prayers]!). These chants are invocations to the Almighty, to Prophet Muhammad, and to the Friends of God seeking their blessings for the Shidis.

The procession led by the elders must reach the crocodile pond near the shrine before the call for midday prayers (*zuhr*). The elders move towards Mor Sahib. Then *tikko* starts and meat, first placed in a dervish begging bowl (*kashkol*), is fed by the pond's keeper to the chief of the crocodiles with the help of a stick. The best pieces, for instance a goat's head, is offered to him.[62]

For dessert, he gets a special unleavened bread mixed with *ghī*, sugar, and dried fruit called *kuttī* as well as *badāmī halwā* (almond sweet). When Mor Sahib accepts the sacrificial food, one of the elders blows a conch and people dance joyously.

After *tikko*, those who participated in *dhamāl* now rest and are served sweet drinks. For the dance resuming after *zuhr*, men, women, and children move towards the shrine. Climbing the stairs, they praise Mangho Pir and Bava Ghor. They sing: *Shīdī bhaī dūr se āyā – sawā mūñ sindūr lāyā – sēwā kare mēwā khāwe – Shīdī bashāh dūr se āya.*[63] This mix of Urdu and Gujarati can be translated as: 'The Shidi brother has come from afar – on so many faces he puts vermilion – doing worship, eating fruits – the Shidi king has come from afar.' Inside the shrine, they first offer *fātiha* at the tomb.

After a while, *maidānī dhamāl* starts, performed by designated dancers for two to three hours to enter into *hāl* (a state of spiritual rapture and ecstasy). *Maidānī* means the union of lovers. Dancers inhale the blessed smell of aromatic frankincense. The journalist Adil Rashdi observed: 'At this point, quite a few devotees have attained various stages of *wajd* or spiritual ecstasy. Some faint while others continue dancing all the way to the end. Such men and women are then considered *wajd bābā* or *bībī*, from whom other devotees seek solutions to their problems.'[64]

Afterwards, all participants return to the place where *dhamāl* had started in the morning and continue with *amrī* until late in the night. After sunset, the chief of the combined 'four houses' visits every hut to collect money called *niyāz chanda* in a dervish begging bowl. This money is used for the expenses incurred for preparing sweet rice for the evening meal.[65]

During the *mēlā*, there is a strong feeling of togetherness, 'we-ness,' and camaraderie among the participants which anthropologists call *communitas*. Apart from the general sense of spiritual devotion warming the hearts of our people, old disputes are resolved and betrothals are arranged. In fact, the festival can be interpreted as a ritual of intensification as it intensifies the emotional bonds within African diasporic communities. Through the celebration of their cultural traditions, it also periodically restores their unity and ensures the continuity of their distinct culture. It can be assumed that for Shidis, Afro-Baloch, and Afro-Sindhis the crocodile cult at Mangho Pir brings back memories from a distant past in Africa. Nevertheless, there are indications of crocodile worship in tribal regions in west India which point to a more widespread ancient cult.[66]

Chapter 5

The Power of Rituals I: Remembering Benevolent Saints

In an insightful article, rich in theory and interpretation, the German anthropologist Helene Basu investigated the relationship between memory and kinship among Africans in Pakistan as reflected and expressed through ritual performances.[67] Drawing on an idea by Guilio Camillo, an Italian philosopher of the Renaissance, she calls these rites a 'theatre of memory' staged at major Shidi shrines in Karachi. She examines an annual ritual, called *Maī jo bhōja* (literally 'weight of the mother'), held in the name of Mai Mishra. Its rich symbolism is clearly focused on fertility. Mai Mishra and other Shidi saints, as well as Shidi *faqīr*s, act as *murshid*s (spiritual guides), a term taken from Sufi terminology, by initiating male and female disciples as ritual sons (*bālkā*) and daughters (*bālkī*) in the form of a ritual kinship relation. The collective memory in Mai Mishra is grounded in bodily practices in the sense that 'the body is transformed into a site of memory through possession by the ancestors.'[68] This gendered ritual was said to take place at Lasi *makān* in the old Shidi Goth of Karachi. The following sequences or 'memorial clusters' are expressed mainly through singing, playing drums, and dancing:[69]

1. *bismillāh*: invoking God, Prophet Muhammad, and the saints.
2. *maidānī*: drumming of 'seven rhythms,' each associated with one female saint;
   remembrance of the 'absent child' (*bālkā*). *Maidān* is also the name of the dance floor in the
   cult of the *zār* spirits in Sudan.
3. *Mā'ī Gōmā*: chants and dancing venerating the female ancestor Mai Goma (one of the sisters of Bava Ghor), with female body rhythms, also invoking the imagery of the bride.
4. *nazrāna*: offering ritual gifts to Mai Mishra.
5. *mishrī*: initiation of ritual daughters of female ancestor saints; they tie cotton strings around each other's wrists symbolizing the bonds of kinship; they eat bread with ghee and sugar.
6. *sat zikr*: chanting 'seven songs.'
7. *pyālā Shīdī Mukhtiar*: initiation of the ritual sons of male ancestor saints; each man drinks a bowl filled with water mixed with almonds and poppy seeds.
8. *bhōja*: placing clay pots upon the heads of seven initiated women outside under the tree; in Basu's words, it becomes apparent that the preceding acts of initiation served to create a pool of actors

Fig. 46 Nocturnal procession by Shidis from Lasi *makhan* to Kharadar *makan*, Karachi (May 2016)

Fig. 47 Women carrying clay pots in the name of Mai Mishra during the procession, Karachi (May 2016)

eligible for assuming the roles of 'brothers' and 'sisters' (all played by women).
9. *julūs*: procession of seven women, representing the brother and sister *murshid*s, each carrying three clay pots in the company of their spiritual children (*bālkā*s). The seven women thus become living and moving images of the brother and sister saints on their journey; *muggarmān* drummers accompany the procession; all participants are barefoot; the nocturnal procession moves to Kharadar *makān* to pay respects to Bava Ghor (Figs. 46-47).
10. *dhamāl*: 'hot' state of dancing and collective possession after returning to the shrine; Basu notes: 'For about two hours the seven actresses, still loaded with clay pots, remain in a fixed position under the tree, while a changing crowd of men and women continues to dance expressively to the rhythms, inducing experiences of possession by ancestors and ancestresses.'[70]
11. *niyāz*: distribution of the blessed sweet food (*kichāḍī*, food defined as female), that is to say the contents of the clay pots moved around during the procession.

Basu concludes: '[...] wedding symbolism is also used to carve out the main character of the whole event – the female saint Mai Mishra. By alluding to life cycle rituals from the perspective of women, the gender identity of the saint is stressed. This suggests that elements of kinship and marriage serve as mnemonic devices for remembering women of the African diaspora. The Shidi theatre of memory implies two different strands of remembering – one anchored in the body, in movements, gestures, limb controls; the other visualised through images that symbolically express cultural categories of thought.'[71]

Some of the ritual sequences discussed above are also part of other dramatic scripted performances which express collective memory revolving around the African past of our people. Thus, purifying the ritual arena and especially the sacred drum with incense, drumming, dancing, and drinking from a bowl are basic elements of Shidi rituals. 'Offering the *pyālā*' means the commitment to participate; only those belonging to the same *makān* are supposed to drink. There is a difference between a *pakkā pyālā*, a 'pure' drink consumed in the name of Bava Ghor, and a *kachchā pyālā*, a 'raw' drink with a disgusting taste consumed to learn more about an evil spirit ruling over a patient. The ingredients of the 'pure' drink vary somewhat from one ritual to another, but, in general, water is mixed with raw sugar and cardamom, anise seed, poppy seed, black pepper, and pistachio are added.

Drinking a bowl of milk, on the contrary, means to cool down the effects of 'hot' spirits disturbing the patient. Wedding ceremonies also include a procession to a shrine and invocation of the saints.

While the ritual in the name of Mai Mishra focuses on the 'weight of the mother' and ends with the consummation of sweet food defined as female, in comparison, the focus of the *'urs* of Bava Ghor is on the sacrifice of a male goat and on listening to the voice of the saint through the *muggarmān*. The ritual traditionally held at Kharadar *makān* starts with *bismillāh* followed by drumming, singing, and dancing of both men and women in a segregated space under a *tambū* (tent) or *shamiāna* (awning) in front of the shrine. Close to the *muggarmān* four smaller barrel-shaped drums are put on the ground (see also Chapter VI).

The songs are *sifātaiñ* praising the qualities of God. Next, veiled female dancers consecrate the goat. After the sacrifice, drumming and dancing is resumed in the interior courtyard of the shrine. For that, two *muggarmān*s are placed in the center and tapped while men beating smaller drums slowly circle around them. It is said that during *dhamāl* the *mōkil* of Bava Ghor (or of another saint) comes from behind, puts his right hand on the shoulder of the dancer, and guides him. A *mōkil* is a spirit who obeys the benevolent saint and acts as his servant. He usually remains invisible, but on occasions can take on any form. The protective character of African saints in the context of rituals is emphasized by Yaqoob Qambrani who notes: 'Shidis believe that the souls of our elders continue to guide us in all ages, so we take guidance from them when we are in trance.'[72]

Initiated men and women, who maintain a special spiritual connection (*rūhānī*) to a male or female saint, such as Bava Ghor or Mai Mishra, can act as their medium. They go into *hāzrī* or trance. When asked about their experience, they emphasize that their body had been 'heavy' before, but now it feels 'light.' In this state, the *rūh* or soul of the respective saint is said to speak through his or her mouth and is also able to diagnose illness and to heal patients. The *rūh* is the organ with which a Sufi saint communicates with God.

Shidi processions and dances are also performed in contexts where prominent Sufi saints, such as La'l Shahbaz Qalandar, are venerated. Thus, during the annual *'urs* of La'l Shahbaz Qalandar in the Islamic month of Sha'ban, for three days a *julūs* is led through Sehwan's Makrani neighborhood which ends at the saint's shrine (see the introduction to this book). On 21 Rajab, Shidis regularly perform a nocturnal *dhamāl* in veneration of the Qalandar, for instance in Karachi, whereby both women and men go into trance to the beat of the *muggarmān* and the sound of the *surando*, a nine-stringed lute played with a bow by Baloch musicians. During these ritual practices, Shidis invoke their African ancestor saints, paying homage to the great Sufi masters.

The Power of Rituals II: Warding off Malevolent Spirits

In parts of Sindh and coastal Balochistan, distress and affliction are often articulated within the cultural idiom of spirit possession which means that their causes are identified with the deeds of malevolent beings. People, primarily women, are afflicted by capricious, dangerous, impure, and cunning spirits. These are called *jinn* (either of Muslim, Hindu, Christian, or 'pagan' African denomination), *bālā* (demon, bigger than *jinn*, of local tribal origin), *gwāt* (evil spirit coming from the Arab coast of the Persian Gulf or from Africa), *bhūt* (Hindu spirit of the dead), or *churēl* (spirit in the shape of an ugly woman).

According to the indigenous world-view, these spirits do exist and have their own distinctive character, thoughts, and actions. Evil, 'impure' spirits seize and enter the patient, govern him or her temporarily, and cause illness in mind and body. The patient often cannot fulfill the expected social role. Women often suffer from chronic depression, infertility, seizures, mental disorders and other issues, while others feel *tenshen* (tension). Reasons for such symptoms frequently include the withdrawal of love and affection, separation, greed, jealousy, and in some cases bullying. Much has to do with rigid social control, while other symptoms relate to inferior social status or stigmatization. Healers, who have experienced possession themselves first-hand, try to harness the spirits' powers for the benefit of their patients. In this context rituals help the latter to overcome their fears.

Four regimes of healing are common among various ethnic groups in the named regions: The first ritual is *dhamāl*, already briefly mentioned above; the other three are known as *chotā majlis, chang-sōrūz,* and *gwātī* or *gwāt-i leb*. The religious specialists practicing these rituals often have African roots. It is insightful to learn that, as shown by ethnographic data from many parts of the world, people who appear strikingly different from others (for instance because of their skin color), who are perceived as strangers and marginalized, are generally attributed special magical powers and considered ideal mediators between humans and the world of spirits.[73] The healing rituals in question show similarities to indigenous African religions of possession, such as the *ngōma* practiced along the Swahili coast, the well-studied *zār* cult of peoples living in Ethiopia and in the Nile Valley of Sudan and Egypt, but in particular to rituals dealing with the *ahl-e havā*, literally People of the Wind. These wind-spirits (*bād*) belong to a cult practised by Iranians of African descent in the Persian Gulf region.

The *gwātī* séances are more linked to shamanism and became, in During's words, 'dervishized',[74] while *dhamāl* shows clear influences of Sufi Islam and can be understood as a religious practice which travelled from Africa via Zanzibar to coastal Balochistan, Sindh, and Gujarat.[75] Drawing on I.M. Lewis' sociological approach to forms of ecstatic religion, the rituals briefly described below can be categorized as 'peripheral possession cults' whereby not only the afflicted individuals mostly belong to the poor and downtrodden, but the character of the spirits is peripheral in the sense that they are thought to originate from outside, meaning that they are not Muslim, but Hindu or adhering to 'pagan' religions.[76]

If an evil spirit, or a beautiful male or female spirit driven by love, enters the body, molests the person, and pesters life out of her or him, a therapeutic *dhamāl* is arranged – either at a shrine or in one of the lanes close to the patient's home.[77] The patient is distinctively dressed in white clothes and puts a handkerchief around his or her head. Then the patient as well as other participants inhale the pungent smell of strong frankincense (*lubān*) to lure out the intrusive malevolent spirit. The latter often demands certain food, sometimes also blood which makes an animal sacrifice necessary. When the possessed, 'ridden' by an evil *jinn*, talks in a hoarse or female voice, has a fit, and writhes convulsively in the 'hot' state of *hāzrī* (literally 'presence', 'appearance'), the spirit is questioned and challenged, for instance in the name of Bava Ghor. In the presence of four witnesses, the spirit is asked: 'Who are you? Where do you come from? What do you want?'

This enables ritual specialists, healers and magicians to know more about the evil affecting this state of possession, to control the spirit at least to some extent and to determine proper curing methods to be applied in future. Afterwards, the possessing *jinn* drinks the '*pyālā* of Hazrat Ghaus Pak' (Abdul Qadir Jilani) as this prominent saint of the Muslim world is considered a powerful conqueror of evil spirits. This bowl of milk, a substance used to cool down the dangerous heat in the patient, is supposed to be the spirit's last one as he should henceforward stop molesting the patient. The spirit is pacified and tamed so that in future she or he will be able to answer questions from those who are in need, such as: 'Ask the *jinn* what is wrong with me, my body is hurting all the time!'

What is achieved is an accommodation with the spirit rather than exorcism. At least the spirit in question will probably become less frightening. In other cases the healer manages to fully expel the malevolent being. The ritual ends with *dhamāl* in which the patient wears a piece of cloth (*rūmal*) as a sash tied around his hip. When treatment is successful, the patient is transformed and feels better. Referring to the performance of such *dhamāl* among the population of the Makran coast, Sabir Badalkhan adds: 'It was originally performed by Baluch of African origin but now Baluch of all backgrounds, and of both sexes and of all ages, except for very young children, take part in *dhamāl* rituals.'[78] During this collective trance session the participants are cured in sequence by male and female healers.

In comparison, during the ritual called *chotā majlis*, when Sindhi- and Balochi-speaking spirits have entered the patient's body, the latter also drinks the '*pyālā* of Hazrat Ghaus Pak.' *Qawwals* (professional singers and musicians) play the harmonium and a barrel-shaped drum and sing hymns to various Sufi saints.

During a *chang-sōrūz*, a ritual common among Baloch and Shidis, Sufi saints like La'l Shahbaz Qalandar, Shah Nurani, and others are called upon and people enter a state of trance when possessed by spirits. It used to be common for Baloch musicians to play the iron mouth harp *chang*, but this instrument has long since been replaced by the elongated zither-like *bēnjo*, probably derived from the Japanese *kōtō* in the nineteenth century. They also play the two-stringed lute *sōrūz* and the *dhōlak* (small drum). The ritual specialist 'Apa' explained during our discussion that this ritual has nothing to do with the Ghoriya *silsila*, although some Shidis do participate in both.

Gwātī is a healing ritual typical for coastal Makran, although at times it is also performed in Karachi.[79] It can be compared to the *zār* ritual well-known from Ethiopia, Sudan, Egypt, and the Middle East. The term *gwāt* or *gowāt*, most probably derived from the ancient Indo-European word *vāti* meaning 'wind,' denotes an evil spirit thought to be like a wind, a shadow, or a feeling. It is distinguished from *jinn*, said to have physical characteristics. A *gwāt* mainly attacks women, but also children, affecting their heart and thinking, and finally causing illness. There are different types of healers (*gwāt-i mat*, literally Mother of the Wind), both male and female, either receiving their powers from Sufi saints or from their contact with spirits. Some also perform black magic. Many of them are of African descent.

The healers, who gain their knowledge and healing methods through God and the saints are associated with the Rifa'i Sufi order (see below) and especially venerate the Qadiri saint Abdul Qadir Jilani as well as La'l Shahbaz Qalandar. They perform *zikr* (commemoration of God) as a way of attaining a state of religious ecstasy in which they rise and dance in a circle. The officiating healer then presents the wishes of the participants to Ghaus Pak who challenges the *gwāt* with his divine powers. Spirit-oriented healers, on the contrary, have the power to turn spirits into slaves who then serve them and help to treat patients. They can understand the language of the spirits.

Gwāt-i leb (*leb* is derived from Arabic *la'ab* meaning 'game' or 'performance') is an elaborate healing ritual lasting from a few hours to several days in which music plays a prominent role. The expenses for this musical seance must be paid by the patient's family. Farhat Sultana elaborates: 'For the *leb* itself, the *gwāt-i mat* makes arrangements for music and food as required by the *gwāt* possessing the patient or the *gwat-i mat*'s slave spirit. For example, some types of *gwat* like drums (*dol*) and oboe (*sorna*), while others prefer bells and bowed lute (*chango-saroz*), and yet others ask only for two-stringed lute (*saz*) or the rhythmic chanting of religious poetry and Qur'anic verses (*zikr*).'[80]

Monotonous, trance-inducing tunes are played late into the night to find the right one which will please the spirit. When the patient begins to tremble, it is a sign the *gwat* is entering him or her; the tune in question is then repeated again and again until the patient dances in ecstasy.[81] After the latter collapses, the spirit is interrogated speaking through the mouth of the patient. The *gwat* will then demand certain things, for instance that the patient should wear anklets, a finger ring, a red kerchief, etc. 'On this condition he will consent to leave the sufferer in peace for a year, for five, seven, eleven years, after which the sacrifice and the bargain will have to be renewed.'[82] The food, cooked during the ceremony and distributed at the end to the participants, usually includes meat and rice. Farhat Sultana adds, that the type of meal served depends on the nature of the patient's *gwat*. 'Some spirits demand a big feast before leaving the patient, while others only ask for few kilos of *halwa* (wheat pudding). [...] The *gwat*'s share of the food is thrown into a corner outside the house or into the ocean.'[83] This ritual also includes the sacrifice of a chicken or goat whose blood is rubbed on the patient's forehead and other body parts.

Before arranging elaborate healing rituals of the kind described above performed within a semi-public gathering in the presence of family members and neighbors, in a first step the patient consults a religious expert in a private setting. The latter answers initial questions related to distress, affliction, and prediction of the future. This expert is usually an experienced trance

Fig. 48 Baba, a spiritual healer, in his domestic shrine; Lyari, Karachi (December 2010)

healer (*bābā*), often belonging to one of the African diasporic communities to whom people commonly attribute special abilities in the magic-religious sphere.[84]

During the consultation, the healer functions as a medium, seer, and magician. Through inhaling frankincense and subsequent hyperventilation, he enters a trance. In it the practitioner incorporates an African ancestor saint, for instance Bava Ghor, who then communicates with the spiritual forces effecting the problems, and he also summons his own helping spirits (*mōkil*). Thus, for a period, the healer's own body becomes the site of ritual power. He identifies the source of illness and counters its effects through magical practices. Only if this procedure is unsuccessful and the malevolent spirits refuse to leave the patient will the latter be treated through an elaborate healing ritual of the kind described above.

The role of African ancestor saints in such spirit possession cults proves that, apart from African musical instruments, rhythms and dance, the memory of Africa is maintained.

People of African Descent in the Rifa'i Sufi Order

(by Aliya Iqbal Naqvi and Hasan Ali Khan)

Introduction

Many Africans in Pakistan are members of the Rifa'iyya and Qalandariyya, both major Sufi orders. Being at the same time followers of Abdul Qadir Jilani, the founder of the Qadiriyya, they emphasize this affiliation to the largest Sufi order of the Muslim world by adding the name Qadri to their personal name. Besides their indigenous African traditions, Sufi Islam affords them an additional religious idiom and organizational model to express their faith within Pakistani Muslim society. Of foremost importance is therefore the veneration of Prophet Muhammad whose *sunna* is, additionally to the Qur'an, the fountain source of the Sufi tradition. Our people continue to praise the Prophet as the beautiful and exemplary model of man to follow in life in accordance with verse 21 of *sura al-Ahzab* (33). From an ethno-sociological point of view, membership in these Sufi orders helps to counterbalance the process of alienation in the megacity of Karachi. It allows expression of the identity of a practising Sufi Muslim through immediate face-to-face contacts and emotional bonds within a local religious community.

The relation to the Rifa'iyya is particularly strong because Bava Ghor is said to have been the disciple and later the *khalīfa* (literally 'successor') of the Sufi saint Sayyid Ahmad Kabir ar-Rifa'i (d. 1182-83) who lived in a village in the marshland near Basra in Iraq. This oral tradition is related to the historical amalgamation of the Rifa'i Sufi order with the Shidi ritual community and its spirit possession cult centered on African saints.[85] According to some – albeit doubtful – sources, Ahmad ar-Rifa'i was a nephew of Abdul Qadir Jilani. The strictly Sunni order spread widely from its birthplace in Iraq to the west into Syria, Egypt, the Levant, Anatolia, and the Balkans, and to the east into the Caucasus, Iran, and the Indian subcontinent.[86] Its initiated members, the dervishes or *faqīrs* are known for spectacular ecstatic performances (called *zarb*), such as extinguishing fire with their hands, swallowing sabres, red-hot coals, glass, living snakes and scorpions in trance, and especially piercing their body with daggers and iron pins of various sizes.[87]

A branch of the order, retaining its pre-modern organizational structure, is also based in the city of Karachi. It has strong connections to the coastal areas and the hinterland of Pakistani Balochistan, Iranian Balochistan, and the northern coast of Oman. In addition, it has followers on the East African coast and in South Africa, something which may be connected to the old Indian oceanic trade controlled by the Sultanate of Oman before its demise.

Although the Rifa'iyya is mentioned as being present in Muslim India in the Sufi biographical treatise *Akhbār al-akhyār* (Reports on the Pious) compiled by the great Qadiri saint and *hadīth* scholar Shaikh Abd al-Haqq Muhadis al-Dihlawi (d. 1642),[88] our local Rifa'i sub-order migrated a little less than two hundred years ago from Basra to Bombay. One branch later migrated to Karachi on Partition. In this it shares a common migration trend with the first Agha Khan, Hasan Ali Shah (1804-1881),[89] who migrated from Kirman to Bombay at the behest of the British administration in 1842, to subsequently settle and reorganize his Nizari Isma'ili community in India which was in disarray. A fundamental research question that needs to be asked is whether the British played a role in the activities of the Rifa'i order after its migration to India, to counterbalance local spiritual offices and power structures that pre-existed there, especially in Balochistan in the shape of the Khanate of Kalat; just as in the case of the Agha Khan whose arrival facilitated the British takeover of Sindh.

Arrival in India

Until recently, the Rifa'iyya in Karachi was headed by Sayyid Zain al-Abidin Rifa'i (d. 2016), and is now led by his daughter Sayyida Safiya. Today she is the de facto head of this branch along with her brother Muin who lives abroad. The history of the Indian Rifa'i order begins with the migration of Zain al-Abidin's great grandfather, Sayyid Riffat al-Din Rifa'i, to Bombay around the 1840s,[90] the exact date needs to be ascertained from family records. Since the historic mention of the Rifa'iyya in Muslim India in the precincts of Delhi and its surroundings (not in the Iranian borderlands), headed by the Shaikhs who belonged to the social elite, our suborder managed to secure a staunch following amongst coastal Baloch communities. The latter comprise today its major adherents, and are mostly – especially in Karachi – of African descent.

Zain al-Abidin was born on 12 October 1921 in the famed 'Rifa'iyya building' on Ibrahim Rahmatullah Road in Bombay. His mother's name was Pasha Begum; she was the daughter of the Nawab of Pune, hence of royal descent. The Nawab's father Yusuf Saif al-Din's shrine is located in Bombay. His grandfather Muhammad Amin was an honorary magistrate for the British Administration, while his grandfather's brother, Salah al-Din, was the magistrate of Pune and is buried there.[91] These facts imply strong connections to the colonial administration, and a high social status for a

Fig. 49   Sayyid Zain al-Abidin (d. 2016), head of the Rifa'iyya in Karachi

spiritual line that came to have such a large following amongst the lower income Baloch of African descent in Karachi and along the Makran coast.

On the creation of Pakistan, Zain al-Abidin, who was close to Jinnah and a member of the Muslim League's youth wing, left his inheritance in Bombay and migrated with his younger brother Sayyid Imad al-Din to Karachi.[92] The real reason for his migration may have been to promote the Sufi order further, especially amongst the coastal population of Balochistan. His great grandfather, Riffat al-Din, had already gained a large following in Balochistan, both in the Khanate of Kalat as well as in Iran.[93]

Chapter 5

Sayyid Riffat al-Din and the Rifa'i-Afro-Baloch Connections to Sehwan and Karachi

According to the oral history of the order, primarily through the narrations of Khalifa Hajji Ghulam Mustafa (d. 2015), who headed the Lyari *dargah*, the most important one in the order's hierarchy, the Makrani neighborhood in Sehwan was settled roughly around the same time as Riffat al-Din migrated from Iraq to Bombay.[94] Moreover, in an interview with Khalifa Musa, another *khalīfa* from Karachi, he said that the Rifa'i (Baloch) adherents also started coming to Sehwan when the first Makrani settlement was founded in Sehwan, some 150 to 170 years previously.[95] Hasan Ali Khan first learned this information during research with Michel Boivin's French Interdisciplinary Mission in Sindh (MIFS), where the initial work on the Rifa'iyya was completed in 2011. The Makrani or Baloch neighborhood in the city is often frequented by African-descended Baloch from Oman and Iran over the *'urs*. According to oral history, the Baghdadi quarter of Lyari, today the headquarters of the order, was settled by Riffat al-Din himself.[96] If this information is correct, it is worth asking whether the Omani and Irani coastal Baloch connection to the order is equally old.

Context: Historical and Contemporary

The spiritual life of the Rifa'i order in Karachi is centered around Lyari with its mixed Iranian and Pakistani Baloch population, many of whom hold dual nationality. The order's lodges located inside it play host to the Rifa'is visiting from Iran and Oman, in addition to those coming from the Makran coast. They form an intricate nexus in which the Baloch of African descent and the Makrani inhabitants of Lyari play a pivotal role. According to Laurent Gayer, in the second half of the nineteenth century, a large number of Iranian Baloch migrated to Karachi and today form the largest share of its Baloch (this would mean both Shidi and non-Shidi) inhabitants.[97] Although Gayer's assumption is in part accurate, if the oral history of the order is to be believed, which carry credence as the same situation exists with the Makrani settlement of Sehwan, some Iranian Baloch settlers may have migrated earlier, through the proselytism of Riffat al-Din.

In addition, it must be noted that although the Rifa'i order's top hierarchy are Sayyids of Sunni Muslim denomination (as most of its adherents in Lyari and along the Balochistan littoral as well), there is the active element of the Zikri sect followed by many of the inhabitants of Makran (as aforementioned by Frembgen). According to Gayer, many of the Iranian Baloch settlers in Lyari were Sunni Muslims, but in the late 1990s, it is estimated that also around 50,000 Zikris lived in that part of the city.[98] In Sehwan, which the members of the order visit every year on the *'urs* along with their main *khalīfa*s, the largest healing ceremony, known as *bhandāra*, is performed in the Sufi lodge of Murad located in the Makrani neighborhood.[99] It involves the touching of a red-hot iron chain (in Persian *zanjīr*).

Fig. 50   Khalifa Musa performing the healing ritual with the chain, Sehwan

Chapter 5

The Centrality of Lyari: Organizational Hierarchy, the Baghdadi Quarter, and the Performance of Ritual

The organization of the Rifa'iyya lodges plays a central role in the performance of the order's rituals and ceremonies, originating from Karachi and stretching across the entire Makran coast into Iran and Oman. The head *khalīfa* in Lyari in Sayyid Zain al-Abidin's time was Hajji Ghulam Mustafa (Fig. 1), who died in 2015 at over eighty years old. He followed his father in this position. According to Hajji Ghulam Mustafa, although there are many Rifa'i lodges in Balochistan, these are ranked lower in hierarchy than the three main lodges in Karachi. The latter are the *khānqāh* (Sufi lodge) of the Rifa'i Sayyids in Paposh Nagar in the northwest of the city, and two others located in Lyari's Baghdadi quarter. It should be noted that all the *khalīfa*s in Lyari are of African descent. Mustafa asserted that the name 'Baghdadi' and the name of the adjacent 'Basra Colony' were given by Riffat al-Din himself when he set up the main Rifa'i *dargāh* or *astāna* and presumably settled the surrounding area with his Makrani followers.[100]

This shrine, which contains a turban symbolizing Ahmad ar-Rifa'i placed on a pedestal in the sanctuary, is situated in the neighborhood of Juna-Baghdadi. Every day, women from Baghdadi and surrounding areas visit this sacred place attended by old Shidi women acting as *mujāwir*s. Every Thursday evening a group of men gathers there for *zikr* under the guidance of the *khalīfa*.

There is a degree of uniformity amongst the Rifa'is on the matter, as a similar narrative was given to us by Hira Shakir Ali Beg, a young female office bearer trained by Zain al-Abidin when a teenager. She asserted that it had been the performance of a spiritual retreat by Riffat al-Din which resulted in the founding of this main Lyari *dargāh* and the adjacent Baghdadi quarter.[101]

Hajji Ghulam Mustafa stated in our interview that his *dargāh* in Baghdadi was as old as Lyari itself, which means it was established around the second half of the nineteenth century. In this he implied that not only Baghdadi, but all of Lyari was set up by Sayyid Riffat al-Din – something which seems far-fetched. Nevertheless, he did make some historic sense in suggesting that both, Baghdadi and Basra Colony, and many of the names of the streets inside them, take their names from places in Iraq. The reader is reminded that Riffat al-Din migrated to Bombay from Basra. Thus, pending further research, Riffat al-Din and his descendants may have played a hitherto unknown role in the history of Lyari, possibly settling in parts of Karachi's oldest quarter.

The second most important *khalīfa* in Lyari in recent times was Khalifa Musa, who administered the second Rifa'i *dargāh* in Baghdadi (Fig. 50). Due to Hajji Ghulam Mustafa's old age, Musa used to lead the *majlis* in Sehwan at the time of La'l Shahbaz Qalandar's *'urs*.[102] In fact, Ghulam Mustafa was his teacher. After Ghulam Mustafa's death in 2015, his son Saeed became his successor. There are at present four *khalīfa*s in Lyari, of which Musa is now first in the hierarchy. The others are Salim Ansari (the first non-Shidi *khalīfa* in Lyari), Muhammad Fazl, and the youngest is Saeed.

Hira Shakir Ali Beg told us that the main Rifa'i lodges in Balochistan are located in Turbat, Pasni, Ormara, Jiwani, and Gwadar, all along the coast, each with their own *khalīfa*.[103] She stated that there were two *khalīfa*s in Oman, but due to the restrictions of the Omani state, they were neither allowed to perform the healing rituals with the chain (Fig. 50) nor to engage in piercing rituals. In Oman, the head *khalīfa* is Abd al-Rasul who works in Oman Shipping.[104]

In conversation with Safiya al-Abidin, Sayyid Zain al-Abidin's successor, on the issue of *khalīfa*s in Iran, she said she had many followers and had instituted successors in the Chahbahar region herself. The main office bearer in Chahbahar is a Rifa'i by the name of Umar who frequently travels to Pakistan to meet her. She mentioned going to Oman to visit her followers, but not to Iran. Safiya al-Abidin also asserted she had followers among notable Pakistani Baloch clan chiefs, in the central and northern parts of the province, which we did not follow up on.[105] But her most devoted followers, indeed the backbone of the Rifa'i order, are primarily of African descent. They constitute almost its entire organisational hierarchy.

Endnotes

1 Pastner & Pastner 1977: 125-126; cf. Hughes 1877: 44.
2 Green 2012: 126.
3 Cf. Larsen 2004: 14.
4 On the following, see Basu 1995: 36, 71-74; Basu 2000: 256; Basu 2003: 235-241; Abbas 2002: 41-42; Kenoyer & Bhan 2004: 48-49; Basu 2005: 184; Basu 2008b: 234-235; Khalique 2009: 24-26; Varadarajan 2020.
5 Qambrani 2017: 31-33.
6 Catlin-Jairazbhoy 2004: 185; Graves 2020: 97-98.
7 Qambrani 2017: 31, 33.
8 Graves 2020: 101.
9 The slaying of Makhan Devi constitutes a more widespread motif in popular South Asian hagiography as, for instance, also the Sufi saint Shah Madar (15th c.) is said to have killed an evil spirit by the name of Makan Deo who had

devastated the area of today's Makanpur in Uttar Pradesh (de Tassy 1997: 66).
10   Kenoyer & Bhan 2004: 55-56; cf. Basu 1995: 49, 126; Basu 2003: 235-236; Alpers 2004: 28, 30; Catlin-Jairazbhoy 2004: 185; Varadarajan 2020: 67-71.
11   On the shrine of Bava Ghor, see in detail Basu 1995: 125-134.
12   Basu 1995: 21.
13   In the following, concerning the Shidi saints in Indian Gujarat, see: Basu 1995: 8, 74-75; Basu 2000: 251; Basu 2005: 184.
14   Basu 2008b: 232.
15   Basu 2000: 261; Basu 2008b: 241.
16   My friend 'Baba,' a local Afro-Baloch trance healer of spirit possession, has the names of altogether eight saints (five belonging to the Shidi pantheon) written on a signboard in his domestic shrine. Some names, which are double-barrelled, show how the veneration of Shidi saints is inscribed into the vernacular form of saints-and-shrines-centered Sufism. Thus, it is written: 'Hazrat Mubarak Nur Shah *urf* Bava Ghor Data' (the first name was probably misunderstood by the craftsman as Bava Ghor's real name was Sidi Mubarak Nobi) and 'Hazrat Ismail Shah *urf* Shidi La'l Data.'
17   For more information on Darya Shah, see Khan 1997 (p. 229), Boivin 2009, and especially Khan 2008.
18   Khan 2008: 75.
19   Boivin 2015: 204.
20   Basu 2000: 260, footnote 11.
21   Basu 1995: 118, 123, 132; Basu 2008b: 243; cf. Frembgen 2006 a: 243-244.
22   On the following, see Basu 2008b: 244, 251.
23   Personal communication by M. H. Qambrani (22 January 2019, Nayabad in Lyari/Karachi).
24   Basu 2000: 254.
25   Basu 2000: 244.
26   Photograph in Frembgen 2020: 160.
27   Cf. Frembgen 2006 b: 45-47.
28   Basu 2000: 256-257.
29   Basu 1995: 74, 80, 138-141, 153.
30   Basu 1995: 49-54; Basu 2000: 250.
31   Photograph in Frembgen 2020: 160.
32   Photograph in Frembgen 2020: 160.
33   Cf. Basu 2000: 245.
34   Mahdihassan 1981: 3 (In his short article the author, who was a chemist by profession, pursues a very strange and speculative etymology of the word *mangho* trying to derive it from Chinese language; in addition, he also claims that 'Sufism originated in China.' [sic!]); Suvorova 2004: 14.
35   Kenoyer & Bhan 2004: 48.
36   Boivin 2015: 177.
37   Khan 2008: 225-227; cf. Lari 2000: 8.6.

38 The following short notes on the setting of the shrine are based on a visit to Mangho Pir by J.W. Frembgen in February 1989.
39 Ross 1883: 17-18; cf. Bari 1995: 44; Paracha 2018: 72-73.
40 Cf. Khalique 2009: 38-42.
41 Lari 2000: 8.6. Cf. Baillie 1890: 180.
42 Suvorova 2004: 14. On the following, see Shah & Lalvani & Mahdihassan 1984 and Rafiquzzaman & Mahdihassan 1984; Ahmed & Nawab 2015.
43 Ahmed & Nawab 2015: 47.
44 Shah & Lalvani & Mahdihassan 1984: 3; cf. Rafiquzzaman & Mahdihassan 1984: 7.
45 Husain 2010: 25 (based on a legend told by a Shidi lady who called the bandit Mangho Wasa). The following notes are based on Qambrani 2017: 40-49. Cf. Rashdi 1992: 142.
46 Personal communication by the late Hajji Ghulam Akbar Shidi (cf. Qureshi 1993: IV).
47 Husain 2010: 25; Husain 2020: 146; cf. Boivin 2015: 211.
48 Legend told to J.W. Frembgen by 'Nawab' from Lyari; cf. Bhutto 2010: 231; Zaheer 2018: 125.
49 Baillie 1890: 179; Rashdi 1992: 142; Suvorova 2004: 14, 22; Khalique 2009:35; Bhutto 2010: 231; Boivin 2015: 211.
50 Boivin 2015: 211.
51 In 2012, the German film-maker Till Passow shot a 20 minutes documentary 'Mor Sahib. The Crocodile Saint' showing the feeding of the crocodiles, the sacrifice of a goat, the trance dance of women and men, processions, as well as an interview with 'Apa.' This film on the Mangho Pir *mēlā* could not have been made without the support of Hajji Ghulam Akbar Shidi.
52 Actually, in Urdu, Hindi, and Persian, this word denotes a chief police officer or a magistrate, but also 'the porter of a castle.'
53 Qureshi 1993: V.
54 Cf. Gayer 2014: 187, 189.
55 Husain 2010: 25; Husain 2020: 147.
56 Husain 2010: 23; Husain 2020: 143.
57 Qureshi 1993: IV.
58 Husain 2010: 25.
59 Frembgen 2012 (see especially footnote 48 on page 92 concerning the dance of the Shidis); cf. Catlin-Jairazbhoy 2004: 185-186.
60 Cf. Basu 2000: 257.
61 Qureshi 1993: IV.
62 Cf. Rashdi 1992: 141; Husain 2010: 25.
63 Rashdi 1992: 140.
64 Rashdi 1992: 142.
65 Rashdi 1992: 142.
66 Randhawa 1996: 54-55 (photo No. 20).
67 On the following, see Basu 2000.

68	Basu 2000: 248.
69	Cf. Basu 2000: 258-259. Some notes and additional observations, inserted in the following, are my own.
70	Basu 2000: 263.
71	Basu 2000: 264.
72	Qambrani 2017: 49.
73	Müller 1987: 255-256, 364; Haller 2016: 80-81.
74	On possession cults along the Persian Gulf and in Iranian Balochistan, see During 1981; During 1997; Bashiri 1983; Fartacek 2014; Beeman 2015; cf. Basu 2008 b: 236-240.
75	Cf. Basu 2005: 173.
76	Lewis 1989: 27-29.
77	The musicologist Jean During detailed such a séance in Lyari (1997). The following short description of such a ritual is based on my own observations in Baghdadi/Lyari on 18 February 2012.
78	Badalkhan 2008: 282.
79	On the following, see Sultana 1996: 31-43; During 1997: 39-41; Badalkhan 2008: 282; Beeman 2015: 3; Boivin 2015: 146; cf. Jamali 2020: 176. Fartacek (2014: 570) and Beeman (2015: 2) both clearly emphasize that such kind of possession rituals have nothing to do with exorcism; thus, the evil spirit is only tamed and placated, but not expelled.
80	Sultana 1996: 38.
81	During 1981.
82	During 1981.
83	Sultana 1996: 38.
84	Cf. Frembgen 2020: 164-165 (with photographs of an expert healer in Baghdadi).
85	We owe this information to J.W. Frembgen. Cf. Basu 2005: 172, 180.
86	Trimingham 1971: 20-21, 37-40, 280-281; Luizard 1999: 293, 307-308; Frembgen 2008: 116-118, 172-177.
87	Cf. Frembgen 2008: 109-110.
88	Rizvi 1983: 6, 19, 75, 509 (index); Green 2012: 55.
89	On the Agha Khan I's life, see in more detail Daftary 1990: 462-476.
90	Husain 2014: 10. On the history of the Rifa'i in the kingdom of Baroda in Gujarat, see Basu 2005: 179-180.
91	Husain 2014: 8-9. Also confirmed in an interview with Khalifa Hajji Ghulam Mustafa (13 November 2014, Lyari/Karachi).
92	Husain 2014: 19.
93	Interview with Khalifa Hajji Ghulam Mustafa (13 November 2014, Lyari/Karachi).
94	Interview with Khalifa Hajji Ghulam Mustafa (17 June 2014, Sehwan).
95	Interview with Khalifa Musa (22 July 2011, Sehwan).
96	Interview with Khalifa Hajji Ghulam Mustafa (13 November 2014, Lyari/Karachi).

97	Gayer 2014: 128.
98	Gayer 2014: 128.
99	Interview with Khuda Bakhsh Baloch (18 June 2014, Makrani Mohalla/Sehwan).
100	Interview with Khalifa Hajji Ghulam Mustafa (13 November 2014, Lyari/Karachi).
101	Interview with Hira Shakir Ali Beg over WhatsApp (7 April 2020, Karachi).
102	Interview with Khalifa Musa (22 July 2011, Sehwan).
103	Interview with Hira Shakir Ali Beg at the house of Safiya Zain al-Abidin (1 March 2020, Karachi).
104	Interview with Hira Shakir Ali Beg over WhatsApp (7 April 2020, Karachi),
105	Interview with Safiya Zain al-Abidin at her house (1 March 2020, Karachi).

6

Facets of Culture and Everyday Practices: From Music and Dance to Sports and Pastimes

Introduction

Imagining the situation of our people when most of them were forced to leave Africa as slaves, 'they were,' in the words of Shihan De Silva Jayasuriya, 'stripped of all their possessions and they had no property, no homeland and no human rights. Yet what nobody could take away from them was their talents in music and dance.'[1] The latter are dominant drivers of their cultures, embodying their 'spirit.' Like their African ancestor saints, these cultural expressions embody 'voices from distant lands.'

Although aspects of expressive culture, such as ritual music, dance, and poetry, were already discussed in the previous chapter, they are not restricted to the religious domain. They also form part of happy occasions, such as weddings, the entertainment of guests, and times of merrymaking on board ships. Therefore, the 'African idiom' of indigenous music making and dance belong both to the spheres of the sacred and the secular. They constitute important dimensions of creative imagination in times when leisure and pleasure are often suppressed by normative, scriptural Islam. Despite difficult living conditions, a remarkable sense of cheerfulness has been observed among Africans in Pakistan.[2]

Our focus will be first on musical instruments, particularly on the sacred drum *muggarmān*, which is the key component of most rituals. As De Silva

Fig. 51 Consecrating the *muggarman* with sacrificial blood from a dervish bowl, Mangho Pir (July 2010)

Jayasuriya aptly emphasizes: 'Music, dancing and singing provide more than entertainment. They also contribute to a collective social identity.'³ Such cultural practices help to experience body and mind in spontaneity.⁴ After discussing various musical celebrations and the role of performers, notes on sports, such as boxing and football, as well as on everyday pastimes and amusements will conclude this final chapter. Among Shidis, Afro-Baloch, and Afro-Sindhis, as elsewhere in Pakistan, such activities beyond the realm of work belong to the spheres of leisure and hobby; they affirm and generate sociality. These remarks on rather mundane pleasures related to the senses are informed by the following research questions: When do people make a breach in the monotony of their daily life and work? When do they celebrate sociable moments of leisure and pleasure? And how do people think about the element of play in their life, about ludic practices?

The muggarmān and Other Musical Instruments

The sacred tall drum called *muggarmān* (Balochi *mugulmānī*) is an integral part of the cultures of our people and is played above all in the region of Lower Sindh (Figs. 51-52).⁵ In fact, it is an essential source of their identity and the main link to their African past. All of those venerating African ancestors saints feel a spiritual bond with the *muggarmān*.⁶ Its sound is perceived as the voice of Bava Ghor, a voice from the wilderness in distant Africa. Therefore, the drum is also known as *dādā* (grandfather).⁷ It has thus a mystical and spiritual power. Apart from specific ritual contexts in which it is played, while dancing to its rhythm, in the words of Yaqoob Qambrani, 'Shidis forget their miseries and feel united.' Somewhat poetically Qaimkhani writes: 'It is as if they had a spiritual connection with the beat of the drum, and when they danced together at its intoxicating sound, they would forget any enmities, hearts would be cleansed and all the people would be joined together as if they were parts of a secret chain full of love.'⁸

According to Shidi elders, *muggarmān* means 'the caller' and 'the one who unifies.' Hearing the beat of this drum brings Shidis together. Its sound is a call attracting everyone. During religious rituals only men are allowed to play *muggarmān* as well as other drums. Women play smaller drums during weddings when also the larger three-footed drum called *pīp* is used. Before the *muggarmān* is played, it is purified by incense and on ritual occasions also with the blood of a sacrificial goat. Once a year, each *muggarmān* is given ritual cleansing in sea water. As there is no evidence that such drums were brought by slaves from Africa (although they could have been brought by African seamen, merchants, and soldiers), we assume that they were constructed later based on the personal experiences of migrants and their inherent knowledge of music.

The *muggarmān* is played in the names of Bava Ghor, Mai Mishra, and other saints during a dance called *dhamāl* or *gōma*. In many parts of Sub-Saharan Africa where drumming often plays a significant role, the Swahili term *ngōma* denotes the drum as well as dance and singing.[9] Thus, 'among Bantu-speaking populations of central, east-central and southern Africa, *ngōma* may refer to drums of various sizes, shapes and types, to drum ensembles or to individual drums or else to specific music and dance styles.'[10] The latter belong to secular, therapeutic, and religious celebrations.[11]

Fig. 52 Beating the four-footed *muggarman* during a procession around Makrani neighborhood; *'urs* of La'l Shahbaz Qalandar, Sehwan (July 2010)

Muggarmān is a cylindrical four-footed drum open at one end (cf. the introduction to this book). Its membrane is beaten with both hands, not with sticks. During *dhamāl* dance performances in Karachi, membranophones of various sizes are played in ensemble. Usually, four double-headed drums placed on the ground accompany the main footed drum.[12] Two of these drums, called in Sindhi *musīndo*[13] and in Balochi *rahmānī*, are bigger and the other two, called in Sindhi *jalápar* and in Balochi *purkash*, are smaller. Each time, two drums of the same size are placed side by side opposite each other. The drummers, who are all males, tap and stroke both sides of the drum with their hands, not with drumsticks. There is another smaller drum, called in Sindhi *kesar*[14] and in Balochi the 'little *purkash*.' The smallest is the *timbok* (a term derived from Swahili) played both with hands and sticks. When the *maidānī* rhythm is played during a *dhamāl* between *ʿasr* and *maghrib* prayers and the women sing in full throated and high-pitched voices, the number of drums is reduced to three.

There are three major modes of *muggarmān* drumming and dance tunes performed on numerous ritual occasions:

1. *Ketuvīrho*[15] is based on three beats. This rhythm, called *mawái* or *muai*, includes words in Swahili narrating painful events of the past. It starts with a ritual chant praising God, Prophet Muhammad, Hazrat Bilal, as well as Bava Ghor: *Bāvā Ghōr salāmwale, Allāh ho – Nabī, Allāh ho – Nabī, Nabī āle, sal āle, Nabī yā le, Māmā Ghor sal vāle, Māmā Ghor sal vāle, Shīdī bhaī Makke se āye, bāre shān se, Bilāl Makke se āye, bāre shān se.*[16]
2. *Las* is a simple rhythmic pattern also called *maidānī*; after a repetitive sequence, it switches to a joyous mood; at the height of this rhythm dancers thump the ground with their feet and go into trance.
3. *Dhamāl* or *gōma* is a rhythm considered the mother of *laywā* beat.

Today, *muggarmān*s are no longer made in Karachi, but only by an expert in Thatta. The four-footed body is carved out of a single piece of either mango wood or rosewood (*shīsham*) because of its association with sweetness. The single head of the drum itself (*bam*) is made from skin taken from the neck of a camel. A noted player of the *muggarmān* famous throughout Sindh was Vikyo alias Gumbu Shidi.[17] He lived in Tando Muhammad Khan and produced many students who learned from him. Another expert drummer, especially in accompanying songs of praise, was Dada Dino (d. 1982) from village Sahib Khan Marirani close to Hyderabad. He used to travel widely in Sindh whenever a *dhamāl* or *gōmā* took place. Usually, *muggarmān*s are kept in shrines, but sometimes also in private homes.[18] Not every Shidi community in interior Sindh has such a drum.

The barrel-shaped *dūhl*, which is smaller than the Punjabi *dhōl*, is made from wood of *bhēr* or mango tree and both heads are covered with goatskin. At weddings, our people also play the small *dhōlak* (or small-sized *dūhl*), a drum common in the lowlands of Pakistan. During lifecycle rituals, chants are performed to invoke the blessings of the saints and to make wishes become fulfilled. They are accompanied by beating frame drums (*daf* or *daflī*) and/or copper dishes (*thālī*).[19]

During religious rites, the sound of the various drums is rhythmically augmented by a coconut rattle played by women. This rattle of obvious African origin is called *misr* (Egypt) and dedicated to Bava Ghor's sister Mai Mishra.[20] Among our people, the rhythmic dimension of music is very pronounced. Unlike in India, stringed instruments are not used. Indian Sidis, on the other hand, play a one-stringed instrument of evidently African origin, namely a braced musical bow called *malunga*.[21] At the shrine of Bava Ghor in the quarter of Dongri in Mumbai, four bowl-lyres of African, or to be more precise of Ethiopian type, are kept close to the memorial tomb.[22] They are considered sacred, carry female names, and are thought to have reached India miraculously floating on the sea. In fact, the lyre is a common music instrument of the indigenous music of East Africa and the horn of Africa.[23] The same instrument is also used in rites of possession performed in Iran by people of African descent to drive out spirits coming from Nubia.[24]

Music Making and Entertaining

Throughout Sindh and coastal Balochistan, music plays an integral part in the life of our people. In Sindh, women of local African communities are invited by other ethnic groups to sing and dance during joyful festive occasions, such as weddings, birthdays, ceremonies of circumcision, and *aqīqa* (first shaving of a baby's hair), as well as on the auspicious first Thursday of a new month. When Shidi women entertain female guests with the chorused singing of wedding songs (*sehrā*), they play *dhūl* or *dhōlak*, clap their hands, and tie bells around their feet while dancing. Songs follow typically the call-and-response pattern. On such occasions, female participants also raise characteristic shrill, high-pitched trills.

In places like Hyderabad, Karachi Mori near Jamshoro, and Matli, Shidi women do this semi-professionally to generate monetary gain, but in other towns, as I learned, they are often just given food and a little money. Since the late 1970s, when Islamic fundamentalism started growing rapidly in Pakistan, being a professional musician is frowned on among Shidis as it has become associated with the performance of courtesans.[25] Therefore, younger women often prefer other occupations to contribute to their family's income, such as teaching and nursing.

Often both women and men jointly perform at weddings and other rites of passage as well as at Eid celebrations and encourage guests to join in the dance. The traditional wedding songs common in Lower Sindh, consisting of questions and answers, are called *heŕa*. Today, due to the omnipresent electronic media, these folk songs are increasingly being replaced by modern popular songs. As reported from the Sufi shrine of Jhok Sharif in interior Sindh, Shidi musicians also contribute to Shi'a Muharram ceremonies by singing devotional poetry and praise songs.[26]

On joyous occasions within their own community, such as weddings, the birth of a son, circumcision, or when God grants a wish, Shidis visit Sufi shrines and tap the *muggarmān,* singing their famous hymn which goes in Sindhi:

tūñ be Shīdī, māñ be Shīdī – Shīdī mūnjo shān ā – jeko chaweto māñ ahiyāñ Shīdī, tenkeñ ke mūnjo salām ā.

'You are Shidi, I am Shidi. Being Shidi is my pride. To all those who claim to be Shidi, my salute to them!'

One of the most popular lighthearted folk songs of Sindh is called *Ho Jamālo!,* called after its exclamatory refrain. It is sung by Shidis in chorus accompanied by the clapping of hands and stamping with feet. According to their own tradition, it is performed to honor their kinsman Jamal ud-Din Shidi from Rohri in Upper Sindh who courageously crossed the newly built railroad bridge between Sukkur and Rohri on the very first train. He had been imprisoned at Sukkur Jail and, as nobody dared to drive the engine, he volunteered to do so. Afterwards, the British released him. Out of joy for their hero, Shidis danced in jubilation and praised him in this song. This song is accompanied by the joyous *jamālo* dance.[27]

A famous singer, widely popular among people in Sindh, was Allahdino Shidi from Mirpur Pathoro, who passed away in the early 1960s. Bilawal Beljium (b. 1929) from Lyari was a renowned singer and *bēnjo* player. He made innovations in this particular instrument of Balochi folk music and also performed abroad.[28] He died in the 1980s. The period from the early

1980s to the mid-1990s, when the cassette industry boomed in Pakistan, also marked the golden age of Balochi 'disco beats' from Lyari, a new wave of street music in which Shidis, Afro-Baloch, and Afro-Sindhis significantly contributed as singers and percussionists.[29] Thus, the pop song *bhoro bhoro shīdī jambo*, performed by a group named 'Shidi Baloch,' became one of the Balochi 'top twenty' hits. The urban blend of disco and folk tunes produced at that time in Lyari was immensely popular and danceable. Later, at the turn of the century, Mukhtiar Ali Shidi from interior Sindh became a well-known performer who also sings praise songs of La'l Shahbaz Qalandar. Today, there are noted singers like Imam Bakhsh Tiri, Nasir Baloch, and Shahjahan Dauti (all living in Karachi), as well as Aslam (from Thatta).

The famous folk song *Shīdī badshāh ham badshāh* (in common pronunciation: *Shīdī bashāh ham bashāh*) meaning 'Shidi is king, Shidi is king' is followed by the verses: 'Where he puts his foot, there is peace. Our lips are like the parrots, and we are proud of our nose.' As Muhammad Siddiq Musafir critically comments, these lines are also about how other people view them as the 'happy-go-lucky Negro.'[30] This song, accompanied by the sound of *muggarmān* and *dhōl* while men dance the *ham bashāh*, is also called the Las Bela song.[31] It was handed down through oral tradition and popularized some decades ago by Gul Muhammad Pilpli, widely known as GM Pilpli, who performed at weddings and festivals throughout Sindh. Qambrani notes about this artist and his circle: 'He started his career as a comedian from Radio Pakistan, Hyderabad. He was an expert at imitating the voices of birds and animals. Through his Mombasa Art Circle, he promoted performing arts in Sindh. Ghulam Haider Qambrani, Kado Shidi, the actor Abu Bilawal, and other Shidi artists were his associates. The Sindhi film *Badal aein Barsat* (Clouds and Rain), released in 1976, was based on the lives of Shidis. In it the artists of Mombasa Art Circle played a major role. The title song of the film was the ancient folk song of the Shidis.'[32]

Recently, in 2017, the young Abid Brohi from Sibi in Balochistan, performing rap with hip-hop verses sung in Sindhi language, received the prestigious Lux Style Award as the Best Singer of the Year for his 'Sibi song.' Hip-hop and rap is the favorite form of musical expression these days, particularly in Lyari.

It was a traditional form of income for people of African descent to entertain people, especially feudal lords, by acting as court jesters and comedians as well as by performing spectacular dances.[33] This role of entertainers was ascribed to them from the time of their migration to Balochistan, Sindh,

and Gujarat.³⁴ It became an essential part of their social identity. Basu notes that in all likelihood the East African *ngōma* dances form the background of Shidi/Sidi performances in South Asia where they are accompanied by Indian drums, rattles and the blowing of the conch shell. In his work on the history of Sindh, Burton described this dance as follows: 'The males and females are either mixed together, or placed in two bodies opposite each other. The dance is a monotonous one at first, the ladies merely advance and retire, performing occasional pirouettes: the males look on and admire till it becomes their turn to amuse the assembly with jumping and distortions of the limbs.'³⁵ In Makran, Las Bela, and Karachi, the spectacular form of African dance to the beat of drums, derived from *gōma* or *dhamāl*, is the open air collective dance called *laywā* (Fig. 53). This rejoicing style of singing and dancing to the sound of the *sornā* (bass oboe) and percussion instruments, performed on demand, is similar to the Balochi *lewā* of Oman and said to have been common among seamen on the ships navigating between Oman and Africa.³⁶ It is characterized by spacious body movements, high jumps, and extraordinary gestures, for instance by jumping over fire. During this dance, whose aim is nowadays merry-making and not going into a trance (as it was in its original form), performers would also mock and make fun of the audience.³⁷

In the 1970s, there were famous dancers, such as Malang Charlie and Zahur Azad.³⁸ Today, Ustad Ghulam Abbas Baloch and Husain Dada, disciple of the legendary Baba Malang Waja, are well-known performers. In an interview on 'African dancers of Lyari,' Husain Dada explained: 'We basically belong

Fig. 53   *Laywa* dancers during performance, Karachi (March 2006)

to the Sheedi community. We are the direct descendants of sailors who came to the city some 200 years ago from Africa. Since we have African features, we decided to learn Liwa to earn a livelihood.'[39]

When they are invited by the rich of Karachi to perform as *laywā* dancers and fire-breathers at parties, weddings, the opening of a new restaurant, sports events, and in films, dancers paint their bodies and faces, tie bird feathers around their arms, put on distinctive Africanized costumes, for instance skirts made of grass, and fanciful headdresses (Fig. 54). Such performances, at times advertised as 'Black dancers from Makran,'[40] correspond to the racist and kitschy stereotypes about 'African animal-like wilderness' and 'Africans as minstrels born for public entertainment.'[41] Non-Shidis call this commercialized dance *janglī dāñs* (jungle dance). This is reminiscent of the exoticized shows in which Africans were expected (and forced) to sell their 'African body' in zoos and circus across Europe in the late nineteenth and early twentieth century to underline a hierarchy of 'races.' They were exhibited like animals in 'human zoos' and encouraged to play savages and cannibals.

The reader should keep this caricature-like image in mind when our people are invited to perform such 'cultural events' as folk dancers, even abroad. Some decades ago Zahur Azad was sent to the United States to perform. Today, troupes of Indian Sidi musicians tour the United States as well as

Fig. 54   Shidi fire-breather and dancer, Karachi (March 2006)

India where they perform at various national and folk festivals.⁴² Reflecting on such performances in which allegedly 'authentic' African heritage is shown, the art historian Prita Sandy Meier critically comments: 'In this role they are allowed to perform as entertainers for an audience not aware of the sacred significance of their performances or their roles as religious specialists. Furthermore, in this context their performances promote an ahistorical image of Sidi culture, encapsulating their "Africanness" without any real reference to their specific lives and histories, which are deeply embedded within local religious and cultural traditions.'⁴³

It would be misleading to think that all the music performed by Africans in Pakistan is about entertainment. There are prayers and sacred hymns directed to God, Prophet Muhammad, and Sufi saints as well as laments through which painful events of forced migration are vividly memorised. These laments are veritable 'voices from distant lands.' On 21 September 1986, Khurshid Qaimkhani attended the anniversary of Muhammad Siddiq Musafir in Tando Bago celebrated through nocturnal songs and dances. He mentioned the lyrics of a song performed to the beat of the *muggarmān*:⁴⁴

> We have remained separated
> Who knows when we will meet again?
> Watoma! Where are they taking us?
> Oh Wachori – help us!
> In the ocean, we will live together, we will die together!

Another couplet went like this:

> Oh brother, we are being separated
> But with the help of Murungu, on Judgement Day we will again be together, forever.

According to Qaimkhani, Wachori is the name of a famous hero in the folk stories of Kenya and Murungu the name of the supreme deity venerated by the Kikuyu tribe in Central Kenya.⁴⁵ In fact, Murungu is known among many peoples in East Africa. The name Watoma also points to Kenya. Another historical reference was made in a *mawái* where Shidis loudly shouted in Urdu: 'Koto is mine! Koto is mine!' Qaimkhani found out that there is a river named Koto in the Central African Republic from whose fertile banks a large number of people were brought as slaves to present-day Pakistan.

In addition to such laments, in coastal Balochistan there are songs accompanying cooperative work which help to synchronise movements of the workers. This genre is known as *amba*.⁴⁶ Badalkhan describes: 'Amba songs are sung in groups by fishermen when they pull or spread their nets in the sea, or pull or push their boats into the sea or out of the sea during the start or end of the fishing/seafaring seasons. It was also performed on board when sails were used for trade and transport and for pulling or releasing anchors.'[47] He further explains the style of responsorial singing: 'The guide/leader of the working team starts singing the first line and the workmen reply singing the second line, or the refrain, with the rhythm of drums and the movements required for performing the work. Usually, drums accompany the working body providing rhythm to their songs and their work. But *amba* may also be sung without the accompaniment of drums. Being basically a work song it has sometimes very short lines and sometimes even single-worded formulas which are repeated again and again, like *hey, yi, ji, ji Allah* ("O, yes, praise be to you, praise be to God"), or *tarma bidey dema* ("put the *tarm* [the wooden block put under the ship when pulled on the shore; author's note, JWF] in front" [of the boat pushed into or pulled out of the sea], and the jawabi respond in chorus, *heywalla* ("yes, with the name of God")'.[48]

Sports

Although in Karachi our people participate in donkey-cart races, held in spring at some places close to the sea, a sport having gone down over the last decades, and are also successful in traditional wrestling competitions held in rural Sindh, they stand out because of their talents and achievements in boxing and football.[49] In general, excelling in sports not only helps our people to overcome the powerlessness endured in everyday life, but also to experience moral victory.

Boxing provides essential experiences of strength and superiority, but also of failure and defeat. Considering the conditions of poverty, economic exploitation, and powerlessness our people are subjected to in their daily lives, this sport with its whirring energy in the boxing ring not only offers an outlet for frustration, but also empowerment. Around 80 per cent of the boxers in Pakistan, who are members of the Pakistan Boxing Federation (IABA) and number in total about seventy to eighty men, are said to be Shidis, Afro-Baloch, or 'Makranis.'[50] They mainly fight in the categories of light and middle weight. Almost all are amateurs as there are only few semi-professional boxers in the country. Our people act also as boxing coaches, judges, and technical officials (also at international tournaments).

Chapter 6

Fig. 55   Ready for a boxing match, Karachi (November 2010)

The journalist Latif Baloch insightfully comments about the role of Lyari in the emergence of boxing in Pakistan, starting before the Partition of the subcontinent in 1947: 'As the major port of the region, Karachi was visited by sailors and officers from around the globe whose vessels were moored here. These sailors and officers, mostly white, would have friendly boxing matches with local laborers at the port. For this purpose, late Ustad Muhammad Satto, who came to be known as the Father of Boxing in Lyari, founded a boxing club at Lyari Labor Welfare Center in 1935. He was followed by his student Ali Muhammad Qambrani, and then late Ustad Abdullah Baloch, who set up the Pak National Boxing Club in 1940.'[51] In fact, Ali Muhammad Qambrani (d. 2009), a Shidi, represented Pakistan during various international championships. His son Muhammad Siddiq Qambrani was also a prominent boxer of his time. Ali's grandson, who was named after him, won a silver medal at the Hiroshima Asian Games in 1994 and a gold medal in 1995 at the Asian boxing championships held in Manila.

Another famous champion from the Afro-Baloch community had been Jan Muhammad Baloch from Kalri/Lyari who in 1972 participated in the Olympic Games in Munich. Suffering from cancer, he died in 2012 at the age of 72. Other well-known boxers were Mehrullah Lasi from Lyari, gold medalist in the feather-weight division at the Asian Games in 2002 in South

Korea, Siddiq Jawless, a Lasi-Shidi living in Baghdadi, and Malang Baloch from Shah Baig Lane/Lyari. There are several boxing clubs in the city, such as Pak Shaheed Boxing Club in Kalri/Lyari, Trance Lyari Boxing Club in Golimar, and Pak Shaheen Boxing Club at Mauripur Road, in which young women have also trained for a few years. But besides their success in boxing, the sportsmen in question were living, and still do live in misery. They work without job security at organizations like Karachi Port Trust, Karachi Electric Supply, Railway, or WAPDA (Water and Power Development Authority). In Latif Baloch's words, 'they are forced to survive on the fringes of the same country where they were once feted as heroes.'[52]

Apart from producing good boxers, our people have proven themselves successful in football as well, a game introduced to the subcontinent by the British in the mid-nineteenth century. During the 1960s and 1970s, many of them were part of Pakistan's national football team. In the words of Latif Baloch, 'Lyari was a nursery of football.'[53] Besides Lyari, at times also called Mini-Brazil, and other working-class areas of Karachi, like Korangi, Malir, Orangi, and Landhi, football is also very popular among our people living in coastal Balochistan.[54]

The Pakistan Football Federation was founded on 5 December 1947 and in the following year it organized the first National Football Championship.[55] Until the early 1950s, teams still played barefoot. Several players from the Shidi, Afro-Baloch, and Afro-Sindhi communities had already become prominent. Thus, legendary midfielder Abdul Ghafur Majna (Fig. 57), known for his

Fig. 56   Street life in Lyari, Karachi (November 2010)

outstanding defensive strategies, was commonly called Pakistan's Pelé in the 1960s.

A biographical sketch focusing on the sports' career of this footballer of African descent is worth quoting at length: 'Majna was born on August 3, 1938, in the Saifi Lane, Baghdadi, a locality of Lyari. He started his career at Saifi Sports Lyari, a local football club, in 1957. He represented the Sindh Government Press in the All Pakistan Presidential Gold Cup Football Tournament held at the KMC Stadium Karachi in 1958. Later that year, he went to Dhaka for the Agha Khan Gold Cup Football tournament. He captained the team to victory in the final. […] Pakistan coach McBride invited him to the national team's camp in 1959 and added him to the squad. Majna toured Burma, India and China with the team. He represented Pakistan's national team at the Asia Cup in India. He was the only Pakistani player to be selected in an "Asian Eleven" team after the tournament.

During this visit to Bombay, he signed a professional contract with Kolkata Mohammadan (football club). In 1961, he was signed on by Dhaka Mohammadan, after which he joined Victoria Club, Dhaka. He played under Captain Umar in a tournament in Kuala Lumpur, Malaysia, where Pakistan reached the final. In 1964, he went on a tour to China with the national team. […] He rejoined Dhaka Mohammadan in 1965 and stayed with them until 1969. He retired from the national team soon afterwards in protest against the biased treatment of footballers from Karachi [because of racist abuse; author's note, JWF]. However, at the request of the president of Pakistan Football Federation, Abdul Sattar Gabol, he agreed to return from retirement and led the national team at the Asian Games in Iran in 1974.

Abdul Ghafoor Majna had a special bond with the people of Dhaka. He married into a respectable family from Allahabad (Uttar Pradesh, India) who were settled in Dhaka. Majna's house was raided by security personnel during General Pervez Musharraf's tenure. His young son Abdul Ghani, a footballer in the national team, was arrested on charges of aiding and abetting the Taliban. He was in custody for two years. A heartbroken Abdul Ghafoor, unable to bear this ignominy, suffered an attack of paralysis and died soon afterwards. To add insult to injury, this legendary footballer was given no support by the football federation or the government during his illness.'[56]

During the 1960s, the 'golden era' of Pakistani football, other renowned players with African roots besides Abdul Ghafur Majna, included Murad Bakhsh Makwa, Turab Ali, Yusuf Junior, Maula Bakhsh, as well as later Muhammad Siddiq, Muhammad Umar Baloch, Ghulam Abbas, Abdullah Rahim, Ali Nawaz, and Ustad Shidu.[57] When, after the war of 1971,

Fig. 57 The legendary footballer Abdul Ghafur Majna, a Baloch of African descent; poster put up in a club in Baghdadi; Lyari, Karachi (March 2020)

Chapter 6

East Pakistan (which had a much better football infrastructure) became Bangladesh, Pakistani football slowly but steadily declined in the 1970s. Additionally, since 1977, that is to say at the beginning of Zia ul-Haq's Islamist regime, interest in football (and other sports as well as amusements) was discouraged. The enthusiasm for football finally revived in the early 1980s, although on the international level the national team met with many defeats. In the 1990s, Pakistani football, in the words of Ali Ahsan, 'fell once again into an era of political incompetence, mismanagement and lethargy,' which also included a lack of long-term sponsorship.[58] In 2004, a major step was taken in promoting football by establishing the Pakistan Premier League (PPL). Many players in this league as well as in the national team belong to populations of African descent.

In the mid-2000s, grass-roots level football was promoted in Karachi with several regular competitions and free football academies in Lyari, Korangi, and other parts of the city. Nowadays in Karachi there are many football clubs in which sportsmen from our people are active. In Lyari alone 109 clubs are

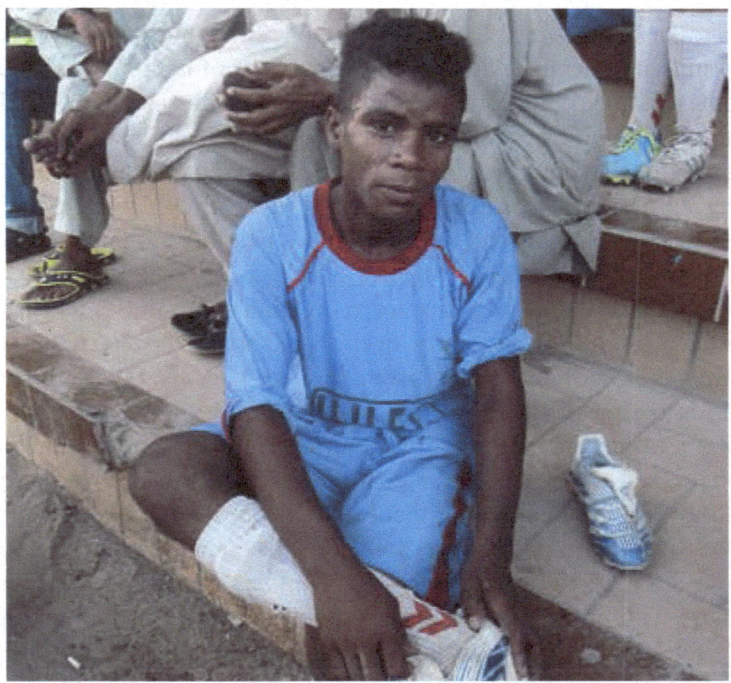

Fig. 58   Arslan, a young gifted footballer from Lyari, Karachi (November 2016)

registered and many others remain non-registered. In a conversation with the journalist Saeed Jan Baloch, an executive member of Saifi Club, until ten to fifteen years ago, there were some fourteen to sixteen junior teams in their club. After school, young men would play football and cricket. Today, unfortunately, besides one senior team, only one junior football team remains.

Everyday Pastimes

On Lyari's Hajji Pir Muhammad Road between Baghdadi and Shah Baig Lane, a main street where men gather, I often watched men sitting in small groups at the roadside playing games: mainly draughts (checkers), ludo, and cards, but also carom board and dominoes. Draughts is a strategic game, and carom a board game of skill, while others are mostly games of chance. Focusing on their respective game, players and spectators shared the same intention and attentiveness which created trust among them. They chatted, laughed, and at times enjoyed a cup of tea (if they could afford it), thus temporarily forgetting their daily worries and the need to complete tasks. Some immerse themselves in deep play every day for hours, meeting friends within a familial setting. These ludic practices are an integral part of social reality in Lyari in times where such expressions of happiness and joy of life are contested and, if not forbidden, at least seen with suspicion and disregard by orthodox religious scholars and activists from Islamic reformist groups.[59] These scholars and activists promote strict religious behaviour and criticize playing games as a waste of time, as pure 'idleness,' which leads to the neglect of prayer duties and responsibilities towards the family.

Men visit these open locations for recreation and amusement after work in the late afternoons and early evenings. Those who are better off dress in white, the color of purity (used, for instance, by Islamic clerics) and the sartorial sign of those who do not work with their hands, and enjoy a cup of tea at the one and only tea shop on Hajji Pir Muhammad Road. As elsewhere, tea shops serve as men's houses. The unemployed spend most of the day playing games. For them there is hardly anything else to do and they seek escape from boredom. Some men frequent a closed space screened off from the road, a sort of pergola, full of singing birds kept in cages and decorated with portraits of Sufi saints, which forms a unique setting for the leisure activities of smoking and chatting. This is another 'temporary world' of male social intercourse with its own rules and etiquette outside ordinary life. In these shady dens of Lyari, young men also take drugs. Out of poverty

Chapter 6

Fig. 59 Playing draughts in Baghdadi; Lyari, Karachi (November 2016)

and without prospects for the future, some become criminals, join one of the gangs active in Lyari, or become involved in the drug mafia.

In the small narrow lanes of interior Baghdadi where the mood is rather relaxed because there is hardly any traffic, older women sit in front of their homes smoking water pipes. I saw young boys hurling a small spinning top made of wood or metal and tied to a string into the air, skilfully catching it with one hand and letting the top spin further onto the palm before hurling it up again. Other children games include playing marbles (mainly by boys), hopscotch over seven squares (by girls), and jumping over the outstretched arms of two boys crouching opposite each other whereby, after a successful jump, the height is measured by span and increased for the next jump. Additionally, there are noisy little halls in which boys play table soccer, carom board, billiard, and computer games.

Witnessing this articulation of playfulness, I remembered the German poet Friedrich von Schiller's famous sentence in his letters on the aesthetic education of man (published in 1795) where he says that 'man is an entire man only there where he plays.'[60] At the above places, men, whether young or old, Shidi, Baloch, or a member of some other ethnic group, is a veritable *homo ludens* drawing on Johan Huizinga's concept of play as a way to engage with the world. This pursuit of passionate activities belongs to the cultural domain of *shauq*. Its essence is the inner state of pleasure which fulfils basic human needs. As emphasized by the anthropologists Kirin Narayan and Muhammad A. Kavesh, the 'key to the conception of *shauq* is choice: people embrace an activity because they *want* to, not because they have to.'[61] What I observed at least in Baghdadi, the central part of Lyari with which I am most familiar, is that the people sitting in the late afternoons and evenings at the roadside still mostly live in the pre-digital age. They hardly use smartphones, partly due to economic reasons, but also because many are non-literate. Instead, they (still) enjoy life in the public space where they meet friends and acquaintances face-to-face. This in turn often paves the way for practical solidarity.

Endnotes

1. De Silva Jayasuriya 2008: 429.
2. My own observations; see also Basu 1994: 47-49; Albinia 2008: 67 (A young Shidi woman from Badin confessed to the author: '*Humein dukh nahin lagta* – we never feel sorrow – only laughter. Sindhi culture is so sad and gloomy; there are too many problems for women – *karokari* [honour-killing; author's note, JWF], dowry – but there is nothing like that here. We manage to ignore these things and be happy.'); Badalkhan 2008: 278-279; Qambrani 2017: 38-39. Concerning the variety of drums in use among our people, I mainly rely on the excellent information provided by Ustad Abdur Rahman Babu, a renowned expert of the Shidi community who lives in Lyari (conversation with him on 26 February 2020 at Lasi-*makān*).
3. De Silva Jayasuriya 2010: 171.
4. Cf. Frembgen & Rollier 2014: XIII.
5. Baloch 1982: 126.
6. Unfortunately, in my introductory article about the Shidi community of Karachi (Frembgen 2020) my linguistically correct spelling *muggarmān* had been replaced by the editors of the volume in question with the spelling 'magarman' (pp. 161, 163) which is at least wrong with respect to Sindh.
7. Qaimkhani 1996: 75.
8. Qaimkhani 1996: 74; translated from Urdu.
9. On the following, see Teffera 2009. Cf. Basu 2008b: 239.
10. Teffera 2009: 306.
11. Cf. Meier 2004: 90.
12. See photograph No. 28 in Frembgen 2020: 162.
13. *Musundu* is also the name of an African drum (similar to *muggarmān*) used in *lewa* performances in Oman (De Silva Jayasuriya 2010: 162). Basu says that the *musindo* played by Sidis in Gujarat is a kettle-drum (2008 b: 243-244).

14   This term is also used for a smaller drum used in peripheral cults of possession in the strait of Hormuz (Bashiri 1983: 5; Beeman 2015: 5).
15   Qambrani 2018: 39. Baloch writes *ketvorovo* (1966: 42; 1982: 126).
16   Cf. Abbas 2002: 40, 44.
17   Qaimkhani 1996: 75.
18   During my visit to Tando Bago on 13 February 2018 in the company of Aslam Khwaja, I learned that for many years the local Shidi community possessed four *muggarmān*s, kept at the shrine of the local saint Nazarmun Shah Jilani adjacent to their neighborhood. One day, two of these sacred drums were stolen. Later the local community donated the third one to a Shidi community in another town in Sindh. In order to protect their last drum, the Councillor representing the community in Tando Bago, now keeps the last *muggarmān* at his home.
19   Nizamani 2006: 71.
20   Cf. Catlin-Jairazbhoy 2004: 193; Varadarajan 2020: 67, footnote 1.
21   Catlin-Jairazbhoy 2004: 187-189.
22   Visit by J.W. Frembgen on 23 January 2018. Graves (2020) has done an excellent in-depth study of this highly interesting type of lyre found in Mumbai. Cf. Robbins & McLeod 2006a: 20-21 (paintings and drawings of Sidi musicians playing a lyre).
23   De Silva Jayasuriya 2010: 157.
24   Bashiri 1983: 10.
25   Abbas 2002: 38-39.
26   Boivin 2012: 102.
27   Nizamani 2006: 64.
28   Ahmed 1989: 27; Khwaja 2013: 43.
29   On this topic, see Aslam 1990.
30   Ahmed 1989: 29 (quoting from Muhammad Siddiq Musafir); Albinia 2008: 77-78.
31   Nizamani 2006: 64, 67, 69.
32   Qambrani 2017: 62-63; cf. Albinia 2008: 78.
33   Rahman 1976: 4; Basu 1995: 47-49.
34   Cf. Basu 1995: 47-49; Badalkhan 2008: 279-280.
35   Burton 1851: 256.
36   During 1997: 39; Badalkhan 2008: 279-281; De Silva Jayasuriya 2010: 162; Khalique 2009: 37; Ali 2011: 20.
37   Basu 1995: 48; Badalkhan 2008: 280-281.
38   Bhutto 2010: 241.
39   Ousat 2013.
40   Badalkhan 2008: 286.
41   See, for instance, the figure of a dark-skinned man (fat, thick-lipped, laughing, dancing, and holding a mug of coffee) used since 1996 as the lucky mascot called 'Lu' by the Italian coffee company Lucaffé. This logo is not only in poor taste, but racist in content.

42 Robbins & McLeod 2006a: 22; cf. Badalkhan 2008: 286; De Silva Jayasuriya 2008: 431; De Silva Jayasuriya 2010: 163.
43 Meier 2004: 92.
44 On the following, see Qaimkhani 1996: 77.
45 Qaimkhani 1996: 78.
46 Badalkhan 2008: 280-281, 283-286; cf. Frishkopf 2006: 165.
47 Badalkhan 2008: 284.
48 Badalkhan 2008: 286.
49 See the chapter 'Sportsmen of Lyari' in Baloch 2017, pp. 154-173, in which the author relies on reports by the renowned sports reporter Ishaq Baloch.
50 Conversation with Akbar Yezdani (30 November 2017, Karachi), who in 2012 briefly established a boxing league for amateurs in Karachi.
51 Baloch 2017: 158.
52 Baloch 2017: 161.
53 Baloch 2017: 101.
54 Ahsan 2010, Part I: 4, Part II: 4.
55 The series of articles by Ali Ahsan (2010, 2011) in the daily *Dawn* provides a good overview of the history of football in Pakistan. See also the photographs in Frembgen 2020: 157.
56 Baloch 2017: 156-157; cf. Ahsan 2010, Part I: 11, Part II: 1.
57 Information gathered in conversations with footballers in Lyari. Cf. Ahsan 2010, Part II: 3-4, 7.
58 Ahsan 2010, Part III: 9.
59 Cf. Frembgen & Rollier 2014: XV-XVI, 147-149.
60 Schiller 1795.
61 Narayan & Kavesh 2019: 5.

Afterword

The present ethnographic study is only a first step towards appreciating the cultural traditions of African communities in Pakistan and a first endeavor to show that their history, society, religion, and everyday practices can be a source of pride for them instead of shame and denial. Especially Shidis emphasize their symbolic and cultural capital to compensate for their small economic capital. This is important to note considering the sense of deprivation and the feelings of inferiority prevalent among them in consequence of the *longue durée* of suppression and fragmentation when dehumanizing slavery disrupted their African culture(s). As frequently underlined by Achille Mbembe, an important contemporary thinker of postcolonialism and influential intellectual of the African continent, the wounds of racism, slavery, and colonialism have not been healed by any means. When Africans, after their colonial dislocation, arrived in South Asia, they were perceived as the physically visible human Other. This status has led to deep-seated, often grotesque prejudices to which they have been subjected to the present day. The effective color-bar makes it very difficult for them to improve their status and to climb the social ladder. Thus, they are often treated as second-class citizens.

The Shidis' distinct African artistic expressions, their music and dances (ethnic markers par excellence and at the same time reservoir of cultural memory), their particular African-derived religious beliefs and practices merged with indigenous Sufi Islam, as well as their own perspectives of history should be valued and preserved. From the perspective of an ethnographer and cultural anthropologist, they constitute a significant contribution to the cultural kaleidoscope and spiritual wealth of Pakistan. In fact, in many respects the community's cohesion depends on the maintenance of their religious identity and cultural roots. Muhammad Siddiq Musafir therefore clearly reminded his people not to lose touch with their traditions and to

Fig. 60 Yaqoob Qambrani (right) and Akhtar Soomro (left) at Press Club, Karachi (January 2014)

pass on their African heritage to the next generations. He did not want the Shidis' African identity and cultural distinctiveness to be silenced. Although a conscious recollection of the past and of one's own values can help to restore self-esteem and cultural identity and create a new self-awareness, it also manifests the status of being perceived as 'foreign' and 'exotic.' As the case of the African-descended population of Balochistan and of the Khaskelis in Sindh shows, a memory of the past which was lost, stolen, or consciously erased, cannot be regained or easily 'repaired.' Nevertheless, renaming helped them to become more readily assimilated into their host societies.

One thing remains undisputed: In view of the neglect and often sheer mistreatment of Africans in Pakistan – in past and present considered as the different and maligned Other, never given the feeling of being welcome in this country after their traumatic forced migration, they deserve above all recognition. They want to be recognized and treated like other Pakistanis. It is incumbent upon every human being to encounter others with tolerance not ignorance, to treat them with respect and dignity. Ethical behavior oriented to the human Other first needs a deconstitution of the self (in the sense of the imperialist and egoist I) to reach out and acknowledge others.[62] Ethics is, of course, not something to be relegated to the state. The latter, however, has the duty to ensure social justice and the betterment of our people's economically depressed conditions. Living among them, making friends with them, and trying to understand their indigenous cultural traditions, created a profound respect in me for their resilience and warmheartedness. I do hope that this book will help to foster their cultural self-esteem.

Endnote

1   Alvi 2020: 161, 173-174.

Bibliography

Abbas, Shemeem Burney: *The Female Voice in Sufi Ritual. Devotional Practices of Pakistan and India.* Karachi 2002 (Oxford University Press).

Ahmed, Feroz: Africa on the Coast of Pakistan. In: *New Directions* 16/4 (1989), pp. 22-31.

Ahmed, Khaled: *Word for Word. Stories behind Everyday Words we use.* Karachi 2010 (Oxford University Press).

Ahmed, Khaled: The Sheedi of Sindh. In: *Newsweek* (Karachi, issue 18 August to 1 September 2018). [https://newsweekpakistan.com/the-sheedi-of-sindh/; accessed on 26 July 2019]

Ahmed, Maqbool: The Oman Connection. In: *The Herald* (Karachi) 43/8 (2011), p. 23.

Ahmed, Maqbool & Zehra Nawab: Harmony springs eternal. Inside an extraordinary Karachi neighbourhood. In: *The Herald* (Karachi) 48/6 (2015), pp. 46-49.

Ahsan, Ali: A History of Football in Pakistan. In: *Dawn* (Karachi), Part I, December 23, 2010 [www.dawn.com/news/593095], Part II, December 23, 2010 [www.dawn.com/news/593096], Part III, December 23, 2010 [www.dawn.com/news/593100], Final part, February 2, 2011 [www.dawn.com/news/603320; all websites accessed on 9 December 2019].

Aitken, Edward H.: *Gazetteer of the Province of Sind.* Karachi 1907 (Repr. Karachi 1986; Indus Publications).

al-Akkad, Abbas Mahmood: *Bilal. The First Muadhdhin of the Prophet of Islam.* Lahore 1978 (Kazi Publications).

Albinia, Alice: *Empires of the Indus. The Story of a River*. New York & London 2008 (W.W. Norton).

Ali, Omar Hamid: *The African Diaspora in the Indian Ocean World*. New York 2011 (Schomburg Center for Research in Black Culture, The New York Public Library).

Ali, Omar Hamid & Kenneth X. Robbins & Beheroze Shroff & Jazmin Graves (eds.): *African Diasporan Communities across South Asia*. Vol. 2 of 'Afro-South Asia in the Global African Diaspora'; Greensboro, NC & Ahmedabad 2020 (The University of North Carolina).

Alpers, Edward A.: The African Diaspora in the Indian Ocean: A Comparative Perspective. In: Shihan De Silva Jayasuriya & Richard Pankhurst (eds.) *The African Diaspora in the Indian Ocean*; pp. 19-50. Trenton & Asmara 2003 (Africa World Press).

Alpers, Edward A.: Africans in India and the Wider Context of the Indian Ocean. In: Amy Catlin-Jairazbhoy & Edward A. Alpers (eds.): *Sidis and Scholars. Essays on African Indians*; pp. 27-41. Noida 2004 (Rainbow Publishers).

Alvi, Anjum: Levinas and ethics: The death of Pope John Paul II. In: *Anthropological Theory* 20/2 (2020), pp. 157-179.

Amin, Mohamed & Duncan Willetts & Graham Hancock: *Journey through Pakistan*. London et al. 1982 (The Bodley Head) & Nairobi (Camerapix).

Asimov, M.S. & C.E. Bosworth: *History of Civilizations of Central Asia*. Vol. 4, Part 1. Delhi 1992 (Motilal Banarsidass Publishing).

Aslam, Ayesha: The Rhythm Revolution. In: *The Herald*, Karachi 21/8 (1990), pp. 85-94.

Awan, A.B.: *Baluchistan. Historical and Political Processes*. London 1985 (New Century Publishers).

Axmann, Martin: *Back to the Future. The Khanate of Kalat and the Genesis of Baloch Nationalism 1915-1955*. Karachi 2008 (Oxford University Press).

Badalkhan, Sabir: On the Presence of African Musical Culture in Coastal Baluchistan. In: Helene Basu (ed.): *Journeys and Dwellings. Indian Ocean Themes in South Asia*; pp. 276-287. Hyderabad/Deccan 2008 (Orient Longman).

Badalkhan, Sabir: *Two Essays on Baloch History and Folklore*. Naples & Rome 2013 (Università degli studi di Napoli & ISMEO).

Bibliography

Baillie, Alexander F.: *Kurrachee: Past, Present and Future*. Bombay & London 1890 (Repr. Karachi 1975 (Oxford University Press).

Baloch, Latif: *The Case for Lyari*. Karachi 2017 (Sindh Independent Media Association).

Baloch, Inayatullah: *The Problem of "Greater Baluchistan": A Study of Baluch Nationalism*. Stuttgart 1987 (Franz Steiner).

Baloch, N.A. (Nabi Bakhsh): *Musical Instruments of the Lower Indus Valley of Sind*. Hyderabad 1966 (Mehran Arts Council).

Baloch, N.A. (Nabi Bakhsh): Folk-Musical Instruments of Mehran Valley. In: Ghulam Ali Allana (ed.), *Folk Music of Sind*; pp. 104-127. Jamshoro 1982 (Institute of Sindhology, University of Sind).

Baloch, Sammi: Bad Blood: Impact of Slavery, Racial Denial and Colourism to Baloch Identity. In: *Balochistan Times*, 23 June 2020. [https://balochistantimes.com/bad-blood-impact-of-slavery-racial-denial-and-colourism-to-baloch-identity; accessed on 23 June 2020]

Baptiste, Fitzroy: From 'Invisibility' to 'Visibility': Africans in India through the Lens of Some Select Sources from the Late Classical Period to the Late 18th Century A.D. In: Kiran Kamal Prasad & Jean-Pierre Angenot (eds.): *Tadia. The African Diaspora in Asia*; pp. 117-166. Bangalore 2008 (Jana Jagrati Prakashana).

Baptiste, Fitzroy & John McLeod & Kenneth X. Robbins: Africans in the Medieval Deccan. In: Kenneth X. Robbins & John McLeod (eds.): *African Elites in India: Habshi Amarat*; pp. 31-43. Ahmedabad 2006 (Mapin).

Bari, Moin: *Saints of Sindh*. Lahore 1994 (Jang Publishers).

Barth, Fredrik: *Sohar. Culture and Society in an Omani Town*. Baltimore & London 1983 (The Johns Hopkins University Press).

Bashiri, Iraj: *Muslims or Shamans: Blacks of the Persian Gulf* [www.angelfire.com/rnb/bashiriGulf.gulf.pdf; accessed on 18 June 2015].

Basu, Helene: *Habshi-Sklaven, Sidi-Fakire: Muslimische Heiligenverehrung im westlichen Indien*. Berlin 1995 (Das Arabische Buch).

Basu, Helene: Theatre of Memory: Ritual Kinship Performances of the African Diaspora in Pakistan. In: Monika Böck & Aparna Rao (eds.), *Culture, Creation, and Procreation: Concepts of Kinship in South Asian Practice*; pp. 243-270. New York & Oxford 2000 (Berghahn).

Basu, Helene: Slave, Soldier, Trader, Faqir: Fragments of African Histories in Western India (Gujarat). In: Shihan De Silva Jayasuriya & Richard Pankhurst (eds.) *The African Diaspora in the Indian Ocean*; pp. 223-249. Trenton & Asmara 2003 (Africa World Press).

Basu, Helene: Geister und Sufis: Translokale Konstellationen des Islam in der Welt des Indischen Ozeans. In: *Zeitschrift für Ethnologie* 130 (2005), pp. 169-193.

Basu, Helene (ed.): *Journeys and Dwellings. Indian Ocean Themes in South Asia.* Hyderabad/Deccan 2008 a (Orient Longman).

Basu, Helene: A Gendered Indian Ocean Site: Mai Mishra, African Spirit Possession and Sidi Women in Gujarat. In: Helene Basu (ed.): *Journeys and Dwellings. Indian Ocean Themes in South Asia*; pp. 227-255. Hyderabad/Deccan 2008 b (Orient Longman).

Basu, Helene: In the Courtroom of Jungle Saints. The Poor and Transcendental Justice. In: William W. S. Sax & Helene Basu (eds.), *The Law of Possession. Ritual, Healing, and the Secular State*; pp. 31-54. New York 2015 (Oxford University Press).

Beeman, William O.: The Zar in the Persian Gulf. Performative dimensions. In: *Anthropology of the Contemporary Middle East and Central Eurasia* 3/1 (2015), pp. 1-12.

Bhatt, Purnima Mehta: Slavery and the Slave Trade. In: Omar H. Ali & Kenneth X. Robbins &

Beheroze Shroff & Jazmin Graves (eds.), *African Diasporan Communities Across South Asia*; pp. 25-46. Greensboro, NC & Ahmedabad 2020 (The University of North Carolina).

Bijarani, Mir Khuda Bakhsh: *Searchlights on Baloches and Balochistan.* Quetta 1974 (Gosh-e-Adab).

Bitterli, Urs: *Alte Welt – Neue Welt. Formen des europäisch-überseeischen Kulturkontakts vom 15. bis zum 18. Jahrhundert.* Munich 1986 (C.H. Beck).

Boas, Franz: *The Mind of Primitive Man.* New York 1922 (Macmillan).

Boivin, Michel: Horsemen and Saviours. Iconography in Hindu Communities of Twentieth Century Sindh. In: Saima Zaidi (ed.), *Mazaar, Bazaar. Design and Visual Culture in Pakistan*; pp. 16-21. Karachi 2009 (Oxford University Press).

Boivin, Michel: The Sufi Center of Jhok Sharif in Sindh (Pakistan): Questioning the *Ziyārat* as a Social Process. In: Clinton Bennett & Charles M. Ramsey (eds.), *South Asian Sufis. Devotion, Deviation, and Destiny*; pp. 95-109. London et al. 2012 (Bloomsbury).

Boivin, Michel: *Historical Dictionary of the Sufi Culture of Sindh in Pakistan and India.* Karachi 2015 (Oxford University Press).

Bourdieu, Pierre: *Die feinen Unterschiede.* Frankfurt a.M. 1982 (Suhrkamp).

Brentjes, Burchard: *Die Söhne Ismaels. Geschichte und Kultur der Araber.* Leipzig 1973 (Koehler & Amelang).

Bürgel, Johann Christoph: *Allmacht und Mächtigkeit. Religion und Welt im Islam.* Munich 1991 (C.H. Beck).

Burton, Richard F.: *Sindh and the Races that inhabit the Valley of the Indus.* London 1851 (Repr. Karachi 1973; Oxford University Press).

Burton, Richard F.: *Sind revisited.* London 1877 (Repr. Karachi 1993; Department of Culture and Tourism, Government of Sindh).

Bhutto, Fatima: Mangho Pir. In: *Granta. The Magazine of New Writing* 112 (2010), pp. 225-241.

Campbell, Gwyn: The African Diaspora in Asia. In: Kiran Kamal Prasad & Jean-Pierre Angenot (eds.): *Tadia. The African Diaspora in Asia*; pp. 43-82. Bangalore 2008 (Jana Jagrati Prakashana).

Catlin-Jairazbhoy, Amy & Edward A. Alpers (eds.): *Sidis and Scholars. Essays on African Indians.* Noida 2004 (Rainbow Publishers).

Catlin-Jairazbhoy, Amy: A Sidi CD? Globalising African Indian Music and the Sacred. In: Amy Catlin-Jairazbhoy & Edward A. Alpers (eds.): *Sidis and Scholars. Essays on African Indians*; pp. 178-211. Noida 2004 (Rainbow Publishers).

Daftary, Farhad: *The Ismāʿīlīs. Their History and Doctrines.* Cambridge 2007 (Cambridge University Press).

Davis, David Brion: *The Problem of Slavery in the Age of Emancipation.* New York 2014 (Alfred A. Knopf).

De Silva Jayasuriya, Shihan: Crossing Boundaries: Africans in South Asia. In: *Afrika Spectrum* 43/3 (2008), pp. 429-438.

De Silva Jayasuriya, Shihan: *African Identity in Asia. Cultural Effects of Forced Migration.* Princeton 2009 (Markus Wiener Publications).

De Silva Jayasuriya, Shihan: *The African Diaspora in Asian Trade Routes and Cultural Memories.* Lewiston 2010 (The Edwin Mellen Press).

De Silva Jayasuriya, Shihan & Richard Pankhurst (eds.): *The African Diaspora in the Indian Ocean.* Trenton & Asmara 2003a (Africa World Press).

De Silva Jayasuriya, Shihan & Richard Pankhurst: On the African Diaspora in the Indian Ocean Region. In: Shihan De Silva Jayasuriya & Richard Pankhurst (eds.) *The African Diaspora in the Indian Ocean*; pp. 7-17. Trenton & Asmara 2003b (Africa World Press).

Doniger O'Flaherty, Wendy: *Women, Androgynes, and Other Mythical Beasts.* Chicago & London 1980 (The University of Chicago Press).

During, Jean: *Iran Vol. 5 & 6. Baloutchistan. Musiques d'extase et de guérison* [longplay record with booklet in French and English]. Paris 1981 (Ocora/Radio France).

During, Jean: African Winds and Muslim Djinns. Trance, Healing and Devotion in Baluchistan. In: *Yearbook of the International Council for Traditional Music* 29 (1997), pp. 39-56.

Eaton, Richard M.: Malik Ambar and Elite Slavery in the Deccan, 1400-1650. In: Kenneth X. Robbins & John McLeod (eds.): *African Elites in India: Habshi Amarat*; pp. 45-67. Ahmedabad 2006 (Mapin).

Edwards, Holly: *Of Brick and Myth. The Genesis of Islamic Architecture in the Indus Valley.* Karachi 2015 (Oxford University Press).

Ehsaei, Mahdi: *Afro-Iran.* Heidelberg & Berlin 2015 (Kehrer).

Elfenbein, J.H.: *The Baluch Language.* London 1966 (Luzac).

Fabietti, Ugo: Equality versus Hierarchy: Conceptualizing Change in Southern Balochistan. In: Paul Titus (ed.), *Marginality and Modernity. Ethnicity and Change in Post-Colonial Balochistan*; pp. 3-27. Karachi 1996 (Oxford University Press).

Fartacek, Gebhard: Besessenheit und Identität. Erkundungen zum *zār*-Kult am Shatt al-Arab (SW-Iran). In: *Anthropos* 109 (2014), pp. 567-582.

Fatah, Sonya: Sidelined Skin. Sheedis continue to struggle against racism in Pakistan. In: *The Herald* (Karachi) 36/10 (2005), pp. 112-114.

Flood, Finbarr Barry: *Objects of Translation: Material Culture and Medieval 'Hindu-Muslim' Encounter.* New Jersey 2011 (Princeton University Press).

Floyer, Ernest Ayscoghe: *Unexplored Balūchistan.* London 1882 (Griffith & Farran).

Forkl, Hermann: Einführung in den schwarzafrikanischen Islam. In: Hermann Forkl & Johannes Kalter & Thomas Leisten & Margareta Pavaloi (eds.), *Die Gärten des Islam*; pp. 298-303. Stuttgart & London 1993 (Edition Hansjörg Mayer).

Freeman-Grenville, G.S.P.: The Sidi and Swahili. In: *Bulletin of the British Association of Orientalists*, N.S. 6 (1971), pp. 3-18.

Frembgen, Jürgen Wasim: *Naswar. Der Gebrauch von Mundtabak in Afghanistan und Pakistan.* Liestal 1989 (Stiftung Bibliotheca Afghanica).

Frembgen, Jürgen Wasim: Divine Madness and Cultural Otherness: Diwānas and Faqīrs in Northern Pakistan. In: *South Asia Research* 26/3 (2006 a), pp. 235-248.

Frembgen, Jürgen Wasim: *The Friends of God – Sufi Saints in Islam. Popular Poster Art from Pakistan.* Karachi 2006 b (Oxford University Press).

Frembgen, Jürgen Wasim: *Journey to God. Sufis and Dervishes in Islam.* Karachi 2008 (Oxford University Press).

Frembgen, Jürgen Wasim: *Dhamāl* and the Performing Body: Trance Dance in the Devotional Sufi Practice of Pakistan. In: *Journal of Sufi Studies* 1 (2012), pp. 77-113.

Frembgen, Jürgen Wasim: The Shidi Community of Karachi: A Brief Pictorial Introduction. In: Omar H. Ali & Kenneth X. Robbins & Beheroze Shroff & Jazmin Graves (eds.), *African Diasporan Communities Across South Asia*; pp. 153-166. Greensboro, NC & Ahmedabad 2020 (The University of North Carolina).

Frembgen, Jürgen Wasim & Paul Rollier: *Wrestlers, Pigeon Fanciers, and Kite Flyers. Traditional Sports and Pastimes in Lahore.* Karachi 2014 (Oxford University Press).

Frishkopf, Michael: Review of audio CD with booklet 'Music of Makran: Traditional Fusion from Coastal Balochistan,' prepared by Anderson Bakewell in collaboration with Sabir Badalkhan. In: *Asian Music* 37/2 (2006), pp. 164-171.

Frye, Richard N.: Remarks on Baluch History. In: *Central Asiatic Journal* 6 (1961), pp. 44-50.

Furlonge, Nigel D.: Revisiting the Zanj and Re-Visioning Revolt: Complexities of the Zanj Conflict – 868-883 AD. In: *Negro History Bulletin* 62/4 (1999), pp. 7-14.

Gabriel, Alfons: *Die religiöse Welt des Iran*. Vienna 1974 (Böhlau Verlag).

Gayer, Laurent: *Karachi. Ordered Disorder and the Struggle for the City*. Noida 2014 (HarperCollins Publishers India).

Gazdar, Haris: My name is Lyari. In: Sehba Sarwar (ed.), *Homes and Histories. Living Room Art*; pp. 18-23. Houston 2012-13.

Gazetteer Balochistan 1906: *Balochistan through the Ages, Vol. I-II (Selection from Government Record)*. Quetta 1979 (Nisa Traders).

Gazetteer Balochistan: *Imperial Gazetteer of India, Provincial Series, Balochistān*. Lahore 1984 (Repr., Sang-e-Meel Publications).

Gazetteer Las Bela: *District Gazetteer Las Bela, 1907*. Karachi 1983 (Indus Publications).

Gazetteer Sindh: *Gazetteer of the Province of Sind. Compiled by E.H. Aitken*. Karachi 1907 (Repr. Karachi 1986, Indus Publications).

Gholi, Ahmad & Masoud Ahmadi Musaabad: Problematized Humanism: Sadi's Racist Tendency in Gulistan. In: *International Journal of Applied Linguistics & English Literature* 4/3 (2015), pp. 39-44.

Graves, Jazmin: Through the Eyes of the Lyre: A Transoceanic Perspective on the Sidi Sufi Devotional Tradition of Western India. In: Omar H. Ali & Kenneth X. Robbins & Beheroze Shroff & Jazmin Graves (eds.), *African Diasporan Communities Across South Asia*; pp. 93-109. Greensboro, NC & Ahmedabad 2020 (The University of North Carolina).

Green, Nile: *Making Space. Sufis and Settlers in Early Modern India*. New Delhi 2012 (Oxford University Press).

Haller, Dieter: *Tanger. Der Hafen, die Geister, die Lust. Eine Ethnographie*. Bielefeld 2016 (transcript).

Halliday, Tony (ed.): *Pakistan. APA Guides*. Berlin et al. 1990 (APA Publications, RV Reise- und Verkehrsverlag). [several editions in English and German]

Harris, Joseph E.: *The African Presence in Asia. Consequences of the East African Slave Trade*. Evanston 1971 (Northwestern University Press).

Harvey, Steven: A New Islamic Source of the *Guide of the Perplexed*. In: A. Hyman (ed.), *Maimonidean Studies*, Vol. 1; pp. 31-60. New York 1990 (Yeshiva University Press).

Hays, J. Daniel: *From Every People and Nation: A Biblical Theology of Race*. Leicester 2003 (Apollos).

Hollister, John Norman: *The Shi'a of India*. London 1953 (Luzac and Co.).

Hopkins, B.D.: Race, Sex and Slavery: 'Forced Labour' in Central Asia and Afghanistan in the Early 19th Century. In: *Modern Asian Studies* 42/4 (2008), pp. 629-671.

Hughes, A.W.: *The Country of Balochistan*. London 1877 (Repr. Karachi 1977; Indus Publications).

Husain, Khalifa Isma'il: *Nur-i Rifa'i, Hayat-i Tayyaba*. Karachi 2014 (Anjuman-i Ashiqan-i Ghaus al-Rifa'i).

Husain, Rumana: *Karachiwala. A Subcontinent within a City*. Karachi 2010 (Jaal).

Husain, Rumana: The Manghopir Mela or Sheedi Mela of the Sheedis of Karachi. In: Omar H. Ali & Kenneth X. Robbins & Beheroze Shroff & Jazmin Graves (eds.), *African Diasporan Communities Across South Asia*; pp. 143-150. Greensboro, NC & Ahmedabad 2020 (The University of North Carolina).

Hussain, Abid: In conversation with Laurent Gayer and Omar Shahid Hamid on Karachi. In: *Herald* (Karachi) 49/10 (2016), pp. 94-103.

Jafri, Syed Husain Mohammad: *The Origins and Early Development of Shi'a Islam*. Karachi 2000 (Oxford University Press).

Jamal al-Din, Nadia: Miskawayh. In: *Prospects. The Quarterly Review of Comparative Education* 24/1-2 (1994), pp. 131-152.

Jamali, Hafeez Ahmed: Shorelines of memory and ports of desire. Geography, identity, and the memory of oceanic trade in Mekran Coast (Balochistan). In: Smriti Srinivas & Bettina Ng'weno & Neelima Jeychandran (eds.), *Reimagining Indian Ocean Worlds*; pp. 165-179. London & New York 2020 (Routledge).

Janmahmad: *The Baloch Cultural Heritage*. Karachi 1982 (Royal Book Company).

Jansen, Michael: *Die Indus-Zivilisation. Wiederentdeckung einer frühen Hochkultur*. Cologne 1985 (DuMont).

Kalhoro, Zulfiqar Ali (ed.): *Studies in Kalhora History, Economy and Architecture.* Karachi 2017 (Sindh Books).

Kalichbeg Fredunbeg, Mirza: *The Chachnamah, an Ancient History of Sind.* Translated from the Persian (originally written in Arabic by Ali Kufi). Lahore 1985 (Vanguard Books).

Kenoyer, J. Mark & Kuldeep K. Bhan: Sidis and the Agate Bead Industry of Western India. In: Amy Catlin-Jairazbhoy & Edward A. Alpers (eds.), *Sidis and Scholars. Essays on African Indians*; pp. 42-60. Noida 2004 (Rainbow Publishers).

Khalidi, Omar: The Habshis of Hyderabad. In: Kenneth X. Robbins & John McLeod (eds.), *African Elites in India: Habshi Amarat*; pp. 245-253. Ahmedabad 2006 (Mapin).

Khalique, Amna: *The Peoples of African Descent in Pakistan. Sheedis and their Role in Sindhi History.* Saarbrücken 2009 (VDM Verlag Dr. Müller).

Khan, Dominique-Sila: *Conversions and Shifting Identities. Ramdev Pir and the Ismailis in Rajasthan.* New Delhi 1997 (Manohar).

Khan, Dominique-Sila: Jhulelal and the Identity of Indian Sindhis. In: Michel Boivin (ed.), *Sindh through History and Representations. French Contributions to Sindhi Studies*; pp. 72-81. Karachi 2008 (Oxford University Press).

Khannous, Touria: *Black-Arab Encounters in Literature and Film.* New York 2022 (Routledge).

Khosronejad, Pedram: Out of focus. Photography of African slavery in Qajar Iran. In: *Anthropology of the Contemporary Middle East and Central Eurasia* 4/1 (2017), pp. 1-31.

Khuhro, Hamida: How it all began. In: Khuhro, Hamida & Anwer Mooraj (eds.), *Karachi. Megacity of Our Times*; pp. 1- 23. Karachi 1997 (Oxford University Press).

Khwaja, Aslam: Forgotten Journeys. In: Sehba Sarwar (ed.), *Homes and Histories. Living Room Art*; pp. 40-42. Houston 2012-13.

Khwaja, Aslam: *People's Movements in Pakistan.* Karachi 2016 (Kitab Publishers).

Kirmani, Nida: Life in a 'No-go Area'. Experiences of Marginalisation and Fear in Lyari. In: Nichola Khan (ed.), *Cityscapes of Violence in Karachi.*

Publics and Counterpublics; pp. 114-132. Karachi 2017 (Oxford University Press).

Klein, Kerwin Lee: On the Emergence of Memory in Historical Discourse. In: *Representations* 69 (2000), pp. 127-150.

Knappert, Jan: *Islamic Legends. Histories of the Heroes, Saints and Prophets of Islam*, Vol. I, Leiden 1985 (E.J. Brill).

Kooria, Mahmood: Introduction: narrating Africa in South Asia. In: *South Asian History and Culture* 11/4 (2020), pp. 351-362.

Lambrick, H.T.: The Sindh Battles, 1843. In: Mubarak Ali (ed.), *Sindh Observed. Selection from the Journal of Sindh Historical Society*; pp.165-204. Lahore 2005 (Fiction House).

Lari, Suhail Zaheer: *An Illustrated History of Sindh.* Karachi 2002 (Heritage Foundation, Pakistan).

Lari, Yasmeen: *Karachi. Illustrated City Guide.* Karachi 2000 (Oxford University Press & Heritage Foundation).

Larsen, Kjersti: Multiculturalism through Spirit Possession. In: *ISIM Newsletter* 14 (2004), pp. 14-15.

Lewis, I.M.: *Ecstatic Religion. A Study of Shamanism and Spirit Possession.* London & New York 1989 (Routledge).

Lieven, Anatol: *Pakistan. A Hard Country.* London 2011 (Allen Lane/ Penguin Books).

Lodhi, Abdulaziz Y.: African Settlements in India. In: *Nordic Journal of African Studies* 1/1 (1992), pp. 83-86.

Luizard, Pierre-Jean: Les confréries soufies en Irak Arabe aux dix-neuvième et vingtième siècles face au chiisme duodécimain et au Wahhabisme. In: Frederick de Jong & Bernd Radtke (eds.), *Islamic Mysticism Contested. Thirteen Centuries of Controversies and Polemics*; pp. 283-309. Leiden et al. 1999 (Brill).

Lynton, Harriet Ronken & Mohini Rajan: *The Days of the Beloved.* Hyderabad 1987 (Orient Longman).

Mahdihassan, S.: On the Place Names: Mangho-Peer near Karachi and Mangloro in Swat. In: *Sindhological Studies*, Summer 1981, pp. 1-7.

Mahdihassan, S. (ed.): *Bazar Drugs and Folk Medicine in Pakistan.* Karachi 1984 (Hamdard Foundation).

Malik, Iftikhar H.: *Religious Minorities in Pakistan.* London 2002 (Minority Rights Group International).

Malik, Mohammad Usman & Annemarie Schimmel (eds.): *Pakistan. Das Land und seine Menschen – Geschichte, Kultur, Staat und Wirtschaft.* Tübingen & Basel 1976 (Horst Erdmann).

Malkani, H.C.: Karachi 150 Years ago, Its Exports, Imports, and Revenue on the Eve of British Conquest. In: *Sindh Quarterly* 8/4 (1980), pp. 34-37.

Masih, Niha: Exposing India's lethal race issue. In: *New York Times,* 18 April 2017, International Edition, p. 1.

Masson, Charles: *Narrative of a Journey to Kalat.* London 1843 (Repr. Karachi 1976, Indus Publications).

Matheson, Sylvia A.: *The Tigers of Baluchistan.* Karachi 1975 (Oxford University Press).

Mills, Margaret A. & Peter J. Claus & Sarah Diamond (eds.): *South Asian Folklore. An Encyclopedia.* New York & London 2003 (Routledge).

Meier, Prita Sandy: Per/forming African Identities. Sidi Communities in the Transnational

Moment. In: Amy Catlin-Jairazbhoy & Edward A. Alpers (eds.): *Sidis and Scholars. Essays on African Indians*; pp. 86-99. Noida 2004 (Rainbow Publishers).

Momen, Moojan: *An Introduction to Shi'i Islam. The History abd Doctrines of Twelver Shi'ism.* New Haven and London 1985 (Yale University Press).

Müller, Klaus E.: *Das magische Universum der Identität. Elementarformen sozialen Verhaltens.* Frankfurt & New York 1987 (Campus).

Müller, Klaus E.: Das Unbehagen mit der Kultur. In: Klaus E. Müller (ed.), *Phänomen Kultur. Perspektiven und Aufgaben der Kulturwissenschaften*; pp. 13-47. Bielefeld 2003 (transcript).

Müller, Klaus E.: *Verfangen im Fadenkreuz Gottes. Eine kulturanthropologische Fabel.* Wiesbaden 2020 (Springer VS).

Murphy, Richard: A Whiter Shade of Pale. In: *The Friday Times* (Lahore), 14 to 20 April 1994, p. 17.

Napier, W.F.P.: *The Conquest of Scinde.* London 1845 (T. & W. Boone).

Narayan, Kirin & Muhammad A. Kavesh: Priceless Enthusiasm: The Pursuit of *Shauq* in South Asia. In: *Journal of South Asian Studies* 42/4 (2019), pp. 711-725.

N'Diaye, Tidiane: *Der verschleierte Völkermord. Die Geschichte des muslimischen Sklavenhandels in Afrika.* Reinbek 2010 (Rowohlt).

Nicolini, Beatrice: The Makran-Baluch -African Network in Zanzibar and East Africa during the XIXth Century. In: *African and Asian Studies* 5/3-4 (2006), pp. 347-370.

Nissen, Hans J.: Frühe Hochkulturen im Nahen und Mittleren Osten. In: Catalogue *Vergessene Städte am Indus. Frühe Kulturen in Pakistan vom 8.-2. Jahrtausend v. Chr.*; pp. 43-49. Mainz 1987 (Verlah Philioo von Zabern).

Nizamani, Sikander Ali: *Sheedi Community of Sindh, Pakistan.* Unpublished M.Sc. thesis, Department of Anthropology, Quaid-i-Azam University Islamabad 2006.

O'Brien, John: *The Unconquered People. The Liberation Journey of an Oppressed Caste.* Karachi 2012 (Oxford University Press).

Ousat, Ali: In the Shadow of Fire and Bullets: African Dancers of Lyari shed New Light on Restive Area. In: *The Express Tribune* (Karachi), 12 August 2013.

Pankhurst, Richard: The Ethiopian Diaspora to India: The Role of Habshis and Sidis from Medieval Times to the End of the Eighteenth Century. In: Shihan De Silva Jayasuriya & Richard Pankhurst (eds.) *The African Diaspora in the Indian Ocean*; pp. 189-221. Trenton & Asmara 2003 (Africa World Press).

Paracha, Nadeem Farooq: *Points of Entry. Encounters at the Origin-Sites of Pakistan.* Chennai 2018 (Tranquebar).

Pastner, Carroll McClure: *Sexual Dichotomization in Society and Culture: The Women of Panjgur, Baluchistan.* Ann Arbor 1971 (Ph.D. thesis, Brandeis University; University Microfilms).

Pastner, Carroll McClure: The Status of Women and Property on a Baluchistan Oasis in Pakistan. In: Lois Beck & Nikkie Keddie (eds.), *Women in the Muslim World*; pp. 434-450. Cambridge, Mass. & London 1978 (Harvard University Press).

Pastner, Stephen: Ideological Aspects of Nomad-Sedentary Contact: A Case from Southern Baluchistan. In: *Anthropological Quarterly* 44/3 (1971), pp. 173-184.

Pastner, Stephen: Conservatism and Change in a Desert Feudalism: The Case of Southern Baluchistan. In: Wolfgang Weissleder (ed.), *The Nomadic Alternative. Modes and Models of Interaction in the African-Asian Deserts and Steppes*; pp. 247-260. The Hague & Paris 1978 (Mouton).

Pastner, Stephen & Carroll McClure Pastner: Adaptations to State-Level Politics by the Southern Baluch. In: L. Ziring & R. Braibanti & W.H. Wriggins (eds.), *Pakistan. The Long View*; pp. 117-139. Durham 1977 (Duke University Press).

Pastner, Stephen & Carroll McClure Pastner: Clients, Camps & Crews: Adaptational Variation in Baluch Social Organization. In: Stephen Pastner & Louis Flam (eds.), *Anthropology in Pakistan: Recent Socio-Cultural and Archaeological Perspectives*; pp. 61-73. Karachi 1982 (Indus Publications).

Patai, Raphael: *Sitte und Sippe in Bibel und Orient.* Frankfurt a.M. 1962 (Ner-Tamid-Verlag).

Pfeffer, Georg: *Pariagruppen des Pandschab*. Freiburg 1970 (dissertation, printed by Klaus Renner, Munich).

Pitts, Johny: *Afropean. Notes from Black Europe.* London 2020 (Penguin).

Popovic, Alexandre: *The Revolt of African Slaves in Iraq in the 3rd/9th Century.* Princeton 1999 (Markus Wiener Publications).

Postans, Thomas: *Personal Observations on Sindh: Manners and Customs of its Inhabitants.* London 1843 (Repr. Karachi 1973; Indus Publications).

Pottinger, Henry: *Travels in Beloochistan and Sinde.* London 1816 (Repr. Karachi 1976, Indus Publications).

Pozdena, Hans: *Das Dashtiari-Gebiet in Persisch-Belutschistan.* Vienna 1978 (A. Schendl).

Prasad, Kiran Kamal & Jean-Pierre Angenot (eds.): *TADIA. The African Diaspora in Asia.* Bangalore 2008 (Jana Jagrati Prakashana).

Prasad, Yuvaraj D. & Miles L. Bradbury: The Kutchi Merchants and the African Slave Trade in the

Persian Gulf. An Appraisal: 1807-1905. In: Omar H. Ali & Kenneth X. Robbins & Beheroze Shroff & Jazmin Graves (eds.), *African Diasporan*

Communities Across South Asia; pp. 49-63. Greensboro, NC & Ahmedabad 2020 (The University of North Carolina).

Qaimkhani, Khurshid: *Bhataktī Naslaiñ* [The Nomadic Peoples; in Urdu]. Lahore 1996 (Fiktion House).

Qamar, Raheel & Qasim Ayub & Aisha Mohyuddin & Agnar Helgason & Kehkashan Mazhar & Atika Mansoor & Tatiana Zerjal & Chris Tyler-Smith & S. Qasim Mehdi: Y-Chromosomal DNA Variation in Pakistan. In: *American Journal of Human Genetics* 70 (2002), pp. 1107-1124.

Qambrani, Sheedi Muhammad Yaqoob: *Sheedi. A Historical Reality.* Oral text recorded in Urdu by Akhtar Soomro in several sessions at Karachi Press Club, translated from Urdu to English by Aslam Khwaja [unpublished manuscript, 2017].

Qazi, Mohammad Ali: Sindhi Music. In: Yakub Mughul (ed.), *Studies on Sind*; pp. 1-17. Jamshoro 1988 (Pakistan Study Centre).

Quddus, Syed Abdul: *The Tribal Baluchistan.* Lahore 1990 (Ferozsons).

Qureshi, Ashfaq-ur-Rahman: The Crocodiles of Manghopir. In: *The News*, Karachi (November 19, 1993), pp. IV-V.

Rafiquzzaman & S. Mahdihassan: Arsenical Spring Waters at Mangho Pir. In: S. Mahdihassan (ed.): *Bazar Drugs and Folk Medicine in Pakistan*; pp. 4-9. Karachi 1984 (Hamdard Foundation).

Rahman, Haseeb-ur: *The Shidis of Sind. A Pilot Study.* Islamabad 1976 (Lok Virsa Institute/National Institute of Folk Heritage). [unpublished manuscript]

Rashdi, Adil: Crocodile Rock. In: *The Herald*, Karachi 23/6 (1992), pp. 140-142.

Randhawa, Tejinder Singh: *The Last Wanderers. Nomads and Gypsies of India.* Ahmedabad 1996 (Mapin).

Raunig, Walter: *Bernstein – Weihrauch – Seide. Waren und Wege der antiken Welt.* Vienna and Munich 1971 (Verlag Anton Schroll).

Raunig, Walter: Foreword. In: *Mare Erythræum* I, p. 5. Munich 1997 (Staatliches Museum für Völkerkunde München).

Richardson, Miles: Anthropologist – the myth teller. In: *American Ethnologist* 2/3 (1975): 517-533.

Rizvi, Saiyid Athar Abbas: *A History of Sufism in India. Vol. II From Sixteenth Century to Modern Century.* New Delhi 1983 (Munshiram Manoharlal Publishers).

Robbins, Kenneth X. & John McLeod (eds.): *African Elites in India: Habshi Amarat.* Ahmedabad 2006a (Mapin).

Robbins, Kenneth X. & John McLeod: Africans in Mughal India and the Princely States. In: Kenneth X. Robbins & John McLeod (eds.): *African Elites in India: Habshi Amarat*; pp. 163-175. Ahmedabad 2006b (Mapin).

Ross, David: *The Land of the Five Rivers and Sindh.* London 1883 (Chapman and Hall).

Rotter, Gernot: *Die Stellung des Negers in der islamisch-arabischen Gesellschaft bis zum XVI. Jahrhundert.* Bonn 1967 (Dissertation, University of Bonn).

Sardar Khan Baluch, Muhammad: *History of Baluch Race and Baluchistan.* Quetta 1958 (Gosh-e-Adab).

Schiller, Friedrich von: Ueber die ästhetische Erziehung des Menschen (2. Teil, 10. bis 16. Brief). In: *Die Horen, 2. Stück.* Tübingen 1795.

Schimmel, Annemarie: *Und Muhammad ist Sein Prophet. Die Verehrung des Propheten in der islamischen Frömmigkeit.* Düsseldorf & Cologne 1981 (Eugen Diederichs).

Shadi Khan Saif: Sheedis – The Lost African Tribe in Pakistan. In: *Fairplanet*, 2 March 2020 [www.fairplanet.org/story/sheedis-the-lost-african-tribe-in-pakistan/; accessed on 10 April 2021]

Shah, Riaz Ali & Mohanlal Lalvani & S. Mahdihassan: Mango Pir Spring Waters. In: S. Mahdihassan (ed.): *Bazar Drugs and Folk Medicine in Pakistan*; pp. 1-3. Karachi 1984 (Hamdard Foundation).

Sheth, Ketaki: *A Certain Grace. The Sidi: Indians of African Descent.* New Delhi 2013 (Photoink).

Shroff, Beheroze: Sidis in Mumbai: Negotiating Identities between Mumbai and Gujarat. In: *African and Asian Studies* 6 (2007), pp. 305-319.

Siddiq Musafir, Muhammad: *Ghulāmi ain azādi ja ibratnāk nazaray.* Hyderabad 1952 (R.H. Ahmed & Brothers). [Dreadful Scenes of Slavery and Freedom; in Sindhi language]

Siddiq Musafir, Muhammad: *Ghulāmi aur azādi ke ibratnāk nazaray.* Karachi 2021 (Progressive Kitab Publishers). [translated from Sindhi into Urdu by Aslam Khwaja]

Siddiq Musafir, Muhammad: *Manzil-e Musāfir. Kulliyāt-e Musāfir.* Hyderabad 1965 (second edition, text completed October 2, 1952). [The Traveller's Journey. The Collected Works of Musafir; autobiography by Musafir in Sindhi language]

Slimbach, Richard A.: Ethnic Binds and Pedagogies of Resistance: Baloch Nationalism and Educational Innovation in Karachi. In: Titus, Paul (ed.), *Marginality and Modernity. Ethnicity and Change in Post-Colonial Balochistan*; pp. 138-167. Karachi 1996 (Oxford University Press).

Snouk Hurgronje, Christiaan: *Mekka in the Latter Part of the 19th Century.* Leyden & London 1931 (E.J. Brill & Luzac).

Sommer, Anton F.W.: *Lehrbuch des Belutschi.* Vienna 1997 (Orientalische Grammatiken und Lexika, Bd. 8).

Southgate, Minoo: The Negative Image of Blacks in Some Medieval Iranian Writings. In: *Iranian Studies* 17/1 (1984), pp. 3-36.

Spooner, Brian: Who are the Baluch? A preliminary investigation into the dynamics of an ethnic identity from Qajar Iran. In: Edmond Bosworth and Carole Hillenbrand (eds.), *Qajar Iran. Political, Social, and Cultural Change 1800-1925*; pp. 93-110. Costa Mesa, CA 1983 (Mazda Publishers).

Steingass, F.: *A Comprehensive Persian-Engish Dictionary.* London 1892 (Routledge & Kegan Paul).

Stöhr, Waldemar: *Lexikon der Völker und Kulturen. Band 1: Abnaki – Hamiten.* Braunschweig 1972 (Georg Westermann & Rowohlt).

Sultana, Farhat: *Gwat* and *gwat-i-leb*: Spirit Healing and Social Change in Makran. In: Paul Titus (ed.), *Marginality and Modernity. Ethnicity and Change in Post-Colonial Balochistan*; pp. 28-50. Karachi 1996 (Oxford University Press).

Suvorova, Anna: *Muslim Saints of South Asia. From eleventh to fifteenth centuries.* London and New York 2004 (RoutledgeCurzon).

Swidler, Nina: Beyond Parody: Ethnography engages Nationalist Discourse. In: Paul Titus (ed.), *Marginality and Modernity. Ethnicity and Change in Post-Colonial Balochistan*; pp. 168-190. Karachi 1996 (Oxford

University Press).al-Tabari, Abu Dja'far: *Tarikh al-Rusul wa al-Malik.* Vol. III. Leiden 1964 (Brill).

Talhami, Ghada Hashem: The Zanj Rebellion Reconsidered. In: *The International Journal of African Historical Studies* 10/3 (1977), pp. 443-461.

de Tassy, Garcin: *Muslim festivals in India and Other Essays.* Translated and edited by M. Waseem. Delhi 1997 (Oxford University Press).

Teffera, Timkehet: Ngoma drums and musical performances of the Wasamba in Tanzania. In: Gisa Jähnichen (ed.), *Studio Instrumentorum Musicae Popularis I*, pp. 305- 318. Münster 2009 (MV-Wissenschaft).

Trimingham, J. Spencer: *The Sufi Orders in Islam.* Oxford 1971 (Oxford University Press).

Vansina, Jan: *Oral Tradition as History.* Madison, Wisconsin 1985 (The University of Wisconsin Press).

Varadarajan, Lotika: Bava Gor and the Creation of Sidi Identity. In: Omar H. Ali & Kenneth X. Robbins & Beheroze Shroff & Jazmin Graves (eds.), *African Diasporan Communities Across South Asia*; pp. 67-75. Greensboro, NC & Ahmedabad 2020 (The University of North Carolina).

Waines, David (ed.): *The History of al-Ṭabarī. Vol. XXXVI: The Revolt of the Zanj, A.D. 869-879/A.H. 255-265.* Albany, N.Y. 1992 (State University of New York Press).

Walker, John: A Rare Coin of the Zanj. In: *The Journal of the Royal Asiatic Society of Great Britain and Ireland* 3 (1933), pp. 651-655.

Wensinck, A.J. & J.H. Kramers (eds.): *Handwörterbuch des Islam.* Leiden 1976 (E.J. Brill).

Wieviorka, Michel: Is it so difficult to be an Anti-Racist? In: Pnina Werbner & Tariq Modood (eds.), *Debating Cultural Hybridity. Multi-Cultural Identities and the Politics of Anti-Racism*; pp. 139-153. London & New Jersey 1997 (Zed Books).

Zaheer, Noor: At Home in Enemy Land. Karachi 2018 (Kitab Publishers).

Zubair, Subaita & Urwah Ali & Zuba'u Akhtar: An Ethnographic Investigation of Women's Perspectives and Cognition Regarding Skin Color in Pakistan. In: Anthropos 115/2 (2020): 405-415.

Contributors

Jürgen Wasim Frembgen, anthropologist, Islamic Studies scholar, and writer, is a retired Senior Curator (Hauptkonservator) and head of Oriental Department at the Museum Fünf Kontinente in Munich, and Adjunct Professor emeritus at the Institute of Near and Middle Eastern Studies, Ludwig-Maximilians-University, Munich.

Hasan Ali Khan, historian of religion, is Principal Investigator (PI) for the research project 'Changes among *Thari* Communities during the Last Decade: Economics and Social Uplift. An Analysis.' He was Assistant Professor at the School of Arts, Humanities, and Social Sciences, Habib University, Karachi, and taught at the Aga Khan University, Karachi, and the Indus Valley School of Art and Architecture. His PhD from SOAS, University of London, 2009, is on the medieval Suhrawardi Sufi order and its related architecture in Multan and Uch.

Aliya Iqbal Naqvi, historian, is Scholar-in-Residence and permanent faculty in the Department of Social Sciences & Liberal Arts at the Institute of Business Administration, Karachi. She previously headed the Liberal Arts Program at the Indus Valley School of Arts and Architecture, Karachi. She holds a Bachelor's and a Master's degree from Harvard University, Cambridge, MA, and is in the process of completing a PhD from the same institution.

Sheedi Yaqoob Qambrani, historian, social activist, and political leader; President of the 'Pakistan Sheedi Ittehad.' He lives in Karachi.

Akhtar Soomro, photojournalist, worked for local newspapers before shooting assignments for international newspapers and magazines. In 2009,

he was part of a *New York Times*'s team that won a Pulitzer for 'International Reporting' for Pakistan and Afghanistan. He lives in Karachi too.

Photography Credit

Akhtar Soomro, Figs. 4-5, 7-9, 11-12, 15-20, 22-23, 27-47, 51, 53-56
Jürgen Wasim Frembgen, Figs. 1-3, 6, 10, 13-14, 21, 24-26, 48, 52, 57-60
Aliya Iqbal Naqvi, Fig. 49
Sophie Reynard (courtesy MIFS, Director Dr. Michel Boivin), Fig. 50